I0448968

American Diplomacy:
A Handbook

American Diplomacy: A Handbook

1776 - 2000

Jerry K. Sweeney

Copyright © 2006 Jerry K. Sweeney
All rights reserved.

ISBN : 1-4196-4291-X

To order additional copies, please contact us.
BookSurge, LLC
www.booksurge.com
1-866-308-6235
orders@booksurge.com

American Diplomacy: A Handbook

TABLE OF CONTENTS

INTRODUCTION

The most important human considerations are undoubtedly death, taxes and the neighbors. Not a great deal can be accomplished with respect to the first two. However, the last are sometimes amenable to reason and occasionally change. Within the history of the human community, therefore, the connections established between empires, kingdoms and nation states are of critical importance.

Obviously, diplomats are more than simply individuals sent abroad to lie, or dine, for their country, and their individual personalities directly affect the diplomatic process. Nevertheless, they needs must function within established parameters, which is to say that individuals should be conscious of their past if for no other reason than to avoid reinventing the wheel. Therefore, familiarity with the diplomatic history of a nation state involves more than efficiency, it is salient to its survival.

This work is concerned with those incidents that shaped the diplomatic history of the United States since the first settlers set foot on the shores of the continent. It consists of six sections, each of which contains a chronology of events, a summary of important treaties, biographic treatments of various personalities, as well as a bibliographic essay. It also includes a glossary of commonly used terms in diplomatic discourse.

The items listed are those found in any general diplomatic history of the United States. This work does not end with the conventional, however, in that it includes a rather exhaustive list of unperfected treaties as well as those agreements concluded with the various tribes indigenous to North America. In most instances, a listing indicates that on that date a particular action occurred, e.g. the signing of a treaty or the creation of an organization. Some consideration is given to events in the domestic history of nations with which the United States was otherwise involved, but no attempt is made to thoroughly discuss the internal history of other nations except insofar as it directly impinges on subsequent diplomatic developments. Obviously, any domestic politico-economic action affects, to one degree or another, the diplomatic relationship between two nations, but to deal comprehensively with such matters would be impractical in a work of this size. Therefore, the reader is encouraged to pursue the bibliographic references at the end of each chapter for detailed appraisals of the factors at work in a given situation.

It is equally true, of course, that incidents seemingly important at the time, do not loom large in the diplomatic relationship over the long term. Moreover, the reverse is also the case, in that some developments assume decades later an importance quite unappreciated when they occurred. Although the authors attempted to occupy a moderate position in this regard and deal with matters immediate and long-term, the focus is more on the former than the latter. Finally, it is easier to assess the distant past than the present. It is for this reason that readers may find the more contemporary period somewhat truncated in comparison to those eras in which time and reflection allow for a more thorough appraisal of that which proved truly significant.

The date listed for a specific treaty is the date of signature, not the date of ratification or approval inasmuch as the latter differ so widely given the legislative processes of the various countries. To the same degree, the establishment of diplomatic relations with other countries becomes the date upon which the American representatives presented their credentials to the government in question. Thus, the phrase "diplomatic relations with France" indicates that on 23 March 1779 a representative of the government of the U.S. presented his credentials to the acknowledged leader of the government of France. In those instances wherein nation states were created from empires, e.g., the Ottoman Empire, the contemporary name, i.e., Turkey, is used. The biographical entries emphasize individuals, usually non-Americans, who made significant contributions but are otherwise one-dimensional figures in anything but comprehensive monographs. It must be noted, with respect to the biographical sections, that not all individuals listed in the chronological section will be found elsewhere. Indeed, in this instance, the two sections are not fully complementary.

The bibliographic statement furnishes a guide to the significant monographs/documentary collections relevant to the period or a particular subject. The works contained in the annotated bibliography were chosen according to their availability to students and lay readers as well as their representative character in addressing the periods and issues focused on in this volume. Numerous other outstanding monographs are regrettably not included, but such works are presented in the bibliographies herein listed. The authors recognize that any published bibliography is immediately out of date. Therefore, the listings herein contained are only the first step toward a comprehensive literature search.

This work seeks to illuminate the transition from a collection of states seemingly united against the rest of the world, to the point at which the nation appeared to be without serious opposition. The coverage is, mayhap most complete through 1990, that transitional year between the verities of the Cold War and the uncertainties of the so-called New World Order. To that extent, the work represents a discrete period in American Diplomatic History, inasmuch as it begins with otherwise unremarkable events that proved of seminal importance, and ends with the apparent close of the most defining process of recent decades. Only in the fullness of time will seemingly trivial events be appreciated as significant turning points whose importance is unquestioned.

REBELLION AND WAR

1686 — 1815

The overlapping territorial claims by Britain, France and Spain were certain to produce conflict in North America. This period of rebellion and war featured Britain and France inasmuch as their colonial focus was on North America. Furthermore, Spain no longer occupied a position as arbiter of European affairs, whereas Britain and France were contending for the honor. In consequence, the first century of American diplomatic activity involved the colonial aspects of the several wars fought to determine who would dominate Europe.

Britain's relative success in frustrating France in Europe, however, created unexpected problems in North America. In 1776, thirteen of Britain's North American colonies embarked on a bid for independence. The French were soon persuaded to offer aid to those who would disrupt the unity of the British Empire. That aid, at first secret and then open, was of inestimable value to the course of the rebellion. Indeed, the American victory in 1783 would be difficult to conceive without the participation, militarily and diplomatically, of France. Although the Americans were predisposed to scorn monarchies, there was no doubt in their minds that any port was refuge in a storm.

Nevertheless, once independence was secured the new nation intended to pursue a policy of isolation from monarchial and despotic Europe. The isolation, physical and intellectual, incumbent upon the Atlantic passage led to the emergence of a society that perceived itself unique in its composition and aspirations. Still, flaws inherent in the Treaty of Paris (1783), and the conflicting national interests of France and Spain, required involvement with Europe, if only, to secure a measure of commercial opportunity and further the nation's territorial aspirations. Fortunately, the United States found individuals capable of capitalizing upon European distractions in such a manner as to achieve those objectives.

Although the Old World came to the rescue of the New during the Revolution, it bid fair to destroy the Republic in the postwar years. The European conflict precipitated by the French Revolution put even innocent bystanders at risk. Therefore, although the United States was relieved of any legal obligation toward France with the abrogation of the Treaty of Alliance in 1800, it nonetheless found itself at war with Britain in 1812. The War of 1812 was most properly the Second War of American Independence. Although some dispute might exist regarding the identity of the victor, the status of the United States as an independent political entity was resolved with the Treaty of Ghent.

CHRONOLOGY

1686
Nov 16 Treaty of Whitehall (France and U.K.)

1689
May 12 King William's War (War of the League of Augsburg)

1697
Sept 30 Treaty of Ryswick (France and U.K.)

1701
Sept 7 Queen Anne's War (War of the Spanish Succession)

1713
Apr 11 Peace of Utrecht (France, Spain and U.K.)

1739
Oct 19 War of Jenkins' Ear (Spain and U.K.)

1740
Dec 16 King George's War (War of the Austrian Succession)

1748
Dec 4 Treaty of Aix-la-Chapelle (France, Spain and U.K.)

1754
Aug 29 French and Indian War (Seven Years' War)

1763
Feb 10 Peace of Paris (France, Spain and U.K.)

1775
Apr 19 Battles of Lexington and Concord
Sept 19 Secret Committee (Continental Congress)
Nov 29 Committee of Secret Correspondence (Continental Congress)

1776
Mar 3 Silas Deane leaves for Europe (first diplomatic envoy)
May 2 France initiates financial aid for American rebels
Jul 2 Continental Congress proclaims an independent political unit
Sept 1 French and Spanish ports opened to American ships
Sept 26 Benjamin Franklin selected to go to Paris

1777
Apr 17 Committee of Secret Correspondence becomes Committee for Foreign Affairs (Continental Congress)
Jul 5 Secret Committee becomes Committee of Commerce (Continental Congress)
Oct 17 Burgoyne surrenders at Saratoga
Dec 17 France recognizes American independence

1778
Feb 6 Treaty of Amity and Commerce (France)
Feb 6 Treaty of Alliance (France)
Apr 6 Carlisle Commission
Jun 17 U.K. declares war on France
Sept 17 Treaty of Fort Pitt (Delaware and U.S.)

1779
Mar 23 Diplomatic relations (France)
Mar 23 Benjamin Franklin—France (first U.S. Minister)
Apr 12 Treaty of Aranjuez (France and Spain)
Sept 29 Diplomatic relations (Spain)
Dec 20 U.K. declares war on The Netherlands

1780
Dec 9 William Palfrey—France (first U.S. consul)

1781
Jan 10 Department of Foreign Affairs (Confederation)
Mar 1 Articles of Confederation ratified
Jun 14 U.S. peace commission appointed
Oct 5 Thomas Barclay—France (first U.S. consul to reach post)
Oct 19 Cornwallis surrenders at Yorktown
Oct 20 Robert Livingston (Secretary of Foreign Affairs)

1782
Apr 19 Diplomatic relations (Netherlands)
Mar 20 North Ministry resigns (U.K.)
Oct 8 Treaty of Amity and Commerce (Netherlands)

1783
Sept 3 Peace of Paris (U.K. and U.S.)

1784
Feb 22 *Empress of China* departs for Canton, China
May 7 John Jay (Secretary for Foreign Affairs)
Jun 27 Spain closes Mississippi River
Jul 29 Consular treaty—France (unperfected)
Oct 22 Treaty of Fort Stanwix (Six Nations and U.S.)

1785
Jan 21 Treaty of Fort McIntosh (Multitribal)
Jun 1 Diplomatic relations (U.K.)
Nov 28 Treaty of Hopewell (Cherokee and U.S.)

1786
Jan 3 Treaty of Hopewell (Choctaw and U.S.)
Jan 10 Treaty of Hopewell (Chickasaw and U.S.)
Jan 31 Treaty of the Great Miami River (Shawnee and U.S.)
Jun 28 Morocco Treaty
Aug 29 Jay-Gardoqui Treaty—Spain (unperfected)

1788
Jun 21 U.S. Constitution achieves final ratification
Nov 14 Consular convention (France and U.S.)
Dec 1 Spain reopens Mississippi River

1789
Jan 9 Treaty of Fort Harmar (Multitribal)
Jan 9 Treaty of Fort Harmar (Six Nations and U.S.)
Jul 14 French revolution
Jul 27 Department of Foreign Affairs (Congress)
Sept 15 Department of Foreign Affairs becomes Department of State
(Congress)

1790
Mar 22 Thomas Jefferson (Secretary of State)
Apr 30 U.S. demands satisfaction from Spain (Nootka Sound Incident)
Aug 7 Treaty of New York (Creek and U.S.)
Oct 28 Nootka Sound Convention (Spain and U.K.)

1791
May 14 Diplomatic relations (Portugal)
Jul 2 Treaty of Holston River (Cherokee and U.S.)

1792
Apr 4 Consular Service (Congress)
Apr 23 Treaty of Philadelphia (Five Nations and U.S.)

1793
Feb 1 State of War—France and U.K. (ends 17 Mar 1802)
Apr 22 U.S. neutrality proclamation
Jun 8 U.K. blockades French-controlled ports in Europe
Aug 23 Edmond Genet declared *persona non grata* by U.S. (first foreign
diplomat so designated)
Nov 6 U.K. extends naval blockade to French colonies

1794
Jan 2 Edmund Randolph (Secretary of State)
Jan 8 U.K. tightens naval blockade of French- controlled ports
Mar 2 *Glass v. The Sloop Betsy* (Supreme Court)
Apr 9 Gouverneur Morris declared *persona non grata* by France (first
U.S. diplomat so designated)
Apr 25 U.S. embargoes trade with U.K. (Congress)
Jun 26 Treaty of Philadelphia (Cherokee and U.S.)
Jul 15 Treaty of Philadelphia—Chickasaw (unperfected)
Nov 11 Treaty of Canandaigua (Six Nations and U.S.)
Nov 19 Jay's Treaty (U.K. and U.S.)
Dec 2 Agency Treaty (Multitribal)

1795
Aug 3 Treaty of Greenville (Multitribal)
Sept 5 Algiers Treaty
Oct 27 Treaty of San Lorenzo (Spain and U.S.)
Dec 10 Timothy Pickering (Secretary of State)

1796
Mar 7 *Ware v. Hylton* (Supreme Court)
Mar 13 Ellsworth Advisory Opinion (Supreme Court)
May 31 Treaty of New York (Seven Nations of Canada and U.S.)
Jun 29 Treaty of New York (Creek and U.S.)
Jul 2 France adopts principles of U.K. naval blockade
Sept 19 George Washington's Farewell Address
Nov 4 Tripoli Treaty

1797
Mar 2 France extends naval blockade regulations of U.K.
Mar 29 Treaty of Albany (Mohawk and U.S.)
Aug 28 Tunis Treaty
Sept 15 Treaty of Genesee River (Seneca and U.S.)
Oct 8 XYZ Affair (France and U.S.)
Dec 5 Diplomatic relations (Prussia)

1798
Jan 18 France further extends naval blockade of U.K.
Apr 3 XYZ dispatches submitted to Congress
May 28 State of War—France and U.S. (ends 30 Sept 1800)
Jun 7 New York Treaty (Oneida and U.S.)
Jul 7 U.S. abrogates Treaties of Amity and Commerce (France)
Oct 2 Treaty of Tellico (Cherokee and U.S.)

1799
Jan 30 Logan Act (Congress)
Nov 9 Napoleon Bonaparte overthrows French government (Directory)

1800
Feb 5 *Polly* decision (U.K.)
Jun 6 John Marshall (Secretary of State)
Aug * *Bas v. Tingy* (Supreme Court)

Sept 30 Convention of Mortefontaine (France and U.S.)
Oct 1 Treaty of San Ildefonso (France and Spain)

1801
May 2 James Madison (Secretary of State)
May 14 State of War—Tripoli and U.S. (ends 4 Jun 1805)
Oct 24 Treaty of Chickasaw Bluffs (Chickasaw and U.S.)
Dec 17 Treaty of Fort Adams (Choctaw and U.S.)

1802
Mar 17 Treaty of Amiens (France and U.K.)
Jun 4 New York Treaty (Oneida and U.S.)
Jun 16 Treaty of Fort Wilkinson (Creek and U.S.)
Jun 30 Treaty of Buffalo Creek (Seneca and U.S.)
Aug 20 New York Treaty (Seneca and U.S.)
Oct 16 Spain revokes right of deposit (New Orleans)
Oct 17 Treaty of Fort Confederation (Choctaw and U.S.)
Dec 4 Treaty of Raleigh—Tuscarora (unperfected)

1803
Mar 1 Spain restores right of deposit (New Orleans)
Apr 30 Louisiana Purchase
May 12 King-Hawkesbury Convention—U.K. (unperfected)
May 16 State of War—France and U.K.
Jun 7 Treaty of Fort Wayne (Multitribal)
Jun 24 U.K. institutes regulation of neutral trade
Aug 7 Treaty of Vincennes (Multitribal)
Aug 13 Treaty of Vincennes (Kaskaskia and U.S.)
Aug 31 Treaty of Hoe-Buckin-too-pa (Choctaw and U.S.)

1804
Feb * Little v. Barreme (Supreme Court)
Apr 9 U.K. blockades French-controlled ports in Europe
Aug 18 Treaty of Vincennes (Delaware and U.S.)
Aug 27 Treaty of Vincennes (Piankeshaw and U.S.)
Oct 24 Treaty of Tellico (Cherokee and U.S.)
Nov 3 Treaty of St. Louis (Multitribal)

1805
Jun 4 Treaty of Tripoli

Jul 4 Treaty of Fort Industry (Multitribal)
Jul 23 *Essex* decision (U.K.)
Jul 23 Treaty of Chickasaw Country (Chickasaw and U.S.)
Aug 21 Treaty of Grouseland (Multitribal)
Sept 23 Treaty of St. Peter's River (Sioux and U.S.)
Oct 21 Battle of Trafalgar
Oct 25 Treaty of Tellico (Cherokee and U.S.)
Oct 27 Treaty of Tellico (Cherokee and U.S.)
Nov 14 Treaty of Washington (Creek and U.S.)
Nov 16 Treaty of Mt. Dexter (Choctaw and U.S.)
Dec 2 Battle of Austerlitz
Dec 30 Treaty of Vincennes (Piankashaw and U.S.)

1806
Jan 7 Treaty of Washington (Cherokee and U.S.)
Apr 23 Non-importation Act (Congress)
Nov 21 France blockades U.K. (Berlin Decree)
Dec 31 Monroe-Pinckney Treaty—U.K. (unperfected)

1807
Jan 7 U.K. refines naval blockade of French- controlled ports
Jun 22 HMS *Leopard* attacks USS *Chesapeake*
Jul 7 Peace of Tilsit (France and Russia)
Jul 9 Peace of Tilsit (France and Prussia)
Nov 11 U.K. tightens naval blockade of French- controlled ports
Nov 17 Treaty of Detroit (Multitribal)
Dec 17 France tightens blockade of U.K. (Milan Decree)
Dec 23 Embargo Act (Congress)

1808
Apr 17 France seizes U.S. ships (Bayonne Decree)
Nov 10 Treaty of Fort Clark (Osage and U.S.)
Nov 25 Treaty of Brownstown (Multitribal)

1809
Mar 1 Non-Intercourse Act (Congress)
Mar 6 Robert Smith (Secretary of State)
Aug 4 France seizes U.S. ships (Vienna Decree)
Sept 30 Treaty of Fort Wayne (Multitribal)
Oct 26 Treaty of Vincennes (U.S. and Wea)

Nov 5 Diplomatic relations (Russia)
Dec 9 Treaty of Fort Wayne (Kickapoo and U.S.)

1810
Mar 23 France seizes U.S. ships (Rambouillet Decree)
May 1 Macon's Bill #2 (Congress)
Sept 26 Republic of West Florida proclaimed
Oct 27 West Florida annexed by U.S. (executive order)

1811
Apr 6 James Monroe (Secretary of State)
May 16 USS *President* attacks HMS *Little Belt*

1812
Jun 18 State of War—U.K. and U.S.
Jun 23 U.K. suspends interference with U.S. trade
Nov 28 Exchange of naval POWs—U.K. (unperfected)

1813
Mar 11 U.S. accepts Russian mediation with U.K.

1814
Apr 11 Napoleon Bonaparte abdicates as Emperor of France
Apr 24 Diplomatic relations (Sweden)
Jul 22 Treaty of Greenville (Multitribal)
Aug 9 Treaty of Fort Jackson (Creek and U.S.)
Sept 23 Congress of Vienna Protocol
Dec 24 Treaty of Ghent (U.K. and U.S.)
Dec 28 Battle of New Orleans begins (ends 5 Jan 1815)

1815
Feb 28 James Monroe (Secretary of State)
Mar 2 State of War—Algiers and U.S. (ends 3 July)
Jun 18 Battle of Waterloo
Jul 3 Treaty of Commerce (U.K. and U.S.)
Jul 18 Treaty of Portage des Sioux (Potawatomi and U.S.)
Jul 18 Treaty of Portage des Sioux (Piankashaw and U.S.)
Jul 19 Treaty of Portage des Sioux (Teton and U.S.)
Jul 19 Treaty of Portage des Sioux (Sioux and U.S.)
Jul 20 Treaty of Portage des Sioux (Omaha and U.S.)
Sept 2 Treaty of Portage des Sioux (Kickapoo and U.S.)

Sept 8 Treaty of Spring Wells (Multitribal)
Sept 12 Treaty of Portage des Sioux (Osage and U.S.)
Sept 13 Treaty of Portage des Sioux (Sac and U.S.)
Sept 14 Treaty of Portage des Sioux (Fox and U.S.)
Sept 16 Treaty of Portage des Sioux (Iowa and U.S.)
Sept 26 Holy Alliance created (Austria, Prussia and Russia)
Oct 28 Treaty of St. Louis (Kansa and U.S.)
Nov 20 Quadruple Alliance formed (Austria, Prussia, Russia and U.K.)
Dec 5 James Barbour (Senate Foreign Relations Committee)

TREATIES, AGREEMENTS, SUPREME COURT CASES AND ACTS OF CONGRESS

TREATY OF WHITEHALL (1686) France and U.K. Pledges each party to maintain peace in North America regardless of conditions elsewhere between the two nations. Provides for the establishment of a joint commission to settle disputes.

TREATY OF RYSWICK (1697) France and U.K. Ends King William's War (War of the League of Augsburg) by restoring status quo in North America. Joint commission established to deal with Anglo-French disputes in North America.

PEACE OF UTRECHT (1713) France, Spain and U.K. Ends Queen Anne's War (War of the Spanish Succession) and Britain gains Acadia (Port Royal), St. Christopher Island and secures clear title to Hudson Bay and Newfoundland. Spain loses territory in Europe: Gibraltar and Minorca. Joint Commission established to deal with Anglo-French disputes in North America.

TREATY OF AIX-LA-CHAPELLE (1748) France, Spain and U.K. Ends King George's War (War of the Austrian Succession) by restoring the status quo in North America. Joint commission established to deal with Anglo-French disputes in North America.

PEACE OF PARIS (1763) France, Spain and U.K. Ends the French and Indian War (Seven Year's War). France loses Canada and Britain obtains claim to all of North America east of the Mississippi River with the exception of New Orleans. Louisiana passes to the Spanish and the English acquire Florida from Spain in exchange for giving up Cuba.

TREATY OF AMITY (1778) France and U.S. Conforms almost identically with the Plan of 1776. Most-favored-nation privileges stipulated except that when concessions the result of compensation such concessions do not extend to the most-favored party without similar compensation. France also offers certain free ports for American vessels in the West Indies and Metropolitan France. The mutual residence of consuls was to be established by a later convention. See also Convention of Mortefontaine (1800).

TREATY OF ALLIANCE (1778) France and U.S. Designed to come into effect in the event of war between Britain and France, or the interference of French commerce by Britain. Both nations are obliged to fight until American independence is formally or tacitly assured. Neither party can conclude a truce or peace without the formal consent of the other first obtained. France renounces any claim to North America except for those portions not recognized as British by the Treaty of Paris (1763). Both parties guarantee in perpetuity the territory of each, including any territory acquired by either in the course of the war, e.g., the British West Indies. A secret article provides for the adherence of Spain to both the Treaty of Commerce and the Treaty of Alliance. See also Convention of Mortefontaine (1800).

TREATY OF FORT PITT (1778) Delaware and U.S. The agreement is the first treaty concluded on the part of the American people with a tribe resident in North America subsequent to the Declaration of Independence. The Delaware were guaranteed certain territorial rights. See also the Treaty of Greenville (1795).

TREATY OF ARANJUEZ (1779) France and Spain. Spain agrees to participate in the war against Britain in exchange for certain territorial concessions. Both parties agree to continue the war until a peace acceptable to both is achieved. The treaty also binds France to fight until Spain reclaims Gibraltar. The United States is thereby committed to assist Spain's territorial ambitions inasmuch it cannot make a separate peace without French consent.

TREATY OF PARIS (1783) U.K. and U.S. The northern boundary roughly as it now exists, the western boundary the Mississippi River and the southern boundary to begin where the 31st parallel intersects the Mississippi. The Americans obtain the liberty to harvest the North Atlantic fisheries and British creditors are not to be impeded in the collection of prewar debts. The persecution of Americans loyal to the British government is to cease and the states are to be encouraged to return the confiscated property of such loyalists. The British army is to evacuate American territory with all convenient speed and may not carry away any American slaves in its possession.

TREATY OF FORT STANWIX (1784) Six Nations and U.S. First land cession by a tribe resident in North America to the United States. The agreement established the land to be ceded north of the Ohio River and defined the boundaries designating territories reserved to the various tribes. See also the Treaty of Greenville (1795).

TREATY OF HOPEWELL (1785) Cherokee and U.S. The Cherokee ceded land in exchange for specific territorial boundary and acknowledged the right of Congress to regulate their trade. Congress rejected independent treaty making by the states as an intrusion on the power of the central government. Other Americans ignored the treaty provisions and conflict resumed. Subsequent treaties were signed at Hopewell with the Choctaw (3 Jan 1786) and Chickasaw (10 Jan 1786)

TREATY OF FORT MCINTOSH (1785) Delaware, Chippewa, Ottawa and U.S. Those tribes party to the agreement ceded land in exchange for specific territorial boundary and acknowledged the right of Congress to regulate their trade. Tribal hostages were retained until such time as American prisoners were returned. The boundaries of a tribal reserve were established.

JAY-GARDOQUI AGREEMENT (1786) Spain and U.S. This abortive treaty involved exchanging use of the Mississippi River to obtain trading privileges in Spain. Led to the two-thirds requirement for the approval of treaties by the Senate.

TREATIES OF FORT HARMAR (1789) Chippewa, Delaware, Ottawa, Potawatomi, Sac, Wyandot and U.S. These treaties put an end to the practice of acquiring lands from tribes resident in North America by right of conquest. The agreements confirmed the provisions of the Treaties of Fort Stanwix and Fort McIntosh and offered payment for territory previously ceded. Other Americans ignored the treaty provisions and conflict resumed.

GLASS v. THE SLOOP BETSY (1794) Supreme Court avers that federal district courts have complete jurisdiction in admiralty cases.

JAY'S TREATY (1794) U.K. and U.S. British agree to evacuate Northwest forts in exchange for arbitration commissions on boundary questions, debts and spoliations (ships illegally seized). Also established commercial relations on a non-discriminatory basis.

TREATY OF GREENVILLE (1795) Chippewa, Delaware, Eel-river, Kaskaskia, Kickapoo, Miami, Ottawa, Piankashaw, Potawatomi, Shawanoe, Wea, Wyandot and U.S. Ceded most of present-day Ohio to the U.S. Boundaries were drawn to distinguish land reserved for the use of the various tribes from that open for settlement. This treaty was a material factor in the ability of the U.S. to enforce those provisions of Jay's Treaty relating to the British evacuation of Northwest forts.

TREATY OF SAN LORENZO (1795) Spain and U.S. Also known as Pinckney's Treaty. Spain grants freedom to navigate Mississippi River and right of deposit in New Orleans. U.S. accepts a northern boundary at 31 degrees north latitude. Mixed commission established for spoliations and each party agrees to restrain its Indian tribes.

WARE v. HYLTON (1796) Supreme Court rules that treaties take precedence over state law. See also Missouri v. Holland (1920) and Reid v. Covert (1957).

ELLSWORTH ADVISORY OPINION (1796). Chief Justice Oliver Ellsworth avers that the power to make treaties is vested solely in the President and the Senate. Once a treaty is approved and ratified it is the law of the land and therefore binding on the House of Representatives.

TRIPOLI TREATY (1796) Tripoli and U.S. This otherwise unremarkable agreement contained, in the version read before the Senate and signed by the President, an article attesting that the government of the United States was not "founded on the Christian religion." As such, the agreement is the earliest official statement on the secular nature of the American government. The treaty was renegotiated in 1805. The later agreement contained no statement about the religious or secular nature of the government of the United States.

LOGAN ACT (1799) Private citizens may not negotiate with foreign governments on matters affecting the United States without official sanction. To date, no indictments have been filed, although the threat of prosecution is not unknown. Details are found at 18 USC 953. See also George Logan.

BAS v. TINGY (1800) Supreme Court rules that the national government has the constitutional authority to wage war in the absence of a congressional declaration.

CONVENTION OF MORTEFONTAINE (1800) France and U.S. Also known as the Franco-American Convention. France accepts abrogation of Treaty of Amity and Commerce (1778) and U.S. cancels all claims against France. Commercial relations renewed. Abrogates Treaty of Alliance (1778).

TREATY OF SAN ILDEFONSO (1800) France and Spain. Spain retro-
cedes Louisiana in exchange for territory in Italy and six warships.
In a subsequent amendment (22 Jul 1802), Napoleon promises not
to alienate Louisiana to a third power. Franco-Spanish Alliance of
1796 reaffirmed.

LOUISIANA PURCHASE (1803) France and U.S. For $11,250,000 in
gold and $3,750,000 in claims against France U.S. buys the colony
of Louisiana. Napoleon I subsequently transferred ownership of
Louisiana to a British merchant bank (Barings) to receive the purchase price in an expeditious manner.

LITTLE v BARREME (1804) Supreme Court rules that Congress is
constitutionally empowered to participate in the conduct of a limited, undeclared war.

TREATY OF GHENT (1814) U.K. and U.S. Ends War of 1812 on basis
of *status quo ante bellum*. Mixed commissions established to settle
boundary issues.

ANGLO-AMERICAN TREATY OF COMMERCE (1815) U.K. and
U.S. Restores the commercial articles of Jay's Treaty.

BIOGRAPHICAL SKETCHES

BANCROFT, Edward (1744-1821) Born in Massachusetts, studied
medicine in London; he was a double agent *par excellence*. Served as
Franklin's secretary and communicated with London on a regular
basis.

BEAUMARCHAIS, Augustin Caron de (1732-1799) Inventor, watch-
maker, courtier and author of *The Barber of Seville* and *The Mar-
riage of Figaro*, he supervised the operation of Roderique Hortalez
and Company. That company shipped military supplies to America
before France entered the war.

CANNING, George (1770-1827) Served as Foreign Secretary from 1807
to 1809 and 1822 to 1827. His conversations with Richard Rush furnished the impulse for the Monroe Doctrine.

CASTLEREAGH, Robert Stewart, Viscount (1769-1822) Foreign Secretary from 1812 to 1822, he was either a reactionary associate of
despots or one of the most forward-looking statesmen of his day.
A man of uncertain temperament, his feud with Canning was leg-
endary.

CHOISEUL, Etienne-Francois, Duc de (1719-1795) Perceived the benefits to France of an autonomous British North America. His reports

were invaluable to the Comte de Vergennes when he became Foreign Minister.

DEANE, Silas (1737-1789) Dispatched to France to obtain supplies, he was joined by Franklin and Lee to negotiate the Franco-American Alliance. A quarrel with Lee damaged his reputation, and in 1780, he denounced the revolution.

FLORIDABLANCA, Jose Monino y Redona, Conde de (1728-1798) Foreign Minister to Charles III of Spain, he was notorious for having his own way, his suspicion of France and his aversion to the American rebels.

FOX, Charles James (1749-1806) As Secretary for Foreign Affairs (1782) he proposed the unconditional recognition of American independence. He returned to the Foreign Office when the Shelburne Ministry fell (1783), but he was unable to affect the peace settlement.

GENET, Edmond Charles (1763-1834) A French diplomat whose activities led President G. Washington to demand his recall. Facing certain death in France, he sought political asylum and retired to relative obscurity.

HARTLEY, David (1731-1813) Friend and correspondent of Benjamin Franklin, he opposed the American War. He replaced Richard Oswald as the British plenipotentiary in Paris in 1783.

LAURENS, Henry (1724-1792) President of the Continental Congress (1777-78), he was captured while on a mission to The Netherlands in 1779. Released from captivity, he joined the Paris Peace Commission in the closing days of negotiation.

LEE, Arthur (1740-1792) Joined Deane and Franklin in Paris (1776) and quarreled with both. He was recalled in 1779 because of his general unpopularity.

LIVINGSTON, Robert R. (1746-1813) Secretary of the Department of Foreign Affairs (1781-83) and Minister to France (1801-04) where he was instrumental in the purchase of Louisiana.

LOGAN, George (1753-1821) Son of a prominent Pennsylvania Quaker, his attempts to ease Franco-American tensions led to the passage of the Logan Act (1799) that forbids such private diplomacy. He violated the act with a private mission to the U.K. in 1810 but was not prosecuted.

MORRIS, Gouverneur (1752-1816) Minister to France (1792-94), he provided refuge to those fleeing the Terror during the Revolution. Declared *persona non grata*, returned to the U.S. and later opposed the War of 1812.

MURRAY, William Vans (1760-1830) Minister to The Netherlands

(1797-1801). He was a valuable source of information concerning France during the Naval War with France. Joined Oliver Ellsworth and William R. Davies in negotiating the Convention of Morte-fontaine (1800).

OSWALD, Richard (1705-1784) First British plenipotentiary to Paris Peace negotiations, he was a friend and business colleague of Henry Laurens. He had family connections and estates in North America.

PINCKNEY, Charles (1757-1824) Second cousin to C. C. and Thomas Pinckney, he was Minister to Spain (1802-1805).

PINCKNEY, Charles Cotesworth (1745-1825) Brother of Thomas and Minister to France (1796), he was not received by the government and left shortly thereafter. Later joined Elbridge Gerry and John Marshall in the mission that led to the XYZ Affair.

PINCKNEY, Thomas (1750-1828) Brother of C. C., he assisted in the negotiations leading to Jay's Treaty while Minister to the United Kingdom (1792-1796). As Special Commissioner to Spain, negoti-ated the Treaty of San Lorenzo (1796).

SHELBURNE, William P. Fitz-Maurice Lansdowne (1737-1805) Secre-tary for Home Affairs (1782), he was King George III's favorite and Prime Minister from 1782 to 1783. The Jesuit of Berkeley Square was mistrusted by his colleagues and his feud with the Fox family was extreme.

TALLEYRAND-PERIGORD, Charles Maurice de (1754-1839) States-man and diplomat, noted for his capacity for political survival and consummate treachery. He served successively: the Roman Catho-lic Church, the Revolution, Napoleon I, Louis XVIII and Louis Philippe.

TOUSSAINT-L'OUVERTURE, Francois Dominique (1743-1803) Former slave who became virtual dictator of Hispaniola (1784-1801). His overthrow and imprisonment by the French initiated a bloody struggle that led to Napoleon's decision to sell Louisiana.

VERGENNES, Charles Gravier de (1717-1787) Foreign Minister to Louis XVI, his deep hatred of Britain led him to support aid for the American rebels. His primary concern was the security of France and he frequently tried to ignore the interests of the U.S.

WILKINSON, James (1757-1825) A soldier noted for "never winning a battle nor losing a court martial," his devious nature led John Ran-dolph to remark he was from "the bark to the very core a villain." He was a central figure in the continuing Spanish Conspiracy.

ANNOTATED BIBLIOGRAPHY

Pre-Revolutionary American Diplomacy

Works on the pre-revolutionary diplomacy of British American colonies deal primarily with the nature of British colonization in American and British overseas competition with the French. Writers seek to identify the roots of the American Revolution and explain the conditions and events that precipitated it. Useful studies in addressing these issues are:

Jones, Dorothy V. LICENSE FOR EMPIRE: Colonialism by Treaty in Early America (1782). Jones investigates the European treaty system as a means of illustrating the development of the early American model of colonization.

Kaplan, Lawrence S. COLONIES INTO NATION: American Diplomacy 1763-1801 (1972) Kaplan describes the struggle for American independence and maintains that it actually led to isolationism rather than simple anti-French or anti-British sentiment in the early years of the Republic.

Tucker, Robert W. and Hendrickson, David C. THE FALL OF THE FIRST BRITISH EMPIRE (1982). The authors re-examine British colonial policy during the latter half of the eighteenth century and suggest that it was inconsistent objectives that led to the demise of the British Empire in America.

Ubbelohde, Carl. THE AMERICAN COLONIES AND THE BRITISH EMPIRE, 1607-1763 (1975). This concise introduction to British motivations in American colonization approaches the topic from the problems of economics, governance and increasingly contradictory aspirations.

Revolutionary America

Scholarship on revolutionary America focuses largely on the colonists' motivations in rejecting British rule, their alliance with the French and the extent to which the Franco-American liaison influenced revolutionary politics.

Bemis, Samuel F. DIPLOMACY OF THE REVOLUTION (1957). This is a classic study of the American Revolution and its diplomatic aspect. Bemis examines conditions in Europe to describe and assess the extent to which that scenario affected the exercise of revolutionary American diplomacy.

Dull, Jonathon R. FRANKLIN THE DIPLOMAT: The French Mission (1782). Dull's brief treatment focuses on Franklin as a practicing diplomat. The author concludes that Franklin's contributions to the diplomacy of this period were among this statesman's greatest achievements.

Egnal, March. A MIGHTY EMPIRE: The Origins of the American Revolution (1988). Egnal develops the proposition that the American Revolution was generated by revolutionary movements in each colony, that were led by upper class people committed to the rise of the New World.

Hoffman, Ronald and Albert, Peter J., eds. DIPLOMACY AND REVOLUTION: The Franco-American Alliance of 1778 (1981). This volume contains five essays that utilize several different approaches to examine the American-French relationship of the late eighteenth century.

Hutson, James H. JOHN ADAMS AND THE DIPLOMACY OF THE AMERICAN REVOLUTION (1980). Hutson rejects the view of American revolutionary diplomacy as progressive and supports his argument by comparing it to earlier periods of foreign relations and illustrating its conservative character.

Kaplan, Lawrence S. THE AMERICAN REVOLUTION AND A CANDID WORLD (1977). This collection of essays by various experts on the American Revolution offers insights into early American diplomacy with the Old World and its impact on the growth of American isolationism.

Lancelot, Gustavo. CANADA AND THE AMERICAN REVOLUTION, 1774-1783 (1967). Lancelot presents a documentary and narrative account of the late eighteenth century issues that influenced the relationship between American colonials and Canadians. This work analyses the impact of the American invasion of 1775 and the American Revolution on Canadian domestic and foreign policies.

Martin, James Kirby and Lender, Mark Edward. A RESPECTABLE ARMY (1782). This work examines the origins of the American Republic's military from 1763 through 1789 and concludes that Washington's army personified the essence of republicanism to a much greater extent than did the society from which it emerged.

Middlekauff, Robert. THE GLORIOUS CAUSE: The American Revolution 1763-1789 (1982). Middlekauff maintains that the revolutionary experience caused Americans to reconsider the meaning of old truths once associated with the glorious cause.

Pancake, John S. THIS DESTRUCTIVE WAR: The British Campaign in the Carolinas, 1780-1782 (1785). Pancake uses this southern campaign as a vehicle for illustrating his thesis that the British leadership's paralysis of will and lack of energy combined with the overall departure from the pattern of eighteenth century warfare to present the Americans with a considerable advantage.

Stinchcombe, William C. THE AMERICAN REVOLUTION AND THE FRENCH ALLIANCE (1969) Stinchcombe analyses the extent to which the alliance with France influenced the politics of the American Revolution, particularly in regard to domestic American special interest groups. He concludes that Americans considered agreements of this nature to be limited to specific objectives and believed that once such objectives were achieved, the alliance associated with them was ended.

Diplomacy of the Early Republic

The major issues of the early republic centered on forging the peace settlement and the early treaties which emerged from the successful revolution, determining the Constitution's mandates on the execution of foreign policy and achieving workable relations with foreign powers, especially Britain and France. During the period following the revolution, the new nation pursued a course of neutrality and relative isolation and scholars seek to explain the rationale behind these policies. By the mid-1790's, the United States sought increased influence over the territory beyond its borders, an objective which encountered opposition from the British. Works dealing with this later period of the early republic focus on explaining the policy shift of the 1790's and analyzing its implementation.

Bemis, Samuel F. JAY'S TREATY: A Study on Commerce and Diplomacy (1962). This work examines the first treaty negotiated by the newly founded U.S. government.

Bemis, Samuel F. JOHN QUINCY ADAMS AND THE FOUNDATIONS OF AMERICAN FOREIGN POLICY (1949). This work deals with Adams' career as a diplomat and his role in establishing the framework of American foreign policy during the first decades of independence.

Ben-Altar, Doran S. THE ORIGINS OF JEFFERSONIAN COM-
MERCIAL POLICY AND DIPLOMACY (1993). According to
Ben-Altar, Jefferson wanted commerce to act as a messenger of
American republicanism for the agrarian United States.

Bowman, Albert Hall. THE STRUGGLE FOR NEUTRALITY (1974).
This volume analyses Franco-American relations during the Feder-
alist years. Bowman maintains that the domestic conflict over this
period of pro-French policy and the departure from the neutrality
of the previous decade derived from the differing visions of the
American future.

Campbell, Charles S. FROM REVOLUTION TO RAPPROCHE-
MENT: The United States and Great Britain, 1783-1900 (1974).
Campbell traces the stormy course of U.S.-British relations from
the Revolution to the end of the nineteenth century.

Combs, Jerald A. THE JAY TREATY (1970). Combs examines the process involved in forging the Jay Treaty and analyses the influence
of idealism and realism of early American domestic politics on the
final document.

Egan, Clifford. NEITHER PEACE NOR WAR: Franco-American
Relations, 1803-1812 (1983). Egan regards early American relations
with Napoleonic France as largely determined by U.S. relations
with Britain, by commercial competition and by economic restrictions.

Ferrell, Robert H., ed. FOUNDATION OF AMERICAN DIPLO-
MACY, 1775-1872 (1968). This collection of documents from the
first century of U.S. foreign policy is arranged according to the pre-
vailing issues of those years. Ferrell comments on the background
and significance of each document.

Hoffman, Ronald and Albert, Peter J., eds. PEACE AND THE PEACE-
MAKERS: The Treaty of 1783 (1986). This collection of essays
investigates the American Revolutionary War settlement of 1783.
The objectives of the treaty and the personalities who forged it are
the primary focus of this study, but the role of military nationalism
and the long range effects of the agreement are also discussed.

Horsman, Reginald. THE DIPLOMACY OF THE NEW REPUB-
LIC, 1776-1815 (1985). This work provides a very general but useful
orientation to early American diplomacy.

Kaplan, Lawrence S. ENTANGLING ALLIANCES WITH NONE:
American Foreign Policy in the Age of Jefferson (1987). Kaplan
depicts the foreign policy of the early American republic as one

that was primarily focused on survival as a national entity. The author concludes that the isolationism practiced in those years was an abstention from political and military obligations rather than a total withdrawal from world affairs.

Land, Daniel George. FOREIGN POLICY AND THE EARLY REPUBLIC: The Law of Nations and the Balance of Power (1985). Land interprets U.S. foreign policy in the 1780's and 1790's in the context of the then emerging intellectual framework of just war, law of nations and balance of power issues.

Langley, Lester D. STRUGGLE FOR THE AMERICAN MEDITER-RANEAN: United States-European Rivalry in the Gulf-Carib-bean, 1776-1904 (1976). Langley examines U.S. relations with its Caribbean neighbors from the birth of the United States until the nation actually amassed the power to support its claim to prece-dence over European interests in the Caribbean.

Marks, Frederick W. III. INDEPENDENCE ON TRAIL: Foreign Affairs and the Making of the Constitution (1986). Marks' inves-tigates questions of national defense, foreign trade restrictions and public sentiment in shaping the Constitution, concluding that foreign policy was of overwhelming significance in the 1787 docu-ment.

Perkins, Bradford. PROLOGUE TO WAR: England and the United States, 1805-1812 (1961). Perkins' concluded that domestic partisan politics, national honor and the maritime conflict with England were the factors that led to the decision for war in 1812.

Reuter, Frank T. TRAILS AND TRIUMPHS: George Washington's Foreign Policy (1983). Reuter focuses on Washington's contribution to the American foreign policy tradition, both before and after the first president's inauguration.

Ritcheson, Charles R. AFTERMATH OF REVOLUTION (1969). Ritcheson analyses British policy toward the United States in the years immediately following independence. He maintains that any history of U.S. foreign relations during this phase that fails to include the British perspective is nationalistic and overlooks salient issues.

Stuart, Reginald C. UNITED STATES EXPANSIONISM AND BRITISH NORTH AMERICA, 1775-1871 (1988). This work examines American expansionism and its impact on American-Canadian relations, emphasizing the role of cultural dynamics and American values.

Varg, Paul A. FOREIGN POLICIES AND THE FOUNDING
    FATHERS (1963). Varg approaches the early practice of U.S. for-
    eign policy from its ideological and economic perspectives and
    concludes that despite the generous spirit of the founding fathers,
    their aims were distorted by a nationalism that led to a harmful
    unilateralism in foreign affairs.
Varg, Paul A. NEW ENGLAND AND FOREIGN RELATIONS,
    1789-1850 (1983). Varg investigates U.S. foreign policy in the late
    eighteenth and early nineteenth centuries from the point of view of
    the New England region. This study emphasizes the role of foreign
    trade and shipping in U.S. international relations of the period.
Valone, Stephen. TWO CENTURIES OF AMERICAN FOREIGN
    POLICY: The Documentary Record (1995). This collection of
    documents includes not only the usual suspects but also materials
    relating to relations between the U.S. and various North American
    tribes.
Woolery, William Kirk. THE RELATION OF THOMAS JEFFER-
    SON TO AMERICAN FOREIGN POLICY, 1783-1793 (1927).
    Woolery examines the role of particular events outside the United
    States that molded early U.S. foreign policy. He regards Jefferson
    as largely responsible for the policy of neutrality that endured until
    1793.
Wright, James Leitch. BRITAIN AND THE AMERICAN FRON-
    TIER, 1783-1815 (1975). Wright discusses the Anglo-American
    interaction concerning frontier issues from the American Revolu-
    tion until 1815 and concludes that the British aimed at limiting U.S.
    boundaries and bringing about the downfall of the new nation.

The War of 1812

    Works concerning the first war ever declared by the new American
republic examine that conflict for its causes as well as its precedents
in American diplomatic practice. The studies listed here include treatments of the European situation, American domestic issues and the
foreign relations issues that characterized the War of 1812.

Coles, Harry L. THE WAR OF 1812 (1965). This classic study maintains
    that the War of 1812 grew out of the conflicts of a divided Europe
    that thwarted the peaceful attempts by the United States to main-
    tain its international honor and interests.

Hatzenbuehler, Ronald S. and Ivie, Robert L. CONGRESS DECLARES
   WAR (1983). The author's examine the declaration of the War of
   1812 and the extent to which it served as a model for subsequent
   Congressional decisions to go to war. One of the early attempts
   to apply quantitative techniques to historical investigation in the
   diplomatic realm.
Hickey, Donald R. THE WAR OF 1812: A Forgotten Conflict (1989).
   The genesis of this book, according to Donald Hickey, was to
   provide a broader treatment of this conflict that would include
   politics, diplomacy, economics and finance as well as battles and
   campaigns.
Horseman, Reginald. THE CAUSES OF THE WAR OF 1812 (1972).
   Horsman maintains that the roots of the War of 1812 cannot be
   understood apart from the concurrent issues in Europe, particu-
   larly British foreign policy and the Napoleonic conflict.
Perkins, Bradford. CASTLEREAGH AND ADAMS: England and the
   United States, 1812-1823 (1964). Castlereagh, according to Perkins,
   should receive the lion's share of the credit for the improvement in
   Anglo-American relations after the War of 1812.
Updyke, Frank A. THE DIPLOMACY OF THE WAR OF 1812 (1965).
   Updyke discusses Anglo-American relations of the early nineteenth century with particular emphasis on the formulation of
   the Treaty of Ghent. This study also addresses the problems that
   emerged from the subsequent execution of the treaty.
Wright, James Leitch. BRITAIN AND THE AMERICAN FRON-
   TIER 1783-1815 (1975). Wright maintains that post-revolution British foreign policy aimed at limiting U.S. boundaries and sought to
   bring about the downfall of the new nation. His assessment of the
   events of 1812 reflects these views.

Native American Diplomacy

   The diplomatic relationship between the Native American peoples and the United States has been difficult and controversial. During
the colonial era, the desire of English settlers to possess the lands of
the Native Americans led to frequent hostilities. In consequence,
many tribes sought military alliances with the French or Spanish. After
England's decisive victory in 1763, tribes looked to the British government for protection against the land-hungry Americans. During the
American Revolution and the War of 1812 the vast majority of Native

Americans who participated fought for England, further embittering relations.

The first treaties between the United States and Native Americans concerned primarily the issues of war and peace, the sale of land, and trade. With the diminution of the British threat, as well as the United States' growing strength, more attention was paid to civilizing Native Americans on reduced land holdings. Andrew Jackson's removal treaties, for example, were undertaken to free lands east of the Mississippi River for American farmers, while west of the river in the Indian Territory, the native population was supposed to have time to assimilate into white society. In 1871, Congress decided that no new treaties would be concluded, in part because continued recognition of tribal affiliations conflicted with the goal of assimilation. Existing treaties were not affected by this decision and since the United States government did not fulfill the stipulations contained in many of them, Native Americans have increasingly sought redress through the court system.

Calloway, Colin. THE AMERICAN REVOLUTION IN INDIAN COUNTRY: Crisis and Diversity in Native American Communities (1995). Calloway concludes that they sided with the Americans, the British, remained neutral or served both sides. In any event, the American Revolution was a disaster for virtually all Native American communities.

Calloway, Colin. NEW WORLDS FOR ALL: Indians, Europeans, and the Remaking of Early America (1997). Calloway provides an effective synthesis of the interaction between Native Americans and Europeans in the formation of the United States. He argues that human influences were as important as environmental ones in shaping the new America. He also avers that the Indian way of life remained a part of the national experience.

Dowd, Gregory. A SPIRITED RESISTANCE: The North American Indian Struggle for Unity, 1745-1815 (1992). Drawing on ethnographic sources, Dowd examines not only the efforts of the Delaware, Shawnee, Cherokee and Creek nations to undertake an intertribal campaign to resist Anglo-American encroachment, but also the reasons that this resistance failed.

Horsman, Reginald. EXPANSION AND AMERICAN INDIAN POLICY, 1783-1812 (1967). Horsman argues that the founding fathers: "Wanted land, but they also wanted a good conscience." He concludes, however, that the United States failed to find a way to expand that the Native Americans would welcome.

Kappler, Charles (comp. & ed.). INDIAN AFFAIRS: Laws and Treaties (1904-1941). Kappler provides the text of all the treaties concluded between the United States government and Indian nations in the eighteenth and nineteenth centuries.

Nash, Gary. RED, WHITE, AND BLACK: The Peoples of Early America 3rd edition (1992). Nash's work proceeds from the belief that a fuller and deeper understanding of the colonial underpinnings of American history must examine the interaction of many peoples, at all levels of society. His work also discusses a wide range of cultural backgrounds over a period of several centuries.

Prucha, Francis P. AMERICAN INDIAN TREATIES: A History of a Political Anomaly (1994). This work examines the treaty system, to wit, how they were negotiated and the arguments for and against their use.

Prucha, Francis. THE GREAT FATHER: The United States Government and the American Indians (1984). In this two-volume work, Prucha analyses two centuries of federal Indian policy.

Sword, Wiley. PRESIDENT WASHINGTON'S INDIAN WAR (1985). The five-year conflict between the United States and the Native Americans in the Old Northwest, Sword contends, was crucial to securing and sustaining American nationalism. Indeed, in historical perspective, this wilderness conflict looms as the decisive confrontation in the Indian-United States wars that spanned two centuries.

Utley, Robert. THE INDIAN FRONTIER OF THE AMERICAN WEST, 1846-1890 (1984). Utley believes that a great cultural chasm existed in the west that condemned both Indians and whites in that neither really saw or understood each other.

Wallace, Anthony. THE LONG, BITTER TRAIL: Andrew Jackson and the Indians (1993). Wallace provides a brief overview of the origins and repercussions of the Indian removal policy.

White, Richard. THE MIDDLE GROUND: Indians, Empires, and Republics in the Great Lakes Region, 1650-1815 (1991). White argues that the French and Indians of the Great Lakes created between them a middle ground that was an effective vehicle for intercultural exchanges. The fur trade and political alliances with the French and then the British were critical to this process. The emergence of the United States as the dominant power doomed the middle ground because the Americans insisted that maintaining it was no longer possible.

ISOLATION AND EXPANSION

1816 — 1865

The Treaty of Ghent inaugurated an era characterized by an increasingly cordial relationship with Britain. Britain and the United States acted to minimize the possibility of future conflict, adjudicate territorial boundaries and adjust commercial disputes. This Anglo-American detente found renewed expression in the doctrine enunciated by James Monroe. Although President Monroe issued a unilateral statement, his doctrine appeared to support the goals of the British Foreign Office toward Spain and Russia.

The Monroe Doctrine seemingly required the United States to defend the hemisphere against colonial activity. This apparent rejection of the nation's traditional isolationist stance was, however, more honored in the breach than the observance. Britain was allowed, if not encouraged, to assume the anti-colonial burden in South America except insofar as it conflicted with American objectives. Meantime, the Republic pursued a territorial destiny made manifest by the assumption that Americans were selected by a benevolent deity to control the hemisphere, if not the world. Once again, the boundaries of the nation were expanded by astute diplomacy and the exercise of force.

Still, as the frontier pushed ever westward, the Republic was not wholly unaware of that considerable portion of the world beyond North America. In expectation of the day when the nation would be able to fully exploit the resources of the Pacific, the United States sought commercial advantage in East Asia, as well as a transportation link to shorten travel time to the Pacific. In this area, as in so many others, the nation was able to capitalize on European distractions to achieve its objectives. However, in 1861, Americans went to war with themselves. Europe was now able to secure benefits from an American period of distress.

Fortunately, although the France of Napoleon III was disposed to profit from the North American War, Britain was not so inclined. Indeed, notwithstanding several episodes when differences bespoke the possibility of war, Britain remained neutral as the North American experiment in democracy emphasized bullets over ballots. In consequence, the French efforts to reconstitute an empire in the Western Hemisphere proved a less serious challenge to the Monroe Doctrine than otherwise. The new nation that emerged from its ordeal by fire was poised on the threshold of yet another period of expansion. Admittedly, individual and particular emotional ties would remain to bedevil the national experience. Still, the most important legacy of the war was the elevation of a national identity over other loyalties.

CHRONOLOGY

1816

Mar 22 Treaty of Washington (Cherokee and U.S.)
May 13 Treaty of St. Louis (Sac and U.S.)
Jun 1 Treaty of St. Louis (Sioux and U.S.)
Jun 3 Treaty of St. Louis (U.S. and Winnebago)
Jun 4 Treaty of Fort Harrison (Multitribal)
Aug 24 Treaty of St. Louis (Multitribal)
Sept 14 Agency Treaty (Cherokee and U.S.)
Sept 20 Agency Treaty (Chickasaw and U.S.)
Oct 24 Agency Treaty (Choctaw and U.S.)
Dec 10 Senate Committee on Foreign Relations
Dec 13 James Barbour (Senate Foreign Relations Committee)

1817

Mar 30 Treaty of St. Louis (Menominee and U.S.)
Apr 29 Rush-Bagot Agreement (U.K. and U.S.)
Jun 24 Treaty of St. Louis (Oto and U.S.)
Jun 25 Treaty of St. Louis (Ponca and U.S.)
Jul 8 Agency Treaty (Cherokee and U.S.)
Sept 22 John Quincy Adams (Secretary of State)
Sept 29 Treaty of the Miami River (Multitribal)

1818

* * Nathaniel Macon (Senate Foreign Relations Committee)
Jan 1 Commerce and Sea—Argentina (unperfected)
Jan 3 Treaty of Vincennes (Piankeshaw and U.S.)

Jan 22 Treaty of the Flint River (Creek and U.S.)
Apr 29 Ambrister and Arbuthnot Affair (U.K. and U.S.)
Jun 18 Treaty of St. Louis (Grand Pawnee and U.S.)
Jun 19 Treaty of St. Louis (Noisy Pawnee and U.S.)
Jun 20 Treaty of St. Louis (Pawnee and U.S.)
Jun 22 Treaty of St. Louis (Pawnee and U.S.)
Aug 24 Treaty of St. Louis (Quapaw and U.S.)
Sept 17 Treaty of St. Mary's (Multitribal)
Sept 20 Treaty of St. Mary's (U.S. and Wyandot)
Sept 25 Treaty of Edwardsville (Multitribal)
Sept 25 Treaty of St. Louis (Osage and U.S.)
Oct 2 Treaty of St. Mary's (Potawatomi and U.S.)
Oct 2 Treaty of St. Mary's (U.S. and Wea)
Oct 3 Treaty of St. Mary's (Delaware and U.S.)
Oct 6 Treaty of St. Mary's (Miami and U.S.)
Oct 19 Treaty of Old Town (Chickasaw and U.S.)
Oct 20 Convention of 1818 (U.K. and U.S.)

1819
* * James Brown (Senate Foreign Relations Committee)
Feb 22 Adams-Onis Treaty (Spain and U.S.)
Feb 27 Treaty of Washington (Cherokee and U.S.)
Jul 30 Treaty of Edwardsville (Kickapoo and U.S.)
Aug 30 Treaty of Fort Harrison (Kickapoo and U.S.)
Sept 24 Treaty of Saginaw (Chippewa and U.S.)

1820
* * James Barbour (Senate Foreign Relations Committee)
Jun 16 Treaty of Sault de Ste. Marie (Chippewa and U.S.)
Jul 6 Treaty of L'Arbre Croche and Michilimackinac (Multitribal)
Jul 19 Treaty of St. Louis (Kickapoo and U.S.)
Aug 11 Treaty of St. Mary's (U.S. and Wea)
Sept 5 Treaty of Vincennes (Kickapoo and U.S.)
Oct 18 Treaty of Doak's Stand (Choctaw and U.S.)

1821
* * Rufus King (Senate Foreign Relations Committee)
Jan 8 Treaty of Indian Springs (Creek and U.S.)
Aug 29 Treaty of Chicago (Multitribal)

1822

** Jonathan Russell (House Foreign Affairs Committee)
 ** James Barbour (Senate Foreign Relations Committee)
Mar 13 House Committee on Foreign Affairs
Aug 31 Treaty of Marais des Cygnes Factory (Osage and U.S.)
Sept 3 Treaty of Fort Armstrong (Multitribal)
Sept 7 Brazil declares independence from Portugal

1823

** John Forsyth (House Foreign Affairs Committee)
Aug 20 Memorandum (George Canning to Richard Rush)
Sept 3 Treaty of Moscow—Seneca (unperfected)
Sept 18 Treaty of Moultrie Creek (Florida Tribes and U.S.)
Oct 9 Polignac Memorandum (France and U.K.)
Dec 2 Monroe Doctrine
Dec 16 Diplomatic relations (Columbia)
Dec 27 Diplomatic relations (Argentina)

1824

Mar 13 Suppression of the African Slave Trade—U.K. (unperfected)
Apr 17 Treaty of St. Petersburg
Apr 23 Diplomatic relations (Chile)
Aug 4 Treaty at Washington (Iowa and U.S.)
Nov 15 Treaty of Harrington's (Quapaw and U.S.)
Dec 10 Suppression of the African Slave Trade— Columbia (unperfected)

1825

** Nathaniel Macon (Senate Foreign Relations Committee)
Jan 20 Treaty of Washington (Choctaw and U.S.)
Feb 12 Treaty of Indian Springs (Creek and U.S.)
Feb 18 Anglo-Russian Convention
Mar 7 Henry Clay (Secretary of State)
Mar 9 Convention with Columbia for slave trade suppression rejected
by U.S. Senate (first international treaty so treated)
Jun 1 Diplomatic relations (Mexico)
Jun 2 Treaty of St. Louis (Osage and U.S.)
Jun 3 Treaty of St. Louis (Kansa and U.S.)
Jun 9 Treaty of White Paint Creek (Ponca and U.S.)
Jun 22 Treaty of Fort Look-Out (Sioux and U.S.)

Jun 29 Treaty of Broken Arrow—Creek (unperfected)
Jul 5 Treaty of the Teton River (Sioux and U.S.)
Jul 6 Treaty of the Teton River (Cheyenne and U.S.)
Jul 16 Treaty of Arikara Village (Sioux and U.S.)
Jul 18 Treaty of Arikara Village (Arikara and U.S.)
Jul 30 Treaty of Lower Mandan Village (Minitaree and U.S.)
Jul 30 Treaty of Lower Mandan Village (Mandan and U.S.)
Aug 10 Treaty of Council Grove (Osage and U.S.)
Aug 16 Treaty of Sora Kansas Creek (Kansa and U.S.)
Aug 19 Treaty of Prairie de Chien (Multitribal)
Sept 26 Treaty of Fort Atkinson (Multitribal)
Sept 30 Treaty of Fort Atkinson (Pawnee and U.S.)
Oct 6 Treaty of Fort Atkinson (Omaha and U.S.)
Oct 29 Diplomatic relations (Brazil)
Nov 7 Treaty of St. Louis (Shawnee and U.S.)

1826
* * Nathan Sanford (Senate Foreign Relations Committee)
Jan 24 Treaty of Washington (Creek and U.S.)
May 3 Diplomatic relations (Guatemala)
Jun 22 Congress of Panama (ends 15 July)
Jul 10 Treaty of Amity, Commerce and Navigation—Mexico (unperfected)
Aug 5 Treaty of Fond du Lac (Chippewa and U.S.)
Oct 16 Treaty of Wabash River (Potawatomi and U.S.)
Oct 23 Treaty of Wabash River (Miami and U.S.)

1827
* * Edward Everett (House Foreign Affairs Committee)
* * Nathaniel Macon (Senate Foreign Relations Committee
May 21 Diplomatic relations (Peru)
Aug 11 Treaty of Butte des Morts (Multitribal)
Sept 19 Treaty of St. Joseph (Potawatomi and U.S.)
Sept 20 Diplomatic relations (Denmark)
Sept 29 Convention of 1827—U.K. (unperfected)
Nov 15 Agency Treaty (Creek and U.S.)

1828
* * Littleton W. Tazewell (Senate Foreign Relations Committee)
Feb 11 Treaty of Wyandot Village (Miami and U.S.)

Feb 14 Amity, Commerce and Navigation—Mexico (unperfected)
May 6 Treaty of Washington (Cherokee and U.S.)
Aug 25 Treaty of Green Bay (Multitribal)
Sept 20 Treaty of the St. Joseph River (Potawatomi and U.S.)

1829
** William S. Archer (House Foreign Affairs Committee)
Mar 28 Martin Van Buren (Secretary of State)
Jul 29 Treaty of Prairie du Chien (Multitribal)
Aug 1 Treaty of Prairie du Chien (U.S. and Winnebago)
Aug 3 Treaty of Little Sandusky (Delaware and U.S.)
Sept 24 Treaty of the White River (Delaware and U.S.)

1830
May 7 Treaty of Constantinople (Turkey and U.S.)
Jul 15 Treaty of Prairie du Chien (Multitribal)
Aug 31 Treaty of Franklin—Chickasaw (unperfected)
Sept 27 Treaty of Dancing Rabbit Creek (Choctaw and U.S.)

1831
Feb 8 Treaty of Washington (Menominee and U.S.)
Feb 17 Treaty of Washington (Menominee and U.S.)
Feb 28 Treaty of Washington (Seneca and U.S.)
Apr 5 Boundary Agreement (Mexico and U.S.)
May 24 Edward Livingston (Secretary of State)
Jul 4 Claims Convention (France and U.S.)
Jul 20 Treaty of Lewistown (Multitribal)
Aug 8 Treaty of Wapakoneta (Shawnee and U.S.)
Aug 30 Treaty of Miami Bay (Ottawa and U.S.)
Sept 13 Diplomatic relations (Turkey)

1832
** John Forsyth (Senate Foreign Relations Committee)
Jan 19 Treaty of McCutcheonsville (U.S. and Wyandot)
Jan 25 Diplomatic relations (Kingdom of Two Sicilies)
Mar 24 Treaty of Washington (Creek and U.S.)
May 9 Treaty of Payne's Landing (Seminole and U.S.)
Sept 15 Treaty of Fort Armstrong (U.S. and Winnebago)
Sept 21 Treaty of Fort Armstrong (Multitribal)
Sept 25 Diplomatic relations (Belgium)

Oct 11 Treaty of Tallahassee (Appalachicola and U.S.)
Oct 20 Treaty of Camp Tippecanoe (Potawatomi and U.S.)
Oct 20 Treaty of Pontotoc Creek (Chickasaw and U.S.)
Oct 24 Treaty of Castor Hill (Kickapoo and U.S.)
Oct 26 Treaty of Tippecanoe River (Potawatomi and U.S.)
Oct 26 Treaty of Castor Hill (Multitribal)
Oct 27 Treaty of Tippecanoe River (Potawatomi and U.S.)
Oct 27 Treaty of Castor Hill (Multitribal)
Oct 27 Treaty of Washington (Menominee and U.S.)
Oct 29 Treaty of Castor Hill (Multitribal)
Dec 18 Commerce and Navigation Treaty (Russia)
Dec 29 Treaty of Cowskin River (Multitribal)

1833
* * William Wilkins (Senate Foreign Relations Committee)
Jan 23 Peace, Friendship and Amity—Belgium (unperfected)
Feb 14 Treaty of Fort Gibson (Cherokee and U.S.)
Feb 14 Treaty of Fort Gibson (Creek and U.S.)
Feb 18 Treaty of Maumee (Ottawa and U.S.)
Mar 20 Treaty of Amity and Commerce (Thailand)
Mar 28 Treaty of Fort Gibson (Seminole and U.S.)
May 13 Treaty of New Gascony (Quapaw and U.S.)
May 29 Louis McLane (Secretary of State)
Jun 18 Treaty of Fayette County (Appalachicola and U.S.)
Sept 21 Treaty of Platte River (Multitribal)
Sept 26 Treaty of Chicago (Multitribal)
Oct 9 Treaty of Platee River (Pawnee and U.S.)

1834
* * Henry Clay (Senate Foreign Relations Committee)
May 24 Treaty of Washington (Chickasaw and U.S.)
Jul 1 John Forsyth (Secretary of State)
Oct 23 Treaty of the Wabash River (Miami and U.S.)
Dec 4 Treaty of Lake Maxinkuuee (Potawatomi and U.S.)
Dec 10 Treaty of Tippecanoe River (Potawatomi and U.S.)
Dec 16 Treaty of Potawatomi Mills (Potawatomi and U.S.)
Dec 17 Treaty of Logansport (Potawatomi and U.S.)

1835
* * James M. Wayne (House Foreign Affairs Committee)
 * * Edward Everett (House Foreign Affairs Committee)

* * Churchill C. Cambreleng (House Foreign Affairs Committee)
* * John Y. Mason (House Foreign Affairs Committee)
Mar 6 Property Rights— Switzerland (unperfected)
Mar 14 Treaty of Washington— Cherokee (unperfected)
Jun 30 Diplomatic relations (Venezuela)
Jul 1 Agency Treaty (Caddo and U.S.)
Aug 24 Treaty of Camp Holmes (Multitribal)
Dec 26 Claims— Kingdom of the Two Sicilies (unperfected)
Dec 29 Treaty of New Echota (Cherokee and U.S.)

1836
* * James Buchanan (Senate Foreign Relations Committee)
Mar 26 Treaty of Turkey Creek Prairie (Potawatomi and U.S.)
Mar 28 Treaty of Washington (Multitribal)
Mar 29 Treaty of Tippecanoe River (Potawatomi and U.S.)
Apr 11 Treaty of Tippecanoe River (Potawatomi and U.S.)
Apr 22 Agency Treaty (Potawatomi and U.S.)
Apr 23 Treaty of Washington (U.S. and Wyandot)
May 9 Treaty of Washington (Chippewa and U.S.)
Aug 5 Treaty of the Yellow River (Potawatomi and U.S.)
Sept 3 Treaty of Cedar Point (Menominee and U.S.)
Sept 10 Treaty of Cedar Point (Sioux and U.S.)
Sept 17 Treaty of Fort Leavenworth (Multitribal)
Sept 20 Treaty of Chippewanaung (Potawatomi and U.S.)
Sept 22 Treaty of Chippewanaung (Potawatomi and U.S.)
Sept 23 Treaty of Chippewanaung (Potawatomi and U.S.)
Sept 27 Treaty of Rock Island (Multitribal)
Sept 28 Treaty of Rock Island (Multitribal)
Oct 15 Treaty of Bellevue (Multitribal)
Nov 30 Treaty of St. Peter's (Sioux and U.S.)

1837
* * Benjamin C. Howard (House Foreign Affairs Committee)
Jan 14 Treaty of Detroit (Chippewa and U.S.)
Jan 17 Treaty of Doaksville (Multitribal)
Feb 11 Treaty of Washington (Potawatomi and U.S.)
May 26 Treaty of Fort Gibson (Multitribal)
Jul 29 Treaty of St. Peter's (Chippewa and U.S.)
Sept 29 Treaty of Washington (Sioux and U.S.)
Oct 21 Treaty of Washington (Multitribal)

Oct 21 Treaty of Washington (Sioux and U.S.)
Oct 21 Treaty of Washington (Multitribal)
Oct 27 Diplomatic relations (Republic of Texas)
Nov 1 Treaty of Washington (U.S. and Winnebago)
Nov 23 Treaty of St. Louis (Iowa and U.S.)
Dec 20 Treaty of Flint River (Chippewa and U.S.)
Dec 29 SS *Caroline* Incident (U.K. and U.S.)

1838
* * Francis W. Pickens (House Foreign Affairs Committee)
Jan 15 Treaty of Buffalo Creek (New York Indians and U.S.)
Jan 23 Treaty of Saganaw (Chippewa and U.S.)
Feb 3 Treaty of Washington (Oneida and U.S.)
Feb 8 Diplomatic relations (Austria)
May 29 *Sir Robert Peel* Incident (U.K. and U.S.)
Jul 14 Peace, Amity, Commerce and Navigation—Central American
Federation (unperfected)
Sept 10 Adjustment of Claims—Mexico (unperfected)
Oct 19 Agency Treaty (Iowa and U.S.)
Nov 6 Treaty of the Wabash River (Miami and U.S.)
Nov 23 Treaty of Fort Gibson (Creek and U.S.)

1839
Jan 11 Treaty of Fort Gibson (Osage and U.S.)
Feb 7 Treaty of Lower Saginaw (Chippewa and U.S.)
Mar 3 Congress approves military force (Aroostook War)
Aug 26 USS *Washington* seizes *Armistad*
Sept 3 Treaty of Stockbridge (Multitribal)
Nov 3 State of War—China and U.K. (ends 29 Aug 1842)

1840
Mar 29 Commerce and Navigation—Belgium (unperfected)
Sept 15 Diplomatic relations (Italy)
Nov 12 Alexander McLeod arrested for murder (*Caroline* Incident)
Nov 28 Treaty of Wabash River (Miami and U.S.)

1841
* * Caleb Cushing (House Foreign Affairs Committee)
* * William C. Rives (Senate Foreign Relations Committee)
Mar 6 Daniel Webster (Secretary of State)

Mar 9 *U.S. v. Amistad* (Supreme Court)
Oct 12 Alexander McLeod acquitted by New York court
Nov 7 Mutiny aboard *Creole*

1842
* * John Q. Adams (House Foreign Affairs Committee)
 * * William S. Rives (Senate Foreign Relations Committee)
Jan 29 *Creole* Incident
Mar 17 Treaty of Upper Sandusky (U.S. and Wyandot)
May 20 Treaty of Buffalo Creek (Seneca and U.S.)
Jul 30 Treaty of Commerce—Texas (unperfected)
Aug 9 Webster-Ashburton Treaty (U.K. and U.S.)
Aug 29 Treaty of Nanking (China & U.K.)
Aug 29 Foreign National *Habeas Corpus* Act (Congress)
Oct 4 Treaty of La Pointe (Chippewa and U.S.)
Oct 11 Agency Treaty (Multitribal)
Dec 30 Tyler Corollary (Monroe Doctrine)

1843
* * Samuel W. Inge (House Foreign Affairs Committee)
Jul 24 Abel P. Upshur (Secretary of State)
Nov 20 Settlement of Claims—Mexico (unperfected)
Dec 4 President J. Tyler asserts extreme U.S. claim to Oregon Country

1844
Mar 25 Commerce—Prussia and other German states (unperfected)
Apr 1 John C. Calhoun (Secretary of State)
Apr 12 Upshur/Calhoun Annexation Treaty—Texas (unperfected)
Apr 15 Extradition—France (unperfected)
Apr 18 J. Calhoun sends pro-slavery dispatch to British Minister to U.S. (Richard Pakenham)
May 24 First commercial use of telegraph (Baltimore, MD to Washington, DC)
Jun 12 Diplomatic relations (China)
Jul 3 Treaty of Wang-Hsia (China and U.S.)
Sept 29 Vorhees Naval Incident (Argentina and U.S.)
Dec 20 Peace, Friendship, Navigation and Commerce—New Granada (unperfected)

1845
** William Allen (Senate Foreign Relations Committee)
Jan 4 Agency Treaty (Multitribal)
Jan 29 Extradition—Prussia and other German states (unperfected)
Mar 1 Annexation of Texas (President J. Tyler signs joint resolution of congress)
Mar 10 James Buchanan (Secretary of State)
Mar 28 Diplomatic relations suspended (Mexico)
Jul 4 Republic of Texas accepts annexation by U.S.
Oct 29   William A. Leidesdorff (first African American consul—Mexico)
Nov 7 Slidell mission (Mexico)
Dec 2 Polk Corollary (Monroe Doctrine)

1846
* * Ambrose H. Sevier (Senate Foreign Relations Committee)
Jan 14 Methodist Mission Treaty (Kansa and U.S.)
May 2 Droit d'Aubaine and Taxes on Emigration— Hesse-Cassel (unperfected)
May 13 State of War—Mexico and U.S. (ends 2 Feb 1848)
May 15 Treaty of Council Springs (Multitribal)
Jun 5 Treaty of Council Springs & Pottawatomie Creek (Multitribal)
Jun 15 Buchanan-Pakenham Treaty (U.K. and U.S.)
Jun 17 Treaty of Council Springs & Pottawatomie Creek (Multitribal)
Aug 6 Treaty of Washington (Cherokee and U.S.)
Sept 15 Extradition—Switzerland (unperfected)
Oct 13 Treaty of Washington (U.S. and Winnebago)
Dec 12 Bidlack's Treaty (Columbia and U.S.)

1847
* * Truman Smith (House Foreign Affairs Committee)
Jan 13 Treaty of Cahuenga ends hostilities in California
Aug 2 Treaty of Fond du Lac (Chippewa and U.S.)
Aug 21 Treaty of Leech Lake (Chippewa and U.S.)
Aug 24 Armistice of Tacubaya—ends 7 Sept (Mexico and U.S.)
Dec 11 Congress of Lima (ends 1 March 1848)

1848
** Edward A. Hannegan (Senate Foreign Relations Committee)
Feb 2 Treaty of Guadalupe-Hildalgo (Mexico and U.S.)

Feb 9 Peace, Friendship, Commerce and Navigation— Peru (unperfected)
Aug 6 Treaty of Fort Childs (Pawnee and U.S.)
Aug 7 Diplomatic relations (Vatican)
Aug 12 Diplomatic relations (Ecuador)
Aug 21 Ministers and consuls in China and Turkey empowered to punish U.S. citizens who commit criminal acts (Congress)
Oct 18 Treaty of Lake Powawhaykonnay (Menominee and U.S.)
Nov 24 Agency Treaty (Stockbridge and U.S.)

1849
** John A. McClernand (House Foreign Affairs Committee)
** William R. King (Senate Foreign Relations Committee)
Jan 3 Diplomatic relations (Bolivia)
Mar 8 John M. Clayton (Secretary of State)
Mar 17 Diplomatic relations (Egypt)
May 28 Peace, Amity, Commerce and Navigation— Honduras (unperfected)
May 31 Peace, Amity, Commerce and Navigation— Nicaragua (unperfected)
Jun 21 Construction of ship canal—Nicaragua (unperfected)
Sept 3 Amity, Navigation and Commerce—Nicaragua (unperfected)
Sept 9 Treaty of Canyon de Cheille (Navaho and U.S.)
Sept 28 Amity, Navigation and Commerce—Honduras (unperfected)
Oct 22 Amity, Navigation and Commerce—Hawaii (unperfected)
Dec 6 Friendship, Commerce and Navigation—Hawaii (unperfected)
Dec 30 Treaty of Abiquiu (Utah and U.S.)

1850
** Henry S. Foote (Senate Foreign Relations Committee)
Apr 1 Treaty of Washington (U.S. and Wyandot)
Apr 19 Clayton-Bulwer Treaty (U.K. and U.S.)
Jun 20 Passage across Isthmus of Tehuantepec—Mexico (unperfected)
Jul 13 Peace, Friendship, Commerce and Navigation— Peru (unperfected)
Jul 20 Extradition—Mexico (unperfected)
Jul 23 Daniel Webster (Secretary of State)

1851
** Thomas H. Bayly (House Foreign Affairs Committee)
** James M. Mason (Senate Foreign Relations Committee)

Jan 25 Passage across Isthmus of Tehuantepec—Mexico (unperfected)
Mar 19 Treaty of Camp Fremont—Multitribal (unperfected)
Apr 29 Treaty of Camp Barbour—Multitribal (unperfected)
May 13 Treaty of Camp Belt—Multitribal (unperfected)
May 28 Treaty of Stanislaus River—Multitribal (unperfected)
May 30 Treaty of Camp Keyes—Multitribal (unperfected)
Jun 3 Treaty of Camp Burton—Multitribal (unperfected)
Jul 18 Treaty of Camp Union—Multitribal (unperfected)
Jul 23 Treaty of the Traverse des Sioux (Sioux and U.S.)
Aug 1 Treaty of Chico Creek—Multitribal (unperfected)
Aug 5 Treaty of Mendota (Sioux and U.S.)
Aug 16 Treaty of Cotton Wood Creek—Multitribal (unperfected)
Aug 20 Treaty of Russian River—Multitribal (unperfected)
Sept 17 Treaty of Fort Laramie—Multitribal (unperfected)
Oct 6 Treaty of Camp Kalmath—Multitribal (unperfected)
Oct 9 Friendship, Commerce and Navigation—Persia (unperfected)
Nov 4 Treaty of Camp Scott—Multitribal (unperfected)

1852
Jan 5 Treaty of Temecula—Multitribal (unperfected)
Jan 7 Treaty of Santa Ysabel—Dieguino (unperfected)
Jan 24 Passage across Isthmus of Tehuantepec—Mexico (unperfected)
Feb 18 Diplomatic relations (Nicaragua)
Apr 30 Nicaragua and Costa Rica dispute—U.K. (unperfected)
Jun 22 Treaty of Washington (Chickasaw and U.S.)
Jul 1 Treaty of Santa Fe (Apache and U.S.)
Aug 25 Property rights—Belgium (unperfected)
Aug 28 Friendship, commerce and navigations-Uruguay (unperfected)
Nov 6 Edward Everett (Secretary of State)

1853
Jan 2 Individual claim—New Granada (unperfected)
Feb 11 Extradition—Belgium (unperfected)
Feb 17 International copyright—U.K. (unperfected)
Mar 4 Friendship, commerce and navigation—Paraguay (unperfected)
Mar 8 William L. Marcy (Secretary of State)
Mar 21 Passage across Isthmus of Tehuantepec—Mexico (unperfected)
Jun 29 Diplomatic relations (Switzerland)
Jul 6 Diplomatic relations (Hawaii)
Jul 8 Matthew C. Perry, USN, arrives Tokyo (Yedo) Bay

Jul 27 Treaty of Fort Atkinson (Multitribal)
Aug 11 Copyright—France (unperfected)
Sept 8 Treaty of Table Rock—Rogue River (unperfected)
Sept 10 Treaty of Table Rock (Rogue River and U.S.)
Sept 19 Treaty of Cow Creek (Umpqua and U.S.)
Dec 20 Diplomatic relations (Hawaii)
Dec 30 Gadsden Treaty (Mexico and U.S.)

1854
Feb 8 International Copyright—U.K. (unperfected)
Feb 14 Peace, Amity, Commerce, Navigation and Protection—Nicaragua (unperfected)
Feb 28 *Black Warrior* Affair (Spain and U.S.)
Mar 15 Treaty of Washington (Multitribal)
Mar 16 Treaty of Washington (Omaha and U.S.)
Mar 28 State of War—France, Kingdom of Sardina, Russia and U.K. (ends 1 Feb 1856)
Mar 31 Treaty of Kanagawa (Japan and U.S.)
May 6 Treaty of Washington (Delaware and U.S.)
May 10 Treaty of Washington (Shawnee and U.S.)
May 12 Treaty of the Wolf River (Menominee and U.S.)
May 17 Treaty of Washington (Iowa and U.S.)
May 18 Treaty of Washington (Multitribal)
May 18 Treaty of Washington (Kickapoo and U.S.)
May 30 Treaty of Washington (Multitribal)
Jun 5 Marcy-Elgin Reciprocity and Fisheries Treaty (U.K. and U.S)
Jun 5 Treaty of Washington (Miami and U.S.)
Jun 13 Treaty of Washington (Creek and U.S.)
Sept 20 Peace, Friendship, Navigation and Commerce— Venezuela (unperfected)
Sept 30 Treaty of La Pointe (Chippewa and U.S.)
Oct 5 Friendship, Commerce and Navigation—Dominican Republic (unperfected)
Oct 18 Ostend Manifesto (Spain and U.S.)
Nov 4 Treaty of Doaksville (Multitribal)
Nov 15 Treaty of Table Rock (Rogue River and U.S.)
Nov 18 Treaty of Applegate Creek (Multitribal)
Nov 20 Purchase and sale of guano—Ecuador (unperfected)
Nov 29 Treaty of Calapooia Creek (Multitribal)
Dec 9 Treaty of Nebraska City (Multitribal)

Dec 26 Treaty of Medicine Creek (Multitribal)

1855
** Alexander C. M. Pennington (House Foreign Affairs Committee)
Jan 8 Rights of Neutrals at Sea—Mexico (unperfected)
Jan 22 Treaty of Dayton (Multitribal)
Jan 22 Treaty of Point Elliott (Multitribal)
Jan 26 Treaty of Point No Point (Multitribal)
Jan 31 Treaty of Washington (U.S. and Wyandot)
Jan 31 Treaty of Neah Bay (Makah and U.S.)
Feb 22 Treaty of Washington (Chippewa and U.S.)
Feb 27 Treaty of Washington (U.S. and Winnebago)
Mar 10 Neutral rights—Venezuela (unperfected)
Jun 9 Treaty of Camp Stevens (Multitribal)
Jun 9 Treaty of Camp Stevens (U.S. and Yakima)
Jun 11 Treaty of Camp Stevens (Nez Perce and U.S.)
Jun 20   Friendship, Commerce and Navigation—Nicaragua (unperfected)
Jun 22 Treaty of Washington (Multitribal)
Jun 25 Treaty of The Dalles (Multitribal)
Jul 1 Treaty of Quinault River (Multitribal)
Jul 16 Treaty of Bitter Root Valley (Multitribal)
Jul 20 Commercial reciprocity treaty—Hawaii (unperfected)
Jul 31 Treaty of Detroit (Multitribal)
Aug 2 Treaty of Detroit (Chippewa of the Sault Ste. Marie and U.S.)
Aug 2 Treaty of Detroit (Chippewa of Saginaw and U.S.)
Aug 7 Agency Treaty—Shoshoni (unperfected)
Aug 8 Treaty of Abiquiu—Utah (unperfected)
Oct 17 Treaty of the Judith River (Multitribal)
Dec 21 Treaty of Dayton (Molala and U.S.)

1856
Jan 25 Treaty of Olympia (Multitribal)
Feb 5 Agency Treaty (Multitribal)
Feb 11 Treaty of Keshena (Menominee & U.S.)
Mar 8 Peace, Amity, Commerce, Navigation and Extradition—Dominican Republic (unperfected)
Mar 10 Extradition—Baden (unperfected)
Apr 9 Rights of Neutrals at Sea—Ecuador (unperfected)
Apr 16 Declaration of Paris

May 27 Friendship, Commerce, Navigation and Extradition—Chile (unperfected)

May 28 Amity and Commerce (Siam and U.S.)

May 29 Extradition—Netherlands (unperfected)

Jul 10 Amity, Commerce, Navigation and Extradition— Venezuela (unperfected)

Jul 28 U.S. rejects Declaration of Paris

Aug 7 Treaty of Washington (Multitribal)

Aug 18 U.S. consuls become salaried officials (Congress)

Aug 25 Settlement of Questions Relative to Central America—U.K. (unperfected)

Aug 27 Settlement of Questions Relative to Central America—U.K. (unperfected)

Sept 29 Friendship, Commerce and Navigation—Buenos Aires (unperfected)

Oct 17 Settlement of Questions Relative to Central America—U.K. (unperfected)

Dec 1 Rights, Privileges and Duties of Consuls— Chile (unperfected)

1857

* * Thomas L. Clingman (House Foreign Affairs Committee)

Feb 10 Bases for Other Conventions—Mexico (unperfected)

Feb 10 Settlement of Claims, Loans and Anticipation of Duties— Mexico (unperfected)

Feb 10 Postal Convention—Mexico (unperfected)

Feb 10 Commercial Reciprocity across the Frontier— Mexico (unperfected)

Mar 6 Lewis Cass (Secretary of State)

May 25 State of War—China, France and U.K. (ends 14 Nov 1860)

Jun 17 Shimoda Convention (Japan and U.S.)

Aug 21 Extradition—Netherlands (unperfected)

Sept 24 Treaty of Table Creek (Pawnee and U.S.)

Nov 5 Agency Treaty (Seneca and U.S.)

Nov 16 Cass-Yrissarri Treaty—Nicaragua (unperfected)

1858

* * George W. Hopkins (House Foreign Affairs Committee)

Apr 19 Treaty of Washington (Sioux and U.S.)

May 12 Treaty of Washington (Ponca and U.S.)

Aug 5 Trans-Atlantic cable completed (service disrupted within five weeks)

Jun 18 Treaty of Tientsin (China and U.S.)

Jun 19 Treaty of Washington (Sioux and U.S.)

Jul 18 Amity, Commerce, Navigation and Extradition— Venezuela (unperfected)

Jul 29 Treaty of Edo (Japan and U.S.)

Aug 10 Diplomatic relations (Honduras)

1859

* * Thomas Corwin (House Foreign Affairs Committee)

Mar 16 Friendship, Commerce and Navigation—Nicaragua (unperfected)

Apr 15 Treaty of Washington (U.S. and Winnebago)

Apr 20 Interior Commerce between the Frontiers—Mexico (unperfected)

Jun 25 Taku Naval Incident (China and U.S.)

Jul 16 Agency Treaty (Multitribal)

Oct 1 Agency Treaty (Multitribal)

Oct 5 Agency Treaty (Kansa and U.S.)

Nov 5 Diplomatic relations (Japan)

Dec 14 McLane-Ocampo Treaty—Mexico (unperfected)

Dec 14 Enforcement of Treaty Stipulations and Maintenance of Order and Security—Mexico (unperfected)

1860

Mar 5 Claims—Spain (unperfected)

Mar 28 Friendship, Commerce and Navigation—Honduras (unperfected)

May 30 Treaty of Sarcoxieville (Delaware and U.S.)

Dec 17 Jeremiah S. Black (Secretary of State)

1861

* * John J. Crittenden (House Foreign Affairs Committee)

* * Charles Sumner (Senate Foreign Relations Committee)

Feb 18 Treaty of Fort Wise (Multitribal)

Mar 6 Agency Treaty (Multitribal)

Mar 6 William H. Seward (Secretary of State)

Apr 19 U.S. proclaims naval blockade of Confederate States of America (extended on 27 April)

May 6 U.K. proclaims neutrality in regard to conflict in North America

Jul 2 Treaty of Leavenworth (Delaware and U.S.)

Jul 31 Postal Convention—Mexico (unperfected)

Aug 24 Rights of Belligerent and Neutrals in Time of War—Russia (unperfected)

Sept 14 Diplomatic relations (Costa Rica)

Oct 24 First transcontinental telegraph message (San Francisco, CA to Washington, DC.)

Oct 31 Convention of London (France, Spain and U.K.)

Nov 8 SS *Trent* Affair—U.K. and U.S. (ends 26 Dec 1861)

Nov 15 Agency Treaty (Potawatomi and U.S.)

Nov 26 Diplomatic relations (Paraguay)

Dec 3 Annual publication of diplomatic correspondence (*Foreign Relations of the United States* series)

1862

Mar 13 Agency Treaty (Kansa and U.S.)

Apr 7 African Slave Trade Treaty (U.K. and U.S.)

May 29 Amity, Commerce, Consular Privileges and Extradition—Salvador (unperfected)

Jun 9 Regulation of Communication by Post—Costa Rica (unperfected)

Jun 24 Treaty of Washington (Ottawa and U.S.)

Jun 28 Agency Treaty (Kickapoo and U.S.)

Aug 17 CSS *Florida* commissioned

Aug 24 CSS *Alabama* commissioned

Oct 1 Diplomatic relations (Haiti)

1863

** Henry W. Davis (House Foreign Affairs Committee)

Mar 11 Treaty of Washington (Chippewa and U.S.)

Apr 5 SS *Alexandra* seized (U.K.)

May 10 Friendship, Commerce and Navigation—Honduras (unperfected)

Jun 9 Treaty of Lapwai Valley (Nez Perce and U.S.)

Jun 15 Diplomatic relations (El Salvador)

Jun 23 Seizure of SS *Alexandra* invalidated (U.K.)

Jul 2 Treaty of Fort Bridger (Shoshoni and U.S.)

Jul 30 Treaty of Box Elder (Shoshoni and U.S.)

Aug 29 Treaty of Leroy—Osage (unperfected)

Sept 3 Laird Rams seized (U.K.)
Sept 13 Maritime Jurisdiction in Cuban Waters — Spain (unperfected)
Sept 17 Maritime Jurisdiction in Cuban Waters — Spain (unperfected)
Sept 18 Maritime Jurisdiction in Cuban Waters — Spain (unperfected)
Oct 1 Treaty of Ruby Valley (Shoshoni and U.S.)
Oct 2 Treaty of the Red Lake River (Chippewa and U.S.)
Oct 7 Agency Treaty (Utah and U.S.)
Oct 12 Treaty of Tuilla Valley (Shoshoni and U.S.)
Oct 14 Treaty of Soda Springs — Multitribal (unperfected)
Dec 15 Emigration from the U.S. to Surinam of Persons of African Extraction — Netherlands (unperfected)

1864
Feb 23 Diplomatic relations (Liberia)
Apr 10 Archduke Maximilian of Austria proclaimed Emperor of Mexico
Apr 12 Treaty of Washington (Chippewa and U.S.)
Apr 14 State of War — Peru and Spain (ends 9 May 1866)
May 7 Treaty of Washington (Chippewa and U.S.)
Jun 19 USS *Kearsarge* destroys CSS *Alabama*
Jun 20 Consuls recognized as professional staff (Congress)
Oct 7 USS *Wachusett* removes CSS *Florida* from Bahia, Brazil
Oct 14 Treaty of Klamath Lake (Multiltribal)
Oct 18 Agency Treaty (Chippewa and U.S.)
Oct 18 CSS *Shenandoah* commissioned
Nov 14 Congress of Lima (ends 13 March 1865)

1865
** Nathaniel P. Banks (House Foreign Affairs Committee)
Mar 6 Treaty of Washington (Omaha and U.S.)
Mar 8 Treaty of Washington (U.S. and Winneabago)
Mar 10 Treaty of Washington (Ponca and U.S.)
May 1 State of War — Argentina, Brazil, Paraguay and Uruguay (ends 1 March 1870)
Jun 8 Treaty of Spanish Fork — Multitribal (unperfected)
Aug 12 Treaty of the Sprague River (Snake and U.S.)
Sept 13 Treaty of Fort Smith — Multitribal (unperfected)
Sept 29 Agency Treaty (Osage and U.S.)
Oct 10 Treaty of Fort Sully (Sioux and U.S.)
Oct 14 Treaty of Fort Sully (Sioux and U.S.)

Oct 14 Treaty of the Little Arkansas River (Multitribal)
Oct 17 Treaty of the Little Arkansas River (Multitribal)
Oct 18 Treaty of the Little Arkansas River (Multitribal)
Oct 19 Treaty of Fort Sully (Sioux and U.S.)
Oct 20 Treaty of Fort Sully (Sioux and U.S.)
Oct 28 Treaty of Fort Sully (Sioux and U.S.)
Nov 6 CSS *Shenandoah* surrenders (London)
Nov 15 Agency Treaty (Multitribal)
Nov 16 Treaty of Fort Benton—Blackfeet (unperfected)

TREATIES, AGREEMENTS, SUPREME COURT CASES AND ACTS OF CONGRESS

RUSH-BAGOT AGREEMENT (1817) U.K. and U.S. Neither party to maintain any armed naval forces on the Great Lakes except revenue cutters of a stipulated size (one each on Lakes Ontario and Champlain and two on the upper lakes). Approved by U.S. Senate as a treaty 16 April 1818. Amended 6 September 1940, to allow for the construction of warships. The first U.S. arms control agreement and first international instance of reciprocal naval disarmament.

CONVENTION OF 1818. U.K. and U.S. Freedom of commercial intercourse (Canada and West Indies excluded), exchange of consuls, prohibition of discriminating duties, extended northern boundary from Lake of the Woods westward along the 49th parallel to the Rocky Mountains, fishing liberties along the eastern coast of Canada, joint occupation of the Oregon country for ten years and arbitration of claims by Americans for slaves removed by British forces during the War of 1812.

ADAMS-ONIS TREATY (1819) Spain and U.S. Also known as the Transcontinental Treaty. It established the western boundary of the Louisiana Purchase. U.S. renounced claim to Texas and Spain relinquished Florida. U.S. assumed claims of citizens against Spain to a limit of $5 million and Spain abandoned its right to navigate the Mississippi River. A delay in Spanish ratification required a renewed approval by the United States (1821).

TREATY OF ST. PETERSBURG (1824) Russia and U.S. Established the southern boundary of Russian America (Alaska) at 54 degrees 40 minutes north latitude.

ANGLO-RUSSIAN CONVENTION (1825) Russia and U.K. Established boundary between Russian America (Alaska) and British North America (Canada) at roughly what exists today. See Hay-Herbert Treaty (1903)

TREATY OF CONSTANTINOPLE (1830) Turkey and U.S. First treaty according American citizens unrestricted extraterritoriality. Immunity eliminated in 1923.

BOUNDARY AGREEMENT (1831) Mexico and U.S. Mexico accepts Sabine River as boundary betwixt Louisiana and Texas as per Adams-Onis Treaty (1819/21). An earlier treaty (12 Jan 1828) dealt with this issue but approval was not obtained in time so a new treaty was necessary.

U.S. v. AMISTAD (1841) This case involving the mutiny of African slaves on board the Spanish schooner *Amistad*. The ship made landfall on Long Island whereupon the slaves were taken into custody by an American naval officer. The Supreme Court ordered the slaves freed.

CREOLE INCIDENT (1842) The Creole was a U.S. ship carrying a cargo of slaves from Virginia to New Orleans. The slaves mutinied and sailed to Nassau in the Bahamas. When British authorities tried the mutineers but refused to return the others to American jurisdiction a dispute ensued that produced a protest to the British government by the Secretary of State. The controversy led to an extradition provision in the Webster-Ashburton Treaty (1842).

WEBSTER-ASHBURTON TREATY (1842) U.K. and U.S. Compromised disputed boundary between Maine and Quebec as well as adjusted boundary between New York, Vermont and Quebec. U.S. also acquired 6,500 square miles between Lake Superior and Lake of the Woods. Free navigation of St. John, Detroit, St. Clair rivers and Lake St. Clair as well as provided for extradition for all crimes except those of a political nature. Each nation agreed to station a naval squadron on African coast to enforce laws against the slave trade.

FOREIGN NATIONAL *HABEAS CORPUS ACT* (1842) Federal judges were accorded the power to release, under a writ of habeas corpus, any citizen of a foreign country imprisoned for an act committed under a commission, order or sanction of a foreign state or sovereignty under color of international law. This legislation was a consequence of the diplomatic imbroglio that eventuated upon the arrest and trial of a British national in connection with the *Caroline Affair*.

TYLER COROLLARY (1842) Extends the provisions of the Monroe Doctrine (1823) to include the Hawaiian Islands.

TREATY OF WANG-HSIA/WANGHSIA (1844) China and U.S. Modeled on the Treaty of Nanking (1842) it provided for consuls and trade at Canton, Amoy, Ningpo, Foochow and Shanghai as well as most-favored-nation guarantees. Extraterritoriality was established for all crimes save smuggling and opium traffic.

POLK COROLLARY (1845) This expansion of the Monroe Doctrine announced American opposition to voluntary transfers of territory in North America to European control.

BUCHANAN-PAKENHAM TREATY (1846) U.K. and U.S. Division of the disputed Oregon Country at 49 degrees north latitude on land. The ocean boundary passed mid-channel between the mainland and Vancouver Island and south through the Strait of Juan de Fuca to the Pacific. Navigation rights to the Columbia River were granted the U.K. Free navigation of the Strait of Juan de Fuca was guaranteed to both parties. A subsequent dispute over the Juan de Fuca boundary found solution in the Treaty of Washington (1871).

BIDLACK'S TREATY (1846) Columbia and U.S. Also known as the Polk-Mallarino Treaty. General treaty of amity, commerce and navigation which also granted the U.S. transit rights across the Isthmus of Panama in exchange for a guarantee of Columbia's sovereignty over that transit together with the neutrality of the area. Modified by Clayton-Bulwer (1850).

TREATY OF GUADALUPE-HIDALGO (1848) Mexico and U.S. Ended the Mexican-American War, established a boundary on the Rio Grande and ceded the territory between that river and the Pacific Ocean to the U.S. An indemnity of $15 million was granted to Mexico and the U.S. assumed claims by American citizens on Mexico up to $3.25 million.

CLAYTON-BULWER TREATY (1850) U.K. and U.S. Obligated each to renounce exclusive control over a canal through any part of Central America as well as any attempts to occupy, colonize, exercise dominion or erect fortifications therein. The neutrality of any canal built was guaranteed and equal treatment was afforded in the matter of tolls and charges. See also Hay-Pauncefote Treaty (1901).

TREATY OF FORT LARAMIE (1851) Arapaho, Arikara, Assiniboin, Cheyenne, Crow, Gros Ventre, Mandan, Sioux and U.S. This treaty was not perfected but later agreements recognized the treaty as in force. The treaty established formal relations with tribes resident in the northern plains. In an effort to secure passage for emigrants traveling to points west tribal boundaries were established and the U.S. was allowed to build roads and military installations. Travelers were allowed to collect damages for actions by persons connected with the named tribes. The tribes of the southern plains were governed by the Treaty of Fort Atkinson (1853)

GADSDEN TREATY (1853) Mexico and U.S. Provided for the purchase of 19 million acres south of the Gila River for $10 million. Allowed free passage through the Colorado River, the Gulf of California, the Rio Bravo and across the Isthmus of Tehuantepec. (Transit rights across the Isthmus of Tehuantepec canceled by mutual agreement in 1937.)

TREATY OF KANAGAWA (1854) Japan and U.S. Japan promised not to imprison shipwrecked sailors and opened the ports of Shimoda and Hakodate to trade under strict Japanese supervision. A most-favored-nation clause was part of the agreement, but no provision was made for extraterritoriality.

MARCY-ELGIN TREATY (1854) U.K. and U.S. Increased American fishing rights off Canadian coast and allowed Canadians to fish American waters down to Norfolk, Virginia. Certain commodities were reciprocally admitted without duties and free navigation afforded on Lake Michigan and the St. Lawrence River. Abrogated on 17 March 1866.

DECLARATION OF PARIS (1856) The result of a general conference of various European states abolished privateers as well as paper blockades. Neutral ships were allowed to carry enemy goods except contraband and neutral goods aboard enemy ships were immune from seizure, save for contraband. U.S. unsuccessfully attempted to adhere to the declaration after the Civil War began in the hope of denying the Confederacy the right to commission privateers.

SHIMODA CONVENTION (1857) Japan and U.S. Listed the privileges of extraterritoriality, trade and consuls which accrued to the U.S. in consequence of the most-favored-nation clause of the Treaty of Kanagawa. Government supervision of trade and restrictions on travel by the American consul lifted.

TREATY OF TIENTSIN (1858) China and U.S. Opened eleven new Chinese ports to trade and foreign residence, provided for extra-territorially-protected travel throughout China, the right of diplomatic representation in Peiping (Beijing) and the toleration Christian religion, missionaries and converts. The opium trade was legalized and tariffs fixed at five percent were to be collected by the foreign-supervised Imperial Chinese Maritime Customs Service.

TREATY OF EDO (1858) Japan and U.S. Provided for an exchange of diplomatic representation, American consuls at six Japanese ports, unrestricted travel by consuls, residency for Americans within treaty ports, extraterritoriality and a fixed tariff. U.S. agreed to act as mediator whenever requested by Japan and U.S. Navy allowed to keep supplies at three ports.

CONVENTION OF LONDON (1861) France, Spain and U.K. Provided for a joint military expedition to collect debts in default by the government of Mexico. This agreement contained a provision that none of the signatories would attempt to secure any peculiar advantage as well as an article providing for the accession of the U.S.

AFRICAN SLAVE TRADE TREATY (1862) U.K. and U.S. Provided for mutual right of visit and search in specified waters off the coasts of Africa and Cuba as well as mixed courts at New York, Cape Town and Sierra Leone. The mixed courts were comprised of an equal number of judges from each nation to try offenders. Modified in 1870 and terminated 29 April 1923.

BIOGRAPHICAL SKETCHES

BIDLACK, Benjamin A. (1804-1849) Lawyer, newspaper editor, politician, he served as charge d'affaires to New Grenada (Columbia) in 1845. He anticipated Anglo-French machinations in Central America and negotiated a treaty for trans-isthmian communication without instructions.

BULWER, Henry Lytton Earle (1801-1872) Brother to Edward Lytton-Bulwer and ambassador to Spain, Tuscany, Turkey and the U.S. He was the embodiment of the Victorian school of diplomacy and a protege of Palmerston's.

CANNING, George (1770-1827) A follower of William Pitt (the Younger) and a friend of George Fox, Canning served in the House of Commons, with short interruptions, from 1794 to 1827. He served as Foreign Secretary from 1807-1809, and again from 1822-27. Some historians believe his offer of an Anglo-American alliance against the machinations of the Quadruple Alliance in Latin America led John Q. Adams to persuade President J. Monroe to issue the presidential warning now known as the Monroe Doctrine. As for Canning, it was asserted that he "ruled the House of Commons as did Alexander did Bucephalus."

HARRIS, Townsend (1804-1878) New York businessman who became a trader in East Asia, but financial disaster led him to become Consul General to Japan (1855). His success in winning the confidence of the Japanese government led to the Treaty of Edo (1858).

MCLEOD, Alexander (?—?) He was arrested and indicted for the murder and arson in connection with the *Caroline* Affair. It was alleged, although denied by McLeod, that he claimed participation in the destruction of the *Caroline* while serving as the deputy sheriff of Upper Canada. He was acquitted of the charge in that the jury was convinced he was not involved. The British Minister to the U.S. averred that two prosecution witnesses were intimidated by the U.S. government and therefore did not testify. Congress subsequently gave U.S. judges authority over the actions of foreign nationals acting under orders. The war scare which accompanied McLeod's incarceration also led to the commissioning of the USS *Michigan* on 29 September 1844.

PALMERSTON, Henry J. Temple, Viscount (1784-1865) Foreign Minister (1830-41, 1846-51) and Prime Minister (1855-58 and 1859-65) he was first a Tory, then a Whig and finally a Liberal. He was secure in his own rectitude and agreed with Canning that peace was Britain's best policy.

RUSSELL, Lord John (1792-1878) Liberal politician insofar as he supported extending the franchise and eliminating religious intolerance. Prime Minister (1846-52 and 1865-1866) and Foreign Secretary (1852 and 1859-61) he supported a policy of strict neutrality toward the Civil War.

SANTA ANNA, Antonio Lopez de (1794-1876) Professional soldier, he served as President of Mexico in 1833, 1839 and varying times between 1841 and 1844. Exiled to Cuba he assumed the presidency again in 1846 during the Mexican-American War and once again from 1853 to 1855. He was popular, magnetic, opportunistic and many people thought him thoroughly untrustworthy.

SHUFELDT, Robert Wilson (1822-1895) American naval officer responsible for the opening of Korea with his 1882 treaty. The treaty was the result of his initiative, pertinacity and diplomatic skill and ultimately proved Korea's downfall.

TRIST, Nicholas P. (1800-1874) Married to Thomas Jefferson's granddaughter and friend of Andrew Jackson, this highly connected Spanish-speaking State Department Clerk negotiated the peace treaty ending the Mexican-American War. Mr. Trist's treaty was accepted despite the fact he was not an accredited agent at the moment of its conclusion.

WALKER, William (1824-1860) Physician, lawyer and journalist, he forsook the professional existence for that of adventurer. His attempt to conquer Lower California (1853) was followed by his successful operations in Nicaragua (1855) that led to his assuming the presidency (1856). He was overthrown in 1857, and, after two attempts to return to power, the mild-mannered *grey-eyed man of destiny* was executed.

ANNOTATED BIBLIOGRAPHY

U.S. Expansion in the Americas

The chief characteristic of American foreign relations after the War of 1812 was territorial expansion. During this period, the United States extended its borders through purchase, conquest, and annexation of previously unclaimed territories as well as European-held lands. Most studies of the diplomacy of the early nineteenth century describe this process and seek to analyze the policies behind it.

The Monroe Doctrine and its intentions lie at the center of the debate over U.S. territorial expansion. Some studies conclude that it aimed only at limiting additional forceful or illegal acquisitions of American land by European powers. Others maintain that the doctrine sanctioned U.S. intervention against all subsequent European efforts to colonize Western Hemisphere territory. Some analysts support the thesis that it actually promoted a policy of noninvolvement in European political issues.

Brown, Charles H. AGENTS OF MANIFEST DESTINY: The Lives and Times of the Filibusters (1980). Brown investigates the U.S. filibusters of the 1850s against the Antilles, Mexico, and Nicaragua to illustrate the extent to which the ideological framework of Manifest Destiny focused on Central America and the Caribbean.

Goetzmann, William H. WHEN THE EAGLE SCREAMED: The Romantic Horizon in American Diplomacy, 1800-1866 (1966).

Goetzmann's analysis provides a useful overview of early nineteenth century U.S. expansionism.

Graebner, Norman A. EMPIRE ON THE PACIFIC: A study in American Continental Expansion (1983). Graebner discounts the popular
notion that such open-ended mandates as manifest destiny and the
pioneering spirit were crucial in the U.S. expansion to the Pacific,
citing instead a carefully formulated and executed policy designed
to achieve specific geographic limits.

Harlow, Neal. CALIFORNIA CONQUERED: War and Peace on the
Pacific, 1846-1859 (1982). This work recounts the gradual expansion of the United States toward the Pacific shore and its conquest
and annexation of territories along that coast.

Johannsen, Robert W. TO THE HALL OF THE MONTEZUMAS:
The Mexican War in the American Imagination (1985)). The
author examines the political and economic context of America's
first foreign war that he depicts as a rapidly changing environment
in which early nineteenth century romanticism gave way to a more
brazen age of commerce.

Langley, Lester D. STRUGGLE FOR THE AMERICAN MEDITER-
RANEAN: United States-European Rivalry in the Gulf-Carib-
bean, 1776-1904 (1976). Langley examines U.S.-Caribbean relations
from the end of the American Revolution until the United States
actually amassed the power to support its claim to primacy in the
Caribbean.

Lippmann, Walter. U.S. FOREIGN POLICY: Shield of the Republic (1943). This analysis of the Monroe Doctrine assumes that its
framers recognized that United States power was insufficient to
protect the Western Hemisphere.

May, Ernest R. THE MAKING OF THE MONROE DOCTRINE
(1975). May hypothesizes that the Monroe doctrine derived not
only from international but also domestic politics and that dis-
agreements among American policy makers emerged from varied
concepts of the national interest as well as individual interpersonal
styles.

Merk, Frederick. MANIFEST DESTINY AND MISSION IN
AMERICAN HISTORY (1963). Merk viewed Manifest Destiny
and imperialism as traps into which the nation was led in 1846 and
1899. He believed that America's sense of mission, with the expansion of liberty by territorial aggrandizement, to be a better representation of the nation's spirit

Nelson, Anna Kasten. SECRET AGENTS: President Polk and the Search for Peace with Mexico (1988). Nelson describes Polk's unconventional diplomacy in the Mexican War, focusing particularly upon his secretive/executive style of war management.

Olliff, Donothan C. REFORMA MEXICO AND THE UNITED STATES: A Search for Alternatives to Annexation, 1854-1961. The author studies U.S. and Mexican relations during Mexico's La Reforma years and lays particular emphasis on the economic character of that relationship.

Perkins, Dexter. THE MONROE DOCTRINE, 1823-1826 (1927). This work is the classic study of the doctrine.

Stuart, Reginald C. UNITED STATES EXPANSIONISM AND BRITISH NORTH AMERICA, 1775-1871 (1988). The author examines American expansionism and American-Canadian relations, emphasizing the role of cultural dynamics as well as American values.

Weber, David J. THE MEXICAN FRONTIER, 1821-1846 (1982). Weber investigates U.S-Mexican relations during the period between Mexican independence from Spain and the U.S. acquisition of Mexico's northern provinces. This study emphasizes the economic and social elements at work in Mexico and the U.S. frontier.

Weeks, William Earl. JOHN QUINCY ADAMS AND AMERICAN GLOBAL EMPIRE (1992). In his work on the Transcontinental Treaty, Weeks argues that John Quincy Adams acquired not only Florida, a claim to Oregon and a boundary to the Pacific, but also established a foundation for the Monroe Doctrine as well as a dynamic that determined the course of American expansion until the Civil War.

Weinberg, Albert K. MANIFEST DESTINY: A Study of Nationalist Expansionism in American History (1935). Weinberg investigates the various philosophical justifications of the U.S. quest for territory.

U.S. Diplomacy during the Civil War

Studies of American diplomacy during the Civil War focus largely on the role of Confederate and Northern States relations with France and Great Britain. Earlier works criticize British policy *vis-à-vis* the Confederacy, but recent research has sought to evaluate the British and French response to the crisis in terms of pragmatic consideration.

Bernath, Stuart L. SQUALL ACROSS THE ATLANTIC: American Civil War Prize Cases and Diplomacy (1970). Bernath investigates maritime incidents involving Northern, Confederate, and English interests to identify the sources of tension in Anglo-American relations during the Civil War.

Case, Lynn M. and Spencer, Warren F. THE UNITED STATES AND FRANCE: Civil War Diplomacy (1970). This work examines U.S. and French affairs during Civil War years and concludes that this difficult period was beneficial to future relations. The authors maintain that the conflicts resolved in these years laid the groundwork for cooperation in the ensuing decades.

Crawford, Martin. THE ANGLO-AMERICAN CRISIS OF THE MID-NINETEENTH CENTURY (1987). Crawford researches the London *Times'* presentation of Anglo-American relations to determine the roots of hostility between Britain and the U.S. North before the Civil War.

Ferris, Norman B. DESPERATE DIPLOMACY: William M. Seward's Foreign Policy, 1861 (1976). Ferris investigates Seward's handling of the Trent Affair and the heightened domestic concern over Anglo-American hostilities. He concludes that Seward demonstrated considerable diplomatic ability in dealing with the crisis.

Jones, Howard. UNION IN PERIL: The Crisis over British Intervention (1992). Jones provides and excellent analysis of Anglo-American relations during the Civil War.

Merli, Frank J. GREAT BRITAIN AND THE CONFEDERATE NAVY, 1861-1865 (1970). Merli examines the Confederacy's efforts to build naval vessels in British yards and the overall role of British relations with the North and South during the Civil War.

Saul, Norman E. DISTANT FRIENDS: The United States and Russia, 1763-1867 (1991). Saul's book is a comprehensive study covering the first century of relations between Czarist Russia and the United States.

Spencer, Warren F. THE CONFEDERATE NAVY IN EUROPE (1983). This book argues that France and Great Britain followed policies which were based on international law in adopting a neutral stance toward the American Civil War and the Confederacy's efforts to obtain ships from them.

Warren, Gordon H. FOUNTAIN OF DISCONTENT: The Trent Affair and Freedom of the Seas (1981). This work investigates the worst crisis in Anglo-American relations from 1812 until the Civil

War and chronicles the events that complicated a peaceful resolution.

IMPERIALISM AND INVOLVEMENT

1866 — 1914

The North American War (1861-1865) represents a watershed in American history. On the one side, a republic so secure in its own rectitude it could ignore the world, on the other, a democracy torn betwixt isolationist impulses and a penchant for extra-continental exploitation.

In the early days of the Republic the political dominance of the farmer-agrarian group produced a diplomatic focus on territorial expansion. However, the exuberant commercial society of the postwar decades rendered the farmer-agrarians politically irrelevant. Americans by the score came to view the Atlantic and Pacific less as moats behind which to shelter, and more as highways to economic opportunity and national prestige.

Still, the absence of any external threat, ample domestic economic opportunity and the political reconstruction of the nation restricted American interest in affairs external to certain limited opportunities in the Pacific which, although generally ignored at the time, did furnish stepping-stones to the future. A future that became all more apparent when the internal market was perceived as incapable of future expansion.

Accordingly, in the last decade of the century Americans sought salvation and security beyond the national borders. Moreover, the capacity to act now matched past rhetorical statements regarding national power. The result was an irresistible impulse that led to war with Spain. Victory in that conflict gave the United States ample territorial spoils. It also marked the debut of the United States as the dominant element in the Western Hemisphere and a player on the colonial stage.

Americans initially questioned the wisdom of colonial acquisition or participation in the worldwide struggle for power. They insisted such activities were inconsistent with the national commitment to liberty.

Furthermore, they believed the nation had a divinely inspired mandate to serve humanity through example rather than force of arms. With the dawn of the Twentieth-Century, however, Americans determined to spread the benefits of liberty and democracy by active intervention in the many dark corners of the globe. This desire to civilize the brown brethren in the Philippines, and to teach Latin Americans to elect good men, owed much to the American sense of mission. At the same time, the nation's actions represented a new appreciation of the geo-strategically prudent. However, as Americans carried the torch into Caribbean islands, Central American republics, and a newly acquired island empire, Europe finally stumbled into the abyss.

CHRONOLOGY

1866
Mar 8 Extradition—Portugal (unperfected)
Mar 21 Treaty of Washington (Seminole and U.S.)
Mar 29 Treaty of Washington (Potawatomi and U.S.)
Apr 7 Treaty of Washington (Chippewa and U.S.)
Apr 28 Treaty of Washington (Multitribal)
Jun 14 Treaty of Washington (Creek and U.S.)
Jun 25 Convention of Yedo (Multilateral)
Jun 27 State of War—Austria and Prussia (ends 3 July)
Jul 4 Agency Treaty (Delaware and U.S.)
Jul 16 Treaty of Fort Union—Crow (unperfected)
Jul 18 Treaty of Fort Union—Assiniboine (unperfected)
Jul 19 Treaty of Washington (Cherokee and U.S.)
Jul 27 Treaty of Fort Berthold (Arickaree and U.S.)
Jul 27 Trans-Atlantic cable resumes operations
Aug 29 Treaty of Hot Sulpher Springs—Utah (unperfected)
Dec 29 Settlement of Yokohama, Japan—Multilateral (unperfected)

1867
Feb 18 Agency Treaty (Multitribal)
Feb 19 Agency Treaty (Sioux and U.S.)
Feb 23 Treaty of Washington (Multitribal)
Feb 27 Treaty of Washington (Potawatomi and U.S.)
Mar 2 Treaty of Washington—Shawnee (unperfected)
Mar 19 Treaty of Washington (Chippewa and U.S.)
Mar 30 Russian-American Treaty (Alaskan Purchase)

May 13 Naturalization Treaty (U.K. and U.S.)
May 21 Commercial Reciprocity—Hawaii (unperfected)
Jun 19 Emperor Maximilian executed (Mexico)
Jun 21 Dickinson-Ayon Treaty (Nicaragua and U.S.)
Jul 1 Dominion of Canada created
Aug 17 Diplomatic relations suspended (Vatican)
Aug 28 U.S. occupies Midway Island
Oct 21 Treaty of Medicine Lodge Creek (Multitribal)
Oct 21 Treaty of Medicine Lodge Creek (Multitribal)
Oct 24 Cession of St. Thomas and adjacent islands— Denmark (unperfected)
Oct 28 Treaty of Medicine Lodge Creek (Multitribal)

1868
Feb * Lease of the Bay and Peninsula of Samana— Dominican Republic (unperfected)
Mar 2 Treaty of Washington (Ute and U.S.)
Apr 27 Treaty of Washington (Cherokee and U.S.)
Apr 29 Treaty of Fort Laramie (Multitribal)
May 7 Treaty of Fort Laramie (Crow and U.S.)
May 10 Treaty of Fort Laramie (Multitribal)
Jun 1 Treaty of Fort Sumner (Navaho and U.S.)
Jul 3 Treaty of Fort Bridger (Multitribal)
Jul 10 Consular Convention—Mexico (unperfected)
Jul 13 Treaty of Fort Hawley—Gros Ventres (unperfected)
Jul 15 Treaty of Fort Hawley—Crow (unperfected)
Jul 28 Commercial Reciprocity—Hawaii (unperfected)
Jul 28 Burlingame Treaty (China and U.S.)
Aug 13 Treaty of Washington (Nez Perce and U.S.)
Sept 1 Treaty of Fort Benton—Blackfoot (unperfected)
Sept 24 Treaty of Virginia City—Multitribal (unperfected)
Oct 2 Diplomatic relations (Greece)
Oct 15 Cession of St. Thomas and adjacent islands— Denmark (unperfected)
Oct 17 Water Boundary—U.K. (unperfected)
Oct 20 Wounded on the Field of Battle—Multilateral (unperfected)
Nov 10 Water Boundary—U.K. (unperfected)
Nov 10 Settlement of all outstanding claims—U.K (unperfected)
Nov 23 Settlement of all outstanding claims—U.K. (unperfected)

1869
Jan 14 Johnson-Clarendon Claims Convention (unperfected)
Jan 14 Construction of ship canal—Columbia (unperfected)
Jan 14 Water Boundary Arbitration—U.K. (unperfected)
Mar 5 Elihu B. Washburne (Secretary of State)
Mar 17 Hamilton Fish (Secretary of State)
May 8 Commercial Reciprocity—Hawaii (unperfected)
May 10 First transcontinental railroad completed
Sept 4 Annexation—Dominican Republic (unperfected)
Sept 7 Ebenezer Don Carlos Basset—Haiti (first African American minister)
Oct 14 Cession of St. Thomas and adjacent islands— Denmark (unperfected)
Nov 17 Suez Canal opens
Nov 29 Annexation Treaty—Dominican Republic (unperfected)
Nov 29 Annexation—Dominican Republic (unperfected)
Nov 29 Lease of the Bay and Peninsula of Samana— Dominican Republic (unperfected)

1870
Jan 26 Construction of ship canal—Colombia (unperfected)
May 14 Annexation—Dominican Republic (unperfected)
Jul 7 Lease of the Bay and Peninsula of Samana— Dominican Republic (unperfected)
Jul 19 Franco-Prussian War (ends 28 Jan 1871)
Oct 11 Extradition—Guatemala (unperfected)
Dec 15 Friendship, commerce and navigation—Uruguay (unperfected)

1871
* * Simon Cameron (Senate Foreign Relations Committee)
Mar 3 Indian tribes no longer acknowledged as independent political entities (Congress)
Mar 15 Extradition—Honduras (unperfected)
May 8 Treaty of Washington (U.K. and U.S.)

1872
Feb 17 Naval Base at Pago Pago—Samoa (unperfected)
Mar 30 Extradition—Colombia (unperfected)
Sept 14 Arbitration panel awards U.S. $15.5 million in damage claims (Treaty of Washington)
Oct 21 German Emperor selects Haro Channel as boundary between Canada and U.S. (Treaty of Washington)

1873
* * Leonard Myers (House Foreign Affairs Committee)
* * Godlove S. Orth (House Foreign Affairs Committee)
Jun 14 Extradition—Honduras (unperfected)
Oct 31 SS *Virginius* seized by Spain in international waters

1874
Jun * Commerce and trade with Canada—U.K. (unperfected)
Jul 1 Charlotte L. Adams, Kate Goodall, Nellie M. Joselyn, Mary Markoe, Sue Hamilton Owen (first women appointed to a full-time position in Department of State)
Aug 11 Naturalization—Turkey (unperfected)

1875
* * Thomas Swann (House Foreign Affairs Committee)
Mar 18 Hawaiian Reciprocity Treaty

1877
* * Hannibal Hamlin (Senate Foreign Relations Committee)
Mar 12 William M. Evarts (Secretary of State)

1878
Jan 17 Samoan Treaty
Feb 10 Pact of Zanjon (Cuban insurgents and Spain)
Jul 25 Japanese Commercial Treaty

1879
* * Samuel S. Cox (House Foreign Affairs Committee)
* * William W. Eaton (Senate Foreign Relations Committee)
Feb 14 State of War—Bolivia, Chile and Peru (ends 20 Oct 1883)
Sept 2 Town and district of Apia, Samoa—Multilateral (unperfected)
Sept 17 Friendship and commerce—Madagascar (unperfected)
Oct 4 Commerce—Anjouan/Johanna (unperfected)
Nov 1 Extradition—Colombia (unperfected)
Nov 12 President R. Hayes arbitrates territorial dispute betwixt Argentina and Paraguay

1880
Nov 17 Angell Treaty (China and U.S.)
Dec 14 Diplomatic relations (Romania)

1881
** Charles G. Williams (House Foreign Affairs Committee)
 ** William Windon (Senate Foreign Relations Committee)
Feb 17 Trescott Protocol—Santo Domingo (unperfected)
Feb 17 Interoceanic Canal—Colombia (unperfected)
Mar 7 James G. Blaine (Secretary of State)
Apr 11 Commerce and navigation—Romania (unperfected)
Sept 20 Coaling Station in Chimbote—Peru (unperfected)
Oct 7 Protection of trade marks—Romania (unperfected)
Dec 2 Naturalization—Germany (unperfected)
Dec 19 Frederick T. Frelinghuysen (Secretary of State)

1882
May 22 Treaty of Amity and Commerce (Korea and U.S.)
Oct 23 Diplomatic relations (Thailand)
Nov 10 Diplomatic relations (Serbia)

1883
 ** Andrew G. Curtin (House Foreign Affairs Committee)
 ** John F. Miller (Senate Foreign Relations Committee)
Mar 1 Extradition—Luxembourg (unperfected)
Jun 11 Diplomatic relations (Iran)
Sept 29 Town and district of Apia, Samoa—Multilateral (unperfected)

1884
Mar 2 Diplomatic relations (Dominican Republic)
Jun 23 Friendship, commerce and navigation—Argentina (unperfected)
Jun 25 Friendship, commerce and navigation—Argentina (unper-
fected)
Nov 4 Property Rights—Belgium (unperfected)
Nov 18 Commercial reciprocity with Cuba and Puerto Rico—Spain
(unperfected)
Dec 1 Frelinghuysen-Zavala Treaty—Nicaragua (unperfected)
Dec 4 Commercial reciprocity—Dominican Republic (unperfected)

1885
 ** Perry Belmont (House Foreign Affairs Committee)
Feb 14 Trademarks—Switzerland (unperfected)
Feb 20 Extradition—Mexico (unperfected)
Feb 25 Commercial reciprocity with Cuba and Puerto Rico—Spain
(unperfected)

Feb 26 Congo, commerce, slave trade and navigation— Multilateral (unperfected)
Mar 2 Commercial reciprocity with Cuba and Puerto Rico—Spain (unperfected)
Mar 7 Thomas F. Bayard (Secretary of State)

1886
Jun 25 Extradition—U.K. (unperfected)

1887
* * John Sherman (Senate Foreign Relations Committee)
Feb 4 Extradition—Guatemala (unperfected)
Mar 26 Extradition—Argentina (unperfected)
Oct 22 Extradition (Guatemala and U.S.)
Nov 9 Naval Base Agreement (Hawaii and U.S.)

1888
* * James B. McCreary (House Foreign Affairs Committee)
Feb 15 Bayard-Chamberlain Treaty—U.K. (unperfected)
Mar 12 Labor Exclusion Treaty—China (unperfected)
Oct 21 Sackville-West Incident (U.K. and U.S.)

1889
* * Robert R. Hitt (House Foreign Affairs Committee)
Feb 20 Amity, Commerce and Navigation—Japan (unperfected)
Mar 7 James G. Blaine (Secretary of State)
Jun 14 Berlin General Act (Germany, U.K. and U.S.)
Oct 2 International Conference of American States— Washington (ends 19 April 1890)

1890
Apr 28 Arbitration—Multilateral (unperfected)
Oct 20 Blaine-Bond Treaty—U.K. (unperfected)

1891
* * James H. Blount (House Foreign Affairs Committee)
Mar 14 New Orleans Mafia Affair (Italy and U.S.)
Apr 15 Industrial Property Protocol—Multilateral (unperfected)
May 5 SS *Itata* Incident (Italy and U.S.)
Oct 16 True Blue Saloon Affair (Chile and U.S.)

Dec 30 Commercial reciprocity—Costa Rica (unperfected)
Dec 31 Commercial reciprocity—Costa Rica (unperfected)

1892
Feb 29 Bering Sea Arbitration Treaty (U.K. and U.S.)
Mar 25 Extradition—France (unperfected)
Jun 29 John W. Foster (Secretary of State)

1893
* * James B. McCreary (House Foreign Affairs Committee)
* * John T. Morgan (Senate Foreign Relations Committee)
Jan 14 Hawaiian Revolution
Feb 14 Annexation—Hawaii (unperfected)
Mar 1 Congress authorizes the diplomatic rank of ambassador
Mar 7 Walter Q. Gresham (Secretary of State)
Nov 6 Extradition—Venezuela (unperfected)

1894
Mar 17 Gresham-Yang Treaty (China and U.S.)
Jul 4 Republic of Hawaii established
Jul 9 Trademarks—Greece (unperfected)
Aug 1 State of War—China and Japan (ends 17 Apr 1895)
Aug 7 U.S. recognizes Republic of Hawaii
Nov 22 Treaty of Washington (Japan and U.S.)

1895
* * Robert R. Hitt (House Foreign Affairs Committee)
* * John Sherman (Senate Foreign Relations Committee)
Jun 10 Richard Olney (Secretary of State)
Jul 20 Venezuelan Demarche (U.K. and U.S.)

1897
* * Cushman K. Davis (Senate Foreign Relations Committee)
Jan 11 Olney-Pauncefote Convention—U.K. (unperfected)
Jan 30 Boundary—U.K. (unperfected)
Mar 6 John Sherman (Secretary of State)
Jun 16 Annexation—Hawaii (unperfected)
Nov 6 Preservation of the fur seal and sea otter— Multilateral (unperfected)
Dec 14 Industrial Property Protocol—Multilateral (unperfected)

1898
Feb 9 Private letter written by Enrique Dupuy de Lome (Spanish Minister to U.S.) published in *New York Journal*
Feb 15 USS *Maine* sinks
Apr 19 Teller Amendment (Congress)
Apr 20 State of War—Spain and U.S. (ends 10 December)
Apr 28 William R. Day (Secretary of State)
Jun 20 U.S. occupies Guam Island
Jul 4 U.S. briefly occupies Wake Island (reoccupies 17 Jan 1899)
Jul 6 Annexation of Hawaii (Joint Resolution, U.S. Congress)
Sept 30 John Hay (Secretary of State)
Dec 10 Treaty of Paris (Spain and U.S.)

1899
May 18 Hague Peace Conference (ends 29 July)
Sept 6 Open Door Notes (Germany, Russia and U.K.)
Oct 12 Boer War (ends 21 May 1902)
Dec 2 Treaty of Washington (Germany, U.K. and U.S.)

1900
Jan 11 Boxer Rebellion begins—China (ends 12 Sept 1901)
Feb 5 Construction of ship canal—U.K. (unperfected)
Jun 25 Spooner Act (Congress)
Jul 3 Open Door Circular (France, Germany, Japan, Russia and U.K.)
Sept 4 Convention for the Pacific Settlement of International Disputes (Permanent Court of Arbitration)

1901
* * Shelby M. Cullom (Senate Foreign Relations Committee)
Mar 2 Platt Amendment (Congress)
Oct 22 International Conference of American States— Mexico City (ends 31 January 1902)
Nov 18 Hay-Pauncefote Treaty (U.K. and U.S.)
Dec 2 *De Lima v. Bidwell* (Supreme Court)
Dec 9 Construction of ship canal—Nicaragua (unperfected)

1902
Jan 24 Cession of West Indies—Denmark (unperfected)
Jan 28 Extradition and protection against anarchism— Multilateral (unperfected)

Jan 30 Anglo-Japanese Treaty
May 27 Diplomatic relations (Cuba)
Jun 28 Hepburn-Spooner Act (Congress)
Nov 8 Hay-Bond Treaty—U.K. (unperfected)
Dec 9 Venezuelan Crisis
Dec 11 Reciprocity Treaty (Cuba and U.S.)
Dec 29 Drago Doctrine

1903
Jan 3 *Lone Wolf v. Hitchcock* (Supreme Court)
Jan 22 Hay-Herran Treaty—Columbia (unperfected)
Jan 24 Hay-Herbert Treaty (U.K. and U.S.)
Jul 17 Diplomatic relations (Luxembourg)
Sept 19 Diplomatic relations (Bulgaria)
Nov 3 Panamanian Revolution
Nov 6 U.S. recognizes Republic of Panama
Nov 18 Hay-Bunau-Varilla Treaty (Panama and U.S.)

1904
Feb 10 State of War—Russia and Japan (ends 9 Aug 1905)
Jul 22 Diplomatic relations (Panama)
Nov 1 Arbitration—France (unperfected)
Nov 21 Arbitration—Switzerland (unperfected)
Nov 22 Arbitration—Germany (unperfected)
Nov 23 Arbitration—Portugal (unperfected)
Dec 6 Roosevelt Corollary (Monroe Doctrine)
Dec 12 Arbitration—U.K. (unperfected)
Dec 14 Arbitration—Italy (unperfected)
Dec 31 Arbitration—Spain (unperfected)

1905
Jan 6 Arbitration—Austria-Hungary (unperfected)
Jan 18 Arbitration—Mexico (unperfected)
Jan 20 Customs House Treaty—Dominican Republic (unperfected)
Jan 20 Arbitration—Sweden and Norway (unperfected)
Feb 7 Customs House Treaty—Dominican Republic (unperfected)
Feb 11 Arbitration—Japan (unperfected)
Mar 15 Extradition—San Marino (unperfected)
Apr 29 Taft-Katsura Agreement (Japan and U.S.)
May 31 Diplomatic relations (Norway)

Jul 19 Elihu Root (Secretary of State)
Aug 12 Anglo-Japanese Alliance renewed
Sept 5 Treaty of Portsmouth (Japan and Russia)
Oct 30 Diplomatic relations (Montenegro)

1906
Jan 16 Algeciras Conference (ends 7 April)
Apr 6 Extradition—Japan (unperfected)
Jun 27 Merit system for selection and promotion introduced to Consular Service (executive order)
Jul 23 International Conference of American States— Rio de Janeiro (ends 27 August)
Sept 29 Diplomatic relations (Morocco)

1907
* * Robert G. Cousins (House Foreign Affairs Committee)
Feb 8 Debt and finances—Dominican Republic
Feb 24 Gentleman's Agreement (Japan and U.S.)
Jun 15 Hague Peace Conference (ends 18 October)
Oct 18 Porter Convention (Second Hague Convention)
Oct 18 Status of enemy merchant ships—Multilateral (unperfected)
Oct 18 Conversion of merchant ships into war ships— Multilateral (unperfected)
Oct 18 International prize court—Multilateral (unperfected)
Dec 16 Great White Fleet sails (returns 22 Feb 1909)
Dec 20 General Treaty of Peace and Amity (Multilateral)

1908
Apr 16 Extradition—Romania (unperfected)
Apr 16 Commerce—Romania (unperfected)
May 31 Arbitration Convention (U.K. and U.S.)
Nov 30 Root-Takahira Agreement (Japan and U.S.)
Dec 23 Arbitration—Argentina (unperfected)

1909
* * James B. Perkins (House Foreign Affairs Committee)
Jan 7 Arbitration—Bolivia (unperfected)
Jan 9 Canal construction—Colombia (unperfected)
Jan 9 Canal construction—Panama (unperfected)
Jan 11 Boundary Waters Treaty (U.K. and U.S.)

Jan 13 Arbitration — Chile (unperfected)
Jan 27 Robert Bacon (Secretary of State)
Jan 27 Fisheries Arbitration Agreement (U.K. and U.S.)
Feb 26 Declaration of London
Mar 6 Philander C. Knox (Secretary of State)
Mar 13 Extradition — Paraguay (unperfected)
Jul 6 Diplomatic relations (Ethiopia)
Sept 16 Anne H. Shortridge (first woman appointed to professional position in Department of State
Nov 26 Civil service status conferred on all diplomatic officers below the rank of Minister (executive order)

1910
* * David J. Foster (House Foreign Affairs Committee)
May 21 Root-Bryce Treaty (U.K. and U.S.)
Jul 12 International Conference of American States — Buenos Aires (ends 30 August)
Aug 11 Pan-American Union
Sept 7 Decision rendered by Permanent Court of Arbitration (Hague) in fisheries dispute (U.K. and U.S)
Nov 5 Dawson Agreements (Nicaragua)

1911
* * William Sulzer (House Foreign Affairs Committee)
Jan 10 Debt and finances — Honduras (unperfected)
Feb 17 Lowden Act (Congress)
Feb 21 Treaty of Washington (Japan and U.S.)
Jun 6 Debt and finances — Nicaragua (unperfected)
Jul 7 North Pacific Sealing Convention (Japan, Russia, U.K. and U.S.)
Aug 3 Arbitration — U.K. (unperfected)
Aug 3 Arbitration — France (unperfected)
Dec 18 Commerce and Navigation Treaty abrogated (Russia and U.S.)

1912
* * Charles B. Smith (House Foreign Affairs Committee)
Jul 20 Fisheries Convention (U.K. and U.S.)
Aug 2 Lodge Corollary (Monroe Doctrine)
Aug 4 Nicaraguan Intervention (ends 17 Jan 1913)
Aug 24 Panama Canal Act (Congress)
Oct 12 First Balkan War (ends 30 May 1913)

1913
* * Henry D. Flood (House Foreign Affairs Committee)
* * Augustus O. Bacon (Senate Foreign Relations Committee
* * Second Balkan War (ends 10 August)
Feb 8 Chamorro-Weitzel Treaty—Nicaragua (unperfected)
Mar 5 William Jennings Bryan (Secretary of State)
Aug 7 Advancement of peace—El Salvador (unperfected)
Sept 20 Advancement of peace—Panama (unperfected)
Dec 17 Advancement of peace—Nicaragua (unperfected)

1914
* * William J. Stone (Senate Foreign Relations Committee)
Feb 4 Advancement of peace—Iran (unperfected)
Feb 5 Advancement of peace—Denmark (unperfected)
Feb 13 Advancement of peace—Switzerland (unperfected)
Feb 17 Advancement of peace—Dominican Republic (unperfected)
Apr 6 Thompson-Urrutia Treaty (Columbia and U.S.)
Apr 9 Tampico Incident (Mexico)
Apr 21 U.S. forces land Vera Cruz, Mexico (ends 23 November)
May 20 Argentina, Brazil and Chile mediation effort to end Mexican-
U.S. impasse (ends 30 June)
Jun 15 Panama Canal Tolls Act (Congress)
Jul 24 Advancement of peace—Argentina (unperfected)
Aug 4 Great War (armistice 11 Nov 1918)
Aug 5 Bryan-Chamorro Treaty (Nicaragua and U.S.)
Aug 19 U.S. declares neutrality with respect to Great War
Oct 13 Advancement of peace—Greece (unperfected)

TREATIES, AGREEMENTS, SUPREME COURT CASES AND ACTS OF CONGRESS

CONVENTION OF YEDO (1866) Multilateral. This tariff agreement
was modeled on the unequal treaties imposed on China after the
Opium Wars. The convention established a standard five percent
levy on all imports. It was abrogated by the Treaty of Washington
(1894).
RUSSIAN-AMERICAN TREATY (1867) Russia and U.S. Provided
for the purchase of Russian America by the U.S. for $7.2 million.
Although widely criticized, the U.S. recovered the cost of purchase
well before gold was discovered.

DICKINSON-AYON TREATY (1867) Nicaragua and U.S. Primarily a transit agreement providing for passage between the Atlantic and Pacific by U.S. citizens. The agreement also guaranteed U.S. interests in the event Nicaragua concluded an agreement to construct an inter-oceanic canal. The neutrality of any such canal is specifically stipulated.

BURLINGAME TREATY (1868) China and U.S. Anson Burlingame (former U.S. Minister to China,) negotiated this addition to the Treaty of Tientsin in his capacity as Envoy of the Empire to all the Western Powers. Afforded China most-favored-nation status with respect to visit, travel and residence in the U.S. Provoked the Chinese Exclusion Act (1882).

TREATY OF WASHINGTON (1871) U.K. and U.S. Referred the assessment of damages to be paid by Britain for the activities of Confederate commerce raiders (Alabama claims) to an arbitral commission involving Brazil, Italy and the Swiss Confederation. The San Juan boundary dispute was left to a decision by the German Emperor. Reinstated the fishing privileges previously granted in the Marcy-Elgin Treaty. U.K. expresses regret about the activities of the Confederate raiders and accepts responsibility for their activities. Mixed commission to consider claims by U.K. on U.S. Free navigation of St. Lawrence, Yukon, Porcupine, Stikine rivers, free navigation of Lake Michigan and reciprocal transit in bond of goods across U.S. and Canada for ten years.

HAWAIIAN RECIPROCITY TREATY (1875) Hawaii and U.S. Permitted the import of sugar and other products to U.S. duty free in exchange for the export to Hawaii of a long list of American products duty free. Provided that none of the territory of the islands was to be leased or disposed of to a third power and none of the privileges conferred by the treaty should be conferred on any other nation.

PACT OF ZANJON (1878) Cuban insurgents and Spain. Ended the Ten Years' War through a promise of amnesty, changes in the colonial government of Cuba and emancipation of all slaves. The pledge concerning slavery was fulfilled (1886) but the others were not and the war resumed in 1895.

JAPANESE COMMERCIAL TREATY (1878) Japan and U.S. U.S. relinquishes privileges granted by Convention of 1866. See also Treaty of Commerce and Navigation (1894).

SAMOAN TREATY (1878) Samoa and U.S. U.S. obtained right to establish a naval and coaling station on Tutuila (Pago Pago) in exchange for employing its good offices in any dispute between Samoa and a third party. An earlier treaty (1872) rejected by the Senate would have established an exclusive naval base with no commitment to the Samoans.

ANGELL TREATY (1880) China and U.S. Revised open immigration policy established by Burlingame Treaty (1868). Congress restricted Chinese immigration on 6 May 1882. See Gresham-Yang Treaty (1894).

UNITED STATES-KOREA TREATY (1882) Korea and U.S. Provided for trade, residence and most-favored-nation treatment along the model of the Shimoda Convention (1857) and the Treaty of Edo (1858).

PEARL HARBOR TREATY (1887) Hawaii and U.S. This amendment to the renewal of the Hawaiian Reciprocity Treaty (1875) gave the U.S. the exclusive right to fortified naval bases on the island of Oahu.

BERLIN GENERAL ACT (1889) Germany, U.K. and U.S. Tripartite protectorate established over Samoa under a restored native dynasty. See the Convention of 1899.

BERING SEA ARBITRATION TREATY (1892) U.K. and U.S. Dispute over the right of non-Americans to participate in pelagic sealing in Bering Sea. Arbitration panel rules against U.S. on all major points and U.S. ordered to pay damages. See also North Pacific Sealing Convention (1911).

GRESHAM-YANG TREATY (1894) China and U.S. Amended Angell Treaty (1880) to allow limited Chinese immigration to U.S.

TREATY OF WASHINGTON (1894) Japan and U.S. Replaced Treaty of Edo (1858) and the Convention of Edo (1866). Rescinds extraterritoriality, restores control of tariffs to Japan and allowed free travel and immigration. See Treaty of Washington (1911).

TELLER AMENDMENT ((1898) In this amendment to the U.S. declaration of war against Spain. Senator Henry M. Teller (CO) insisted the United States "hereby disclaims any disposition of intention to exercise sovereignty, jurisdiction, or control over said island except for pacification thereof, and asserts its determination, when that is accomplished, to leave the government and control of the island to its people." The U.S. did not annex the island, but American troops remained until 1902. See Platt Amendment (1901).

TREATY OF PARIS (1898) Spain and U.S. Ended the Hispano-American War. Cuba became independent, U.S. acquired Puerto Rico,

Guam and the Philippine Islands. Spain received $20 million for public improvements in the Philippine Islands.

OPEN DOOR NOTE (1899) France, Germany, Japan, Russia and U.K. No discrimination within spheres of influence or any inference with the Imperial Maritime Customs Service collection of tariff duties.

TREATY OF WASHINGTON (1899) Germany, U.K. and U.S. Germany received the islands of Upolu and Savaii and all islets west of 171 degrees west longitude and the U.S. the island of Tutuila and all islets east of 171 degrees west longitude.

SPOONER ACT (1900) Authorizes the president to buy the rights and properties of the New French Canal Company, and "to cause to be constructed" an Isthmian canal that would provide "convenient passage for vessels of the largest tonnage and greatest draft now in use, and such as may be reasonably anticipated."

OPEN DOOR NOTE (1900) France, Germany, Japan, Russia and U.K. The note avowed: "The policy of the Government of the United States is to seek a solution which may bring about permanent safety and peace to China, preserve Chinese territorial and administrative entity, protect all rights guaranteed to friendly powers by treaty and international law and safeguard for the world the principle of equal and impartial trade with all parts of the Chinese Empire."

CONVENTION FOR THE PACIFIC SETTLEMENT OF INTERNATIONAL DISPUTES (1900) The first Hague Peace Conference (1899), convened at the initiative of Czar Nicolas II (Russia), established the Permanent Court of Arbitration. The court was the first global mechanism for the settlement of inter-state disputes. The 1899 Convention was revised at the second Hague Peace Conference (1907). The U.S. acceded, with the reservation that its affiliation did not, in any wise, affect the Monroe Doctrine.

PLATT AMENDMENT (1901) The Platt Amendment allows for U.S. intervention in Cuban affairs. It further permitted the lease of land to establish a naval base (Guantanamo Bay) Under its aegis the United States intervened in Cuban affairs in 1906, 1912, 1917 and 1920. The Platt Amendment was abrogated in 1934, but the United States retained its lease on Guantanamo Bay. See Cuba-U.S. treaty (1934).

HAY-PAUNCEFOTE TREATY (1901) U.K. and U.S. Superseded the Clayton-Bulwer Treaty (1850) insofar as it prohibited the U.S. from building and controlling an isthmian canal. Did not specifically allow the U.S. to fortify such a canal, but did not prohibit such fortifications. An earlier version (5 Feb 1900) was amended by the Senate (20 Dec 1900) in such a manner as to render it unacceptable to the British government.

DE LIMA v. BIDWELL (1901) Supreme Court rules that Puerto Ricans are not *ipso facto* citizens of the United States.

ANGLO-JAPANESE TREATY (1902) Japan and U.K. Provided for the neutrality of either in the event of war on the part of one, except that if an enemy was joined by an ally the neutral status of either would be abandoned. Modified in 1911 to eliminate neutral phase and replaced with active aid. Terminated in 1922 by the Four-Power Pact.

HEPBURN-SPOONER ACT (1902) In accord with the findings of a presidential panel (Walker Commission), the House of Representatives (9 Jan 1902) recommended the construction of an inter-oceanic canal through Nicaragua. An amended version of that legislation was passed as the Hepburn-Spooner Act. It authorized a canal through Nicaragua, if approval of a passage through the Isthmus of Panama was not forthcoming from Columbia. The Columbian Senate rejected the offer (Hay-Herran Agreement) in August 1903. This circumstance led to a revolt and the independence of Panama. See Hay-Bunau-Varilla Treaty (1903).

DRAGO DOCTRINE (1902) Enunciated by Luis Maria Drago, it suggests that nations must not be allowed to collect public debts by armed force or the occupation of territory. Its application was limited to the Western hemisphere. See Roosevelt Corollary (1904) and Porter Convention, (1907).

LONE WOLF v. HITCHCOCK (1903) Supreme Court asserts the plenary authority of Congress over Indian relations and its power to pass laws abrogating treaty stipulations.

HAY-HERBERT TREATY (1903) U.K. and U.S. Provided for tribunal of six impartial jurists of repute (three from each nation) to settle a boundary dispute between Alaska and Canada.

HAY-BUNAU-VARILLA TREATY (1903) Panama and U.S. Conferred upon the U.S. the right to build, fortify and possess a canal zone ten miles wide from Colon to Panama City as if it were sovereign. Panama received $10 million, an annuity of $250,000 (nine years after ratification) and an American guarantee of its independence. Other articles gave the U.S. control over everything necessary to construct and operate a canal.

ROOSEVELT COROLLARY (1904) President Theodore Roosevelt opined that the United States reserved the right to ensure that nations in the Western Hemisphere fulfilled their obligations to international creditors by whatever means it chose. See Drago Doctrine (1902), Porter Convention (1907) and Clark Memorandum (1928).

TAFT-KATSURA MEMORANDUM (1905) Japan and U.S. The Japanese disavowed any designs on the Philippine Island and the U.S. accepted Japan's suzerainty over Korea.

TREATY OF PORTSMOUTH (1905) Japan and Russia. Mediated peace that ended the Russo-Japanese War. Japanese received the southern half of Sakhalin Island, the Liaotung leasehold, the South Manchurian Railway, the economic privileges attached to the least and the Russians got out of the war. Theodore Roosevelt received a Nobel Peace Prize for his efforts (1906).

GENTLEMEN'S AGREEMENT (1907) Japan and U.S. In consequence of domestic fears California would be overrun by Japanese immigrants Elihu Root (Secretary of State) and Tadasu Hayashi (Foreign Minister) sought to limit entry into the U.S. Japanese laborers could not enter the U.S. via Hawaii and Japan would deny passports to laborers seeking passage to Hawaii or the U.S. Japan abrogated the agreement when the Johnson-Reed Immigration Act (1924) forbade Japanese immigration.

PORTER CONVENTION (1907) Second Hague Convention. Modified the proposal made by Luis Drago in his 29 Dec 1902 note on the question of international debts. Although Drago would prohibit any use of force to collect public debts between nations, the Porter Convention, which applies to all contractual obligations, would allow force to be used if a nation refused arbitration or to abide by the ruling of an arbitral panel. See Drago Doctrine (1902) and Roosevelt Corollary (1904).

GENERAL TREATY OF PEACE AND AMITY (1907) Costa Rica, El Salvador, Guatemala, Honduras and Nicaragua. Series of treaties sponsored by the U.S. but to which it is not party. Established the Central American Court of Justice, forbade revolutionary activities against neighbors, agreed to withhold diplomatic recognition from any government established by unconstitutional means (Tobar Doctrine) and proclaimed neutrality of Honduras. See the Estrada Doctrine (1930) and the Convention on the Rights and Duties of States (1933).

ROOT-TAKAHIRA AGREEMENT (1908) Japan and U.S. Both nations agreed to maintain the status quo in the Pacific, respect the territorial possessions of each and support the territorial integrity and independence of China.

BOUNDARY WATERS TREATY (1909) U.K. and U.S. Established a permanent joint commission to settle any disputes over navigation or irrigation rights to lakes and rivers traversing the Canadian-U.S. boundary. Paved the way for the Anglo-American Fisheries Arbitration Agreement (1909) which led to the Anglo-American Fisheries Convention (1912)

DECLARATION OF LONDON (1909) A by-product of the London Naval Conference (1909) that specified the rights of neutrals in wartime, but in the absence of U.K. approval it was of little value. U.S. approved on 24 April 1912.

ROOT-BRYCE TREATY (1910) U.K. and U.S. Establishes a definitive boundary between Canada and U.S. U.S. acquires island in Passamaquoddy Bay.

LOWDEN ACT (1911) This legislation authorized the purchase of sites and buildings for the use of the diplomatic and consular establishments of the United States. Before this act, for the most part, the U.S. operated from rented properties. Some existing diplomatic residences were previously purchased by private individuals and donated to the United States.

TREATY OF WASHINGTON (1911) Japan and U.S. Continuation of trade agreement concluded in 1894. Abrogated by U.S. (26 Jan 1940) and replaced by restrictive trade embargo.

NORTH PACIFIC SEALING CONVENTION (1911) Japan, Russia, U.K. and U.S. Prohibited the practice of pelagic (open sea) sealing and provided for a strictly regulated land kill with Canada and Japan receiving 15% of the proceeds. The agreement also applied to sea otters. Japan abrogated the convention in 1940 although the remaining signatories continued to observe its terms. Canada, Japan, the U.S. and the U.S.S.R. concluded another convention prohibiting pelagic sealing. See Pelagic Sealing Convention (1957).

LODGE COROLLARY (1912) Senator Henry Cabot Lodge (MA) successfully extended the provisions of the Monroe Doctrine to include foreign corporations and nations in Asia.

THOMPSON-URRUTIA TREATY (1914) Columbia and U.S. U.S. paid $25 million (recompense for U.S. involvement in Panamanian revolution of 1903) in exchange for oil concessions to American firms. Ratification delayed (1921) until the death of Theodore Roosevelt (1919) rendered the implicit criticism of Roosevelt's actions in Panama moot.

BRYAN-CHAMORRO TREATY (1914) Nicaragua and U.S. Included a lease of Great Corn and Little Corn islands, a lease for a naval base under American sovereign authority on the Gulf of Fonseca for ninety-nine years and an exclusive option in perpetuity on a prospective canal route through Nicaragua. Nicaragua received $3 million to be spent under American supervision. Abrogated by mutual consent 14 July 1970. Great and Little Corn islands are administered by Nicaragua with the acquiescence of the U.S.

BIOGRAPHICAL SKETCHES

AGUINALDO, Emilio (1869-1964) Filipino patriot, he returned from exile, proclaimed his nation's independence (12 June 1898), became president of the Philippine Republic (23 January 1899) and waged an extensive campaign against the American colonial government until his capture (1901). He retired from public life except for an unsuccessful campaign for the presidency of the Commonwealth (1935).

DIAZ, Porfirio (1830-1915) Mestizo-born and poor, he rose through the ranks of the Mexican Army to become a general (1861). He mounted a successful coup in 1875 and served as president (1876-1880 and 1884-1911) until revolution forced him into exile. He transformed Mexico into a stable, economically progressive nation but economic benefits were not widely distributed and political freedom was unknown.

DRAGO, Luis Marie (1859-1921) Foreign Minister of Argentina (1902-1903) he formulated what became known as the Drago Doctrine. He served on the Tribunal of Arbitration concerned with the North Atlantic Fisheries (1909), and was invited by the Council of the League of Nations to draft the statute for the Permanent Court of Justice.

OLNEY, Richard (1835-1917) A successful corporation lawyer, he served as Attorney General (1893-1895) and Secretary of State (1895-1897) in the second Cleveland administration. He informed the British government (1895) that the U.S. "is practically sovereign on this continent and its fist is law upon the subjects to which it confines its interposition."

PAUNCEFOTE, Julian (1828-1902) Lawyer and diplomat selected as Minister (1889) and later Ambassador (1893) to the U.S. because of his knowledge of international law. He did much to maintain friendly relations between Britain and the U.S.

REED, Thomas B. (1839-1902) Lawyer and politician, he represented Maine in the House of Representatives (1876-1899) and served as Speaker of the House (1889-1890 and 1894-1899). Nicknamed Czar Reed for his exercise of autocratic power as Speaker, he was a vociferous opponent of the war with Spain and the annexation of Hawaii.

SPRING-RICE, Cecil Arthur (1859-1918) British diplomat and, despite his lack of official standing, one of Theodore Roosevelt's kitchen ambassadors. Ambassador to the U.S. (1913-1918), he "steered his course with unfailing judgment and unwearied forbearance, at a time when a single false step might have had the most serious consequences."

STRAIGHT, Willard D. (1880-1918) Although trained as an architect (Cornell, 1901) he served with the Chinese Imperial Maritime Customs Service (1901-1905) until he entered the consular service (1905-1909) and became in 1908 Acting Chief of the Division of Far Eastern Affairs. He was one of the nation's East Asian authorities in public and private affairs until his death.

STRONG, Josiah (1847-1916) Congregational minister and author, his *OUR COUNTRY: ITS POSSIBLE FUTURE AND ITS PRESENT CRISIS* (1885) was not only a pioneer sociological treatise but furnished part of the ideological foundation for the new spirit of manifest destiny which infected the nation in the 1890's.

SUMNER, Charles (1811-1874) Lawyer and politician, he was the most vocal, and often one of the most influential Republicans in the U.S. Senate. As Chairman of the Foreign Relations Committee (1861-71) he was one of the arbiters of America's wartime and postwar foreign policy.

ANNOTATED BIBLIOGRAPHY

American diplomacy from the end of the Civil War to the beginning of World War I pursued a course of expanding territorial holdings beyond the continental United States and amalgamating controlling economic influence over areas throughout the globe.

U.S. Expansionism in the late Nineteenth Century

Studies of late nineteenth century U.S. foreign relations concentrate on the accelerating American influence overseas, examining the goals of expansionism as well as the impact it had abroad. Because this increased international activity was inextricably linked to trade, some works identify economic pursuits as the compelling element. Others focus on military and political aims as the motivating factors. Some authors contend that the U.S. rise to imperialism at the end of the nineteenth century was deliberate while others regard it as a mere by-product of economic growth. Scholars also assumed differing positions on the issue of whether or not imperialism characterized by economic dominance, military intervention or strong cultural influence can be equated with imperialism by colonization.

Beisner, Robert L. FROM THE OLD DIPLOMACY TO THE NEW, 1865-1900 (1986). Beisner discusses American foreign policy in the latter half of the nineteenth century with particular attention to the underlying circumstances, traditions and ideas that determined U.S. diplomacy. This volume also describes the trends leading to the more aggressive and expansionist approach which emerged after 1890.

Bradford, Richard H. THE VIRGINIUS AFFAIR (1980). Bradford explains why the capture of the Virginius, the execution of its crew, and the heated public reaction to the incident did not lead to a military intervention in Cuba by the United States.

Campbell, Charles S. FROM REVOLUTION TO RAPPROCHEMENT: The United States and Great Britain, 1783-1900 (1974). Campbell traces the stormy course of U.S. and British relations from the Revolution to the end of the nineteenth century.

Campbell, Charles S. THE TRANSFORMATION OF AMERICAN FOREIGN RELATIONS, 1865-1900 (1972). This work investigates the transformation of the mid-nineteenth century American foreign policy tradition of missions and anti-colonialism into one of imperialism in the post-Civil War period.

Carstensen, Fred V. AMERICAN ENTERPRISE IN FOREIGN MARKETS: Studies of Singer and International Harvester in Imperial Russia (1984). Carstensen investigates records of two large U.S. companies in the Russian market from 1850 until the beginning of World War I for insights into the impact of private industry on U.S. and Russian relations.

Cohen, Warren I. AMERICA'S RESPONSE TO CHINA: An Interpretative History of Sino-American Relations (1980). Cohen describes U.S. and Chinese relations from the mid-nineteenth century onward.

Drake, Frederick C. THE EMPIRE OF THE SEAS: A Biography of Rear Admiral Robert Wilson Shufeldt, USN (1984). Beyond its first several chapters, this volume deals with U.S. foreign relations with China, Cuba, Mexico, and Korea during the 1860s and 1870s.

Holbo, Paul S. TARNISHED EXPANSION: The Alaska Scandal, the Press and Congress, 1867-1871 (1983). Holbo maintains that the appropriation of Alaska and the scandal that surrounded it substantially inhibited U.S. expansion after 1867.

LaFeber, Walter. THE NEW EMPIRE: An Interpretation of American Expansion, 1860-1898 (1963). LaFeber investigates American expansionism in the latter half of the nineteenth century, concluding that it proceeded gradually and deliberately. He emphasizes the economic forces at work in that process.

Langley, Lester D. STRUGGLE FOR THE AMERICAN MEDITERRANEAN: United States-European Rivalry in the Gulf-Caribbean, 1776-1904 (1976). Langley examines U.S. and Caribbean relations from the American Revolution until the United States actually amassed the power to support its claim to primacy in the Caribbean.

Plesur, Milton. AMERICA'S OUTWARD THRUST, 1865-1890 (1971). Plesur describes this period as one of low political interest in foreign affairs and identifies latent roots for the subsequent expansionist policy.

Stuart, Reginald C. UNITED STATES EXPANSIONISM AND BRITISH NORTH AMERICA, 1775-1871 (1988). The author examines American expansionism and American-Canadian relations, emphasizing the necessity of considering cultural dynamics and American values in reaching an understanding of these two issues.

The United States and Empire

Scholarship on United States diplomacy at the end of the nineteenth and beginning of the twentieth centuries emphasizes the energetic growth of American commercial interests and the expansion of
American influence overseas. Works dealing with this period examine
the increasing role played by domestic politics in the formulation of
foreign policy and give particular attention to U.S. public opinion concerning foreign expansion.

Recent research on this period of diplomacy has been significantly
influenced by ensuing developments in U.S. relations with those areas
touched by American expansion. Historians who before World War
I had defended U.S. expansionism have, for example, often amended
their positions as a result of the devastation wrought by that conflict
and the widely held view that it was precipitated by imperialistic competition. Geography also plays a role in the attitude of scholarship
regarding American intervention abroad. There is a general tendency
for post-World War I writers to adopt a more critical view of intervention in the Western Hemisphere than in other parts of the world.

General

Becker, William H. THE DYNAMICS OF BUSINESS-GOVERN-
    MENT RELATIONS: Industry and Exports 1893-1921 (1982).
    Becker investigates foreign policy as it related to American man-
    ufacturers during the years in which small business first began
    pursuing foreign markets. The work focuses on the role of govern-
    ment in facilitating overseas trade, the creation of the Department
    of Commerce, and the bureaucratic rivalry that ensued between
    DOC and the Department of State.
Brune, Lester H. THE ORIGINS OF AMERICAN NATIONAL
    SECURITY POLICY: Sea Power, Air Power and Foreign Policy
    1900-1941 (1981). Brune provides a history of U.S. sea and air power
    during the first half of the twentieth century. He concludes that
    American separation of force and diplomacy led to bureaucratic
    competition, the development of a separate foreign policy view
    by the military, the heavy modeling of naval techniques in early
    aviation strategy, and difficulties in centralizing national security
    options on the eve of World War II.

Clements, Kendrick A. WILLIAM JENNINGS BRYAN: Missionary Isolationist (1982). Clements coins the phrase missionary isolationist to describe WJB's foreign policy approach and casts the personality of the Christian statesman as a reflection of the values of millions of Americans.

Colin, Richard H. THEODORE ROOSEVELT, CULTURE DIPLOMACY, AND EXPANSION (1985). Collin rejects imperialism and big stick diplomacy as catch words for the type of foreign policy conducted by Theodore Roosevelt. Rather, the author describes turn of the century American diplomacy in terms of the worldwide revolution of modernism and the overall American expansiveness in the arts, diplomacy, technology, and culture.

Dobson, John. RETICENT EXPANSIONISM: The Foreign Policy of William McKinley (1988). Dobson examines the diplomacy of the McKinley Administration and concludes that, although these were times of energetic foreign expansion by the United States, McKinley himself was more a product than a cause of the trends of the period.

Esthus, Raymond A. THEODORE ROOSEVELT AND THE INTERNATIONAL RIVALRIES (1970). Esthus presents Roosevelt as a pragmatic diplomat in world affairs and assesses the effect of U.S. isolationism Roosevelt's ability to achieve his aims in the international arena.

Hildebrand, Robert C. POWER AND THE PEOPLE: Executive Management of Public Opinion in Foreign Affairs, 1897-1921 (1981). Hildebrand investigates the role of public opinion in presidential decision-making from its ascendancy during the McKinley Administration through the public relations failure of the Taft Administration and the foreign policy uses of Wilson's venue.

Scholes, Walter V. and Scholes, Marie V. THE FOREIGN POLICIES OF THE TAFT ADMINISTRATION (1970). This work examines U.S. policy in both Latin America and China during the early decades of the twentieth century and concludes that two basic assumptions of that policy-available capital and British support-confounded U.S. objectives, particularly in China.

Widenor, William C. HENRY CABOT LODGE AND THE SEARCH FOR AN AMERICAN FOREIGN POLICY (1980). This biographical study of Lodge's approach to diplomacy addresses the relationship between foreign and domestic politics during the late nineteenth and early twentieth centuries.

The Hispano-American War

Cosmas, Graham H. AN ARMY FOR EMPIRE: The United States
  Army in the Hispano-American War (1971). Cosmas investigates
  U.S. prosecution of the war with Spain from the perspective of the
  U.S. force that fought it.
Damiani, Brian P. ADVOCATES OF EMPIRE: William McKinley, the
  Senate and American Expansion 1898-1899 (1987). Damiani main-
  tains that McKinley opposed war with the Spanish, but that once
  the course was taken, the president pursued success vigorously.
Gould, Lewis L. THE SPANISH-AMERICAN WAR AND PRESI-
  DENT MCKINLEY (1982). This work constitutes a brief analy-
  sis of McKinley's foreign and domestic policy and its role in the
  American entry into the war with Spain.
Trask, David F. THE WAR WITH SPAIN IN 1898 (1981). This largely
  military history suggests that irrational impulses instead of well
  conceived strategic, economic, or ideological considerations
  brought the United States into a war with Spain.

U.S. Foreign Policy in the Americas

Carr, Raymond. PUERTO RICO: A Colonial Experiment (1984). This
  history of U.S. and Puerto Rican relations from the Hispano-
  American War through the 1980s maintains that Puerto Rico's
  most fundamental difficulties derive primarily from domestic economic problems and not from its relations with the United States.
Crapol, Edward P. AMERICA FOR THE AMERICANS (1973). Crapol
  investigates American competition with Britain in world affairs
  during the latter half of the nineteenth century and explains the
  roots of the early twentieth century turnabout in the American
  attitude toward its rival.
Healy, David. DRIVE TO HEGEMONY (1988). This volume examines U.S. relations with Caribbean countries from 1898-1917. Healy
  maintains that U.S. policy aimed at achieving preeminence in the
  area and was motivated by a desire to prevent European influence
  in the region.
Lael, Richard L. ARROGANT DIPLOMACY: U.S. Policy toward
  Columbia, 1903-1922 (1987). Lael investigates the efforts of early
  twentieth century U.S. Presidents to reconcile national economic
  and strategic interests on the one hand with the rights and sovereignty of Columbia and other Latin American countries on the

other. He concludes that the presidents of that period were not particularly successful resolving the issue and that later presidents fared little better.

Langley, Lester D. THE BANANA WARS: An Inner History of American Empire, 1900-1934 (1983). Langley investigates America's empire in the Caribbean during the early years of the twentieth century and suggests that certain vestiges of that old relationship continue to confound positive progress between the United States and its neighbors in the regions.

Langley, Lester D. THE UNITED STATES AND THE CARIBBEAN, 1900-1970 (1980). Langley presents a chronological and episodic account of U.S. relations with Caribbean nations from the advent of American influence in the Hispano-American war through the demise of the U.S. which characterized early relations continues today: U.S. desire for democracy and progress worldwide on one hand and its custodial treatment of its Caribbean neighbors on the other.

McCullough, David. THE PATH BETWEEN THE SEAS: The Creation of the Panama Canal, 1870-1914 (1977). McCullough identifies the creation of a water passage across Panama as one of the supreme human achievements of all time and tell sits story form the viewpoints of those involved in its development.

U.S. Foreign Policy in the Pacific and the Far East

Breslin, Thomas A. CHINA, AMERICAN CATHOLICISM, AND THE MISSIONARY (1980). Breslin undertakes a study of the impact of Catholic missionaries in China. He concludes that their benevolence, their comparatively opulent life-styles, and their introduction of new ideas contributed to the resurgent of Chinese nationalism and the demise of foreign power in China.

Gates, John M. SCHOOLBOOKS AND KRAGS: The United States Army in the Philippines, 1898-1902 (1973) Gates places the soldier-imperialists of the United States Army within the progressive political tradition. This thorough study is the first stop for any investigation of the Philippine-American War.

Hart, Robert A. THE ECCENTRIC TRADITION: American Diplomacy in the Far East (1976). Hart examines relations between the U.S. and Far Eastern countries from the late eighteenth century through the Vietnam War and suggests that the emotion, extravagance, and high expectations that characterized U.S. policy in that area have significantly impeded productive relations.

Maga, Timothy P. DEFENDING PARADISE (1988). Maga investigates U.S.-Guam relations from 1898 when the United States gained a foothold on the island through the political deliberations concerning decolonization that took place after World War II. This work addresses some of the issues that characterize the present relationship.

Osborne, Thomas J. EMPIRE CAN WAIT: American Opposition to Hawaiian Annexation (1893-1898) (1981). As the title suggests, this volume deals with roots and the rationale of U.S. domestic opposition to the annexation of the Hawaiian Islands.

Reckner, James R. TEDDY ROOSEVELT'S GREAT WHITE FLEET (1988). Reckner investigates the 1907 deployment of the U.S. Atlantic Fleet to the Pacific and concludes that although it was a valuable undertaking for assessing the effectiveness of the battleship fleet, its global impact was diplomatically minimal.

Reed, James. THE MISSIONARY MIND AND AMERICAN EAST ASIAN POLICY, 1911-1915 (1983). Reed investigates the role of the Protestant American missionary in shaping American foreign policy toward East Asia and concludes that the lack of clear-sightedness which characterized the U.S. approach to things Chinese derived significantly from the Protestant missionary movement.

Stanley, Peter W., ed. REAPPRAISING AN EMPIRE: New Perspectives on Philippine-American History (1984). This collection of essays reexamines the widely held notion that the United States had a substantial impact on the Philippines and concludes that American influence has been much less significant than is generally believed.

Welch, Richard E. RESPONSE TO IMPERIALISM: The United States and the Philippine-American War, 1899-1902 (1979). The author investigates the U.S. domestic response to American foreign policy in the Philippines at the turn of the century and assesses its impact on diplomatic behavior.

Empire and Revolution

Breslin, Thomas A. CHINA, AMERICAN CATHOLICISM, AND THE MISSIONARY (1980). Breslin undertakes a study of the impact of Catholic missionaries in China. He concludes that their benevolence, their comparatively opulent lifestyles, and their introduction of new ideas contributed to the resurgence of Chinese nationalism and the demise of foreign influence in China.

Haley, P. Edward. REVOLUTION AND INTERVENTION: The Diplomacy of Taft and Wilson with Mexico, 1910-1917 (1970). Haley examines U.S. foreign policy toward the Mexican Revolution and compares it to the American approach to the revolutions that proliferated after World War II. This work suggests that the policy serves the United States best is one based on its own national interest.

Joseph, Gilbert M. REVOLUTION FROM WITHOUT: Yucatan, Mexico, and the United States, 1880-1924 (1982). This work focuses on the process of revolution in the Yucatan during the early twentieth century, concluding that the failure to achieve a tight urban-rural alliance, the absence of a revolutionary tradition, and the dependency on foreign-dominated markets limited the options of Yucatan revolutionaries.

Leonard, Thomas M. CENTRAL AMERICAN AND UNITED STATES POLICIES, 1820s-1980s: A Guide to Issues and References (1985). Leonard maintains that mid-1980s United States policy on the Central American region is socio-economically incompatible with the objectives of revolutionaries in that area.

Link, Arthur S, ed. WOODROW WILSON AND A REVOLUTIONARY WORLD, 1913-1921 (1982). This series of essays deals with Wilsonian foreign policy toward such international considerations as the Russian and Mexican revolutions, the re-birth of Poland, world order, and world peace.

Noer, Thomas J. BRITON, BOER, AND YANKEE: The United States and South Africa 1870-1914 (1978). Noer investigates U.S. and South African relations and concludes that the United States supported British imperialism in South Africa to insure economic development, progressive government and the westernization of black Africans.

Empire and Race

Anderson, Stuart. RACE AND RAPPROCHEMENT: Anglo-Saxonism and Anglo-American Relations, 1894-1904 (1981). Anderson analyses the cultural and racial aspects of the brief ascendancy of Anglo-Saxonism and its influence on American foreign policy at the beginning of the twentieth century.

Dyer, Thomas G. THEODORE ROOSEVELT AND THE IDEA OF RACE (1980). Dyer investigates Teddy Roosevelt's attitude toward race and its impact on American foreign policy at the turn of the century. This work provides fundamental information on the background of the Anglo-Saxon tradition and its impact on American political life.

Hunt, Michael H. THE MAKING OF A SPECIAL RELATIONSHIP: The United States and China to 1914 (1983). This work analyses U.S-Chinese relations from the economic, social, and racial aspects of conflict and cooperation.

May, Glenn Anthony. SOCIAL ENGINEERING IN THE PHILIPPINES: The Aims, Execution and Impact of American Colonial Policy, 1900-1913 (1980). May argues that U.S. efforts to achieve positive social change in the Philippines during the early twentieth century were not as benevolent as was once thought and were marked by white American ethnocentrism and racism.

McKee, Delber L. CHINESE EXCLUSION VERSUS THE OPEN DOOR POLICY, 1900-1906: Clashes over China Policy in the Roosevelt era (1977). McKee examines the conflicts between the executive's open door policy and the legislature's exclusion policy and concludes that the influence of the labor movement as well as that of racist sentiment are essential in clarifying the roots of this contradiction of policies.

Tsai, Shih-shan Henry. CHINA AND THE OVERSEAS CHINESE IN THE UNITED STATES, 1868-1911 (1983). This book examines the anti-Chinese movement on the U.S. west coast and its impact on U.S. and Chinese relations. Chinese immigrants were active in developing diplomatic relations between the United States and China and in confronting American racism.

WAR AND PEACE

1915-1941

With the outbreak of war in Europe, American editorial writers were wont to give thanks to Columbus and the foresight that led their ancestors to immigrate. However, the United States could no more distance itself from this new major European war than it could remain aloof from the imbroglio of the last century. James Madison and Woodrow Wilson were equally unable to satisfy the national desire to remain neutral. The United States could not escape war with Britain, while Wilson's decisions regarding trade and submarines made war with Germany inescapable.

Save for Latin America and East Asia, the United States held itself aloof from the world for most of the 19th Century. A peaceful Europe and the absence of external threats allowed the populace to concentrate on the construction of a fruitful social and economic order. Still, the new century found the nation forsaking isolation for involvement, imperialism and finally, war. Once victory was at hand, however, the interests of the former allies diverged. The well of conciliation that nurtured the Treaty of Versailles ran dry shortly after the document was created. Moreover, the American willingness to accept additional reconciliatory solutions was scuppered by senatorial intransigence, political duplicity and a monumental presidential ego.

Nevertheless, if the failure of the United States to adhere to the League of Nations indicated a reclusive approach, the brief American experience in putting the world in order had a residual impact. Thus, the United States pursued a curious combination of internationalism and isolation. The Washington treaties assisted in the easing of tensions, while American-sponsored programs did much to ease the effect of German war reparations. The U.S. also participated in many activities under the auspices of the League, while the Pact of Paris represented American idealism at its best. Meantime, the nation restricted immigration and demanded payment of war debts while raising the very tariff barriers that made the payment of such debts difficult.

The trauma of the Great Depression severely diminished what remained of the American commitment to international cooperation. The nation espoused institutional isolation in the guise of neutrality legislation. However, the rise of aggressor nations persuaded the Roosevelt administration to champion order and security in a world grown fractious by chaos and hazard. As the neutrality laws were modified to furnish all aid short of war, and the warlords of Japan placed on notice, the United States increasingly engaged in the practice of belligerent neutrality.

CHRONOLOGY

1915
Feb 4 Germany initiates naval blockade of U.K.
Feb 5 Stone-Flood Act (Congress)
Apr 26 Treaty of London (France, Italy and U.K.)
May 7 SS *Lusitania* torpedoed and sinks
Jun 9 First Secretary of State to openly resign over policy dispute (William J. Bryan)
Jun 24 Robert Lansing (Secretary of State)
Jul 28 U.S. forces land Haiti (ends 15 Aug 1934)
Aug 19 SS *Arabic* torpedoed and sinks
Sept 16 Treaty of Friendship (Haiti and U.S.)
Oct 5 *Arabic* Pledge (Germany)

1916
Feb 17 McLemore Resolution introduced (House of Representatives)
Feb 25 Gore Resolution introduced (Senate)
Mar 3 Gore Resolution rejected (Senate)
Mar 7 McLemore Resolution rejected (House of Representatives)
Mar 14 U.S. forces enter Mexico (ends 7 Feb 1917)
Mar 24 SS *Sussex* torpedoed
May 4 *Sussex* Pledge (Germany)
May 5 U.S. forces land Dominican Republic (ends 16 Sept 1924)
Aug 4 Danish West Indies Acquisition Treaty
Nov 24 Withdrawal of American troops — Mexico (unperfected)

1917
Jan 31 Germany announces resumption of unrestricted submarine war
Feb 1 Germany initiates unrestricted submarine warfare
Feb 3 Diplomatic relations suspended (Germany)
Feb 24 Zimmermann Telegram passed to U.S. (made public 1 Mar 1917)
Feb 26 President W. Wilson requests joint session of Congress
Mar 15 Nicholas II (Russia) abdicates
Apr 6 State of War—Germany and U.S. (armistice 11 Nov 1918)
Nov 2 Lansing-Ishii Agreement (Japan and U.S.)
Nov 6 Bolshevik faction seizes power in Russia
Nov 7 Diplomatic relations suspended (Russia)
Dec 7 State of War—Austria-Hungary and U.S. (armistice 11 Nov 1918)

1918
Jan 8 Fourteen Points speech (President W. Wilson)
Mar 3 Treaty of Brest-Litovsk (Germany and U.S.S.R.)
Apr 10 Webb-Pomerene Act (Congress)
Aug 3 U.S. forces land Archangel (ends 27 Jun 1919)
Aug 15 U.S. forces land Vladivostok (ends 1 Apr 1920)
Nov 11 Armistice ending Great War

1919
** Stephen G. Porter (House Foreign Affairs Committee)
** Henry Cabot Lodge, Sr. (Senate Foreign Relations Committee)
Jan 12 Paris Peace Conference
Mar 2 American Relief Administration created (Executive order)
Mar 4 Round Robin Resolution (Senate)
Mar 25 King-Crane Commission appointed
May 2 Diplomatic relations (Poland)
Jun 11 Diplomatic relations (Czechoslovakia)
Jun 28 Treaty of Versailles—Multilateral (unperfected)
Jun 28 Military assistance—France (unperfected)
Jun 28 German occupation—Multilateral (unperfected)
Jun 28 Treaty regarding Poland—Multilateral (unperfected)
Sept 10 Treaty of St. Germain-en-Laye—Multilateral (unperfected)
Sept 1 Treaty regarding Czechoslovakia—Multilateral (unperfected)
Sept 10 Treaty regarding Yugoslavia—Multilateral (unperfected)
Sept 10 Trade in arms and ammunition—Multilateral (unperfected)
Oct 13 Regulation of aerial navigation—Multilateral (unperfected)

Nov 19 U.S. Senate rejects Treaty of Versailles
Nov 27 Treaty of Neuilly—Multilateral (unperfected)
Dec 9 Treaty regarding Romania—Multilateral (unperfected)
Dec 24 Edge Act (Congress)

1920
Jan 10 League of Nations (Geneva, Switzerland)
Mar 19 U.S. Senate rejects Treaty of Versailles
Mar 19 Diplomatic relations (Finland)
Mar 23 Bainbridge Colby (Secretary of State)
Apr 19 *Missouri v. Holland* (Supreme Court)
May 1 Regulation of aerial navigation—Mulitlateral (unperfected)
Jun 4 Treaty of Trianon—Multilateral (unperfected)
Dec 16 Permanent Court of International Justice—Multilateral (unper-
fected)

1921
Jan 24 Diplomatic relations (Hungary)
Mar 5 Charles Evans Hughes (Secretary of State)
Jul 11 Meta K. Hannay (first woman to take the diplomatic service
examination)
Aug 24 Establishing friendly relations (Austria and U.S.)
Aug 25 Establishing friendly relations (Germany and U.S.) See Treaty
of Berlin, 1921.
Aug 29 Establishing friendly relations (Hungary and U.S.)
Nov 12 Washington Naval Conference (ends 6 Feb 1922)
Dec 13 Four-Power Treaty (France, Japan, U.K. and U.S.)

1922
Jan 24 Diplomatic relations (Hungary)
Feb 6 Five-Power Treaty (France, Italy, Japan, U.K. and U.S.)
Feb 6 Nine-Power Treaty (Belgium, China, France, Italy, Japan, Neth-
erlands, Portugal, U.K. and U.S.)
Feb 6 Use of submarines and noxious gases in warfare - Multilateral
(unperfected)
Feb 11 Japan—U.S. Treaty
Nov 13 Diplomatic relations (Latvia)
Nov 20 Diplomatic relations (Estonia)
Dec 4 Diplomatic relations (Albania)
Dec 5 Diplomatic relations (Lithuania)

Dec 16 Lucile Atcherson commissioned (first woman Foreign Service Officer)

1923
Feb 1 Inter-oceanic canal—Costa Rica (unperfected)
Mar 25 International Conference of American States— Santiago (ends 3 May)
May 26 National Origins Act (Congress)
Aug 6 Treaty of Lausanne—Turkey (unperfected)
Aug 31 Bucareli Agreement (Mexico and U.S.)
Sept 1 Dawes Plan implemented (Allied Reparations Commission)

1924
May 24 Roger's Act (Congress)
Dec 24 No citizen may be excluded from taking the Foreign Service examination by reason of race, gender or national origin (Memorandum— Secretary of State)

1925
* * William E. Borah (Senate Foreign Relations Committee)
Mar 5 Frank B. Kellogg (Secretary of State)
Apr 11 Lucile Atcherson assigned to Berne, Switzerland   (first woman assigned to a foreign post)
Apr 20 Patti H. Field commissioned (first woman Foreign Service Officer commissioned after passage of Rogers Act)
Jun 17 Trade in arms and ammunition—Multilaterial (unperfected)
Jun 17 Protocol for the prohibition of the use in war of asphyxiating, poisonous or other gases and of bacteriological methods of warfare— Multilateral (unperfected)
Nov 2 Patti H. Field takes up duties (first woman to hold a consular appointment)
Dec 1 Treaty of Locarno (Belgium, Czechoslovakia, France, Germany, Italy, Poland and U.K.)

1927
Jan 6 U.S. forces land Nicaragua (ends 3 May 1933)
May 12 Peace of Tipitapa (Nicaragua)
Jun 1 Diplomatic relations (Canada)
Jun 20 Geneva Naval Conference (ends 4 August)
Jul 27 Diplomatic relations (Ireland)
Aug 27 Kellog-Briand Pact (France and U.S.)

1928

Jan 16 International Conference of American States—   Havana (ends 20 February)

Feb 20 Pan American Union—Multilateral (unperfected)

Aug 27 Pact of Paris (Multilateral)

Dec 8 State of War—Bolivia and Paraguay (ends 5 December)

Dec 10 Conference of American States on Conciliation and Arbitration—Washington (ends 5 January 1929)

Dec 17 Memorandum on the Monroe Doctrine (J. Reuben Clark)

1929

Mar 28 Henry Lewis Stimson (Secretary of State)

Sept 14 Permanent Court of International Justice—   Multilateral (unperfected)

1930

Jan 21 London Naval Conference (ends 22 April)

Feb 18 Diplomatic relations (Republic of South Africa)

Apr 22 London Naval Treaty (France, Italy, Japan, U.K.   and U.S.)

May 17 Young Plan implemented (Allied Reparations Commission)

Sept 27 Estrada Doctrine (Genaro Estrada)

1931

* * J. Charles Linthicum (House Foreign Affairs Committee)

Feb 23 Moses-Linthicum Act becomes law

Jun 18 Diplomatic relations (Iraq)

Jun 20 Hoover Moratorium

Sept 18 Mukden Incident (Manchuria)

1932

* * Samuel D. McReynolds (House Foreign Affairs Committee)

Jan 7 Stimson Doctrine

Jan 28 State of War—China and Japan (ends 3 March)

Feb 2 World Disarmament Conference (adjourns July 1932)

Jun 15 State of War—Bolivia and Paraguay (ends 14 Jun 1935)

Jul 18 Great Lakes-St. Lawrence Waterway—Canada and U.S. (unperfected)

Oct 4 Lytton Commission Report (League of Nations)

1933
* * Key Puttman (Senate Foreign Relations Committee)
Mar 4 Cordell Hull (Secretary of State)
May 29 Ruth Bryan Owen—Denmark (first woman envoy extraordinary minister plenipotentiary)
Jun 12 World Economic Conference (ends 27 July)
Oct 11 Suppression of the traffic in women— Multilateral (unperfected)
Nov 16 Roosevelt-Litvinov Agreements (U.S. and U.S.S.R.)
Dec 3 International Conference of American States— Montevideo (ends 26 December)
Dec 13 Diplomatic Relations (Union of Soviet Socialist Republics)
Dec 26 Convention on Rights and Duties of States
(Seventh Pan-American Conference)

1934
Apr 13 Johnson Debt Default Act (Congress)
May 29 Cuba—U.S. Treaty
May 29 World Disarmament Conference (ends 8 June)
Dec 29 Japan announces intention to withdraw from Five Power Treaty (effective 31 Dec 1936)

1935
May 4 Diplomatic relations (Afghanistan)
Aug 31 Neutrality Act (Congress)
Oct 3 State of War—Ethiopia and Italy (ends 5 May 1936)
Oct 5 U.S. embargoes arms shipments to Italy (ends 20 Jun 1936)

1936
Feb 29 Neutrality Act (Congress)
Mar 25 London Naval Treaty (France, U.K. and U.S.)
Jul 17 Spanish Civil War (ends 28 Mar 1939)
Aug 11 U.S. declares neutrality (Spanish Civil War)
Nov 25 Anti-Comintern Pact (Germany and Japan)
Dec 1 Inter-American Conference for the Maintenance of Peace—Buenos Aires (ends 23 December)
Dec 21 *U.S. v. Curtis-Wright Export Corporation* (Supreme Court)

1937
May 1 Neutrality Act (Congress)
May 3 *U.S. v. Belmont* (Supreme Court)
Jul 7 State of War—China and Japan (ends 15 August 1945)
Oct 5 Quarantine Address (Franklin D. Roosevelt)
Nov 3 Brussels Conference (ends 24 November)
Dec 12 USS *Panay* sunk by Japanese aircraft (Nanjing, China)

1938
Jan 10 Ludlow Amendment rejected (House of Representatives)
Mar 13 Germany annexes Austria (Anschluss)
Sept 29 Munich Conference—ends 28 November)
Dec 9 International Conference of American States—   Lima (ends 27 December)
Dec 24 Declaration of Lima

1939
* * Sol Bloom (House Foreign Affairs Committee)
Apr 3 U.S. recognizes government of Francisco Franco (Spain)
Apr 7 Italy conquers Albania
Jun 28 First regular commercial transatlantic flight completed (New York to Lisbon)
Aug 23 Non-Aggression Pact (Germany and U.S.S.R.)
Sept 1 State of War—Germany and Poland
Sept 3 State of War—France, Germany and U.K.
Sept 5 Neutrality Proclamation (U.S.)
Sept 6 U.S. establishes Neutrality Patrol (Atlantic)
Sept 16 Diplomatic relations suspended (Albania)
Sept 21 First Conference of Foreign Ministers of the American Republics (ends 28 September)
Oct 3 Declaration of Panama
Nov 4 Neutrality Act (Congress)
Nov 29 State of War—Finland and U.S.S.R. (ends 12 Mar 1940)

1940
* * Walter F. George (Senate Foreign Relations Committee)
Jan 26 Commercial agreement (Japan and U.S.)
Feb 4 Diplomatic relations (Saudi Arabia)
May 19 Committee to Defend America by Aiding the Allies
Jun 18 No transfer resolution (Congress)

Jul 17 Diplomatic relations (Australia)

Jun 22 France surrenders to Germany

Jul 23 Second Conference of Foreign Ministers of the American Republics (ends 30 July)

Jul 30 Act of Havana

Aug 1 U.S. embargoes aviation gas shipments (Japan)

Sept 2 American First Committee

Sept 3 Destroyers-For-Bases Agreement (U.K. and U.S.)

Sept 5 Diplomatic relations suspended (Estonia)

Sept 5 Diplomatic relations suspended (Latvia)

Sept 5 Diplomatic relations suspended (Lithuania)

Sept 16 Conscription Act (Congress)

Sept 26 U.S. embargoes scrap iron and steel shipments (Japan)

Sept 27 Tripartite Pact (Germany, Italy and Japan)

1941

** Tom Connally (Senate Foreign Relations Committee)

Mar 11 Lend-Lease Act (Congress)

Apr 13 Non-Aggression Pact (Japan and U.S.S.R.)

Jun 22 State of War—Germany and U.S.S.R.

Jul 7 U.S. forces land Iceland

Jul 26 Japanese assets in U.S. frozen

Aug 9 Argentia Bay Conference—U.K. and U.S. (ends 12 August)

Aug 14 Atlantic Charter (U.K. and U.S.)

Aug 18 Congress removes 12-month limitation on draftee   service

Sept 1 U.S. Navy authorized to attack Axis ships anywhere in Atlantic

Sept 4 USS *Greer* attacked by German submarine

Sept 30 Diplomatic relations (Iceland)

Oct 17 USS *Kearny* attacked by German submarine

Oct 31 USS *Ruben James* sunk by German submarine

Nov 17 Neutrality Act (Congress)

Nov 21 U.S. forces land Dutch Guiana

Dec 7 Japan attacks Hawaiian Islands

Dec 8 State of War—Japan and U.S.

Dec 11 State of War— Germany, Italy and U.S.

Dec 11 Diplomatic relations suspended (Hungary)

Dec 12 Diplomatic relations suspended (Romania)

Dec 12 State of War—Romania and U.S.

Dec 13 Diplomatic relations suspended (Bulgaria)

Dec 13 State of War—Bulgaria and U.S.

Dec 22 Arcadia Conference (ends 14 Jan 1942)
Dec 24 St. Pierre and Miquelon Affair (France and U.S.)

TREATIES, AGREEMENTS, SUPREME COURT CASES AND ACTS OF CONGRESS

STONE-FLOOD ACT (1915) This act established a board of examiners and a system of examinations for applicants for the diplomatic and consular services. It also established a promotion system based on merit.

TREATY OF LONDON (1915) France, Italy and U.K. Secret treaty whereby France and U.K. persuaded Italy to abandon the Triple Alliance (Germany, Austria-Hungary and Italy) in exchange for territorial rewards.

DANISH WEST INDIES ACQUISITION TREATY (1916) Denmark and U.S. After abortive attempts to purchase what are now called the Virgin Islands in 1866 and 1902, the U.S. was successful in 1916 at a cost of $24 million.

LANSING-ISHII AGREEMENT (1917) Japan and U.S. U.S. recognized Japan's special interests in China but both nations averred that China's territorial sovereignty and the Open Door principles should be upheld. A special protocol bound each to refrain from obtaining special privileges as a result of the war. Abrogated in 1922 by the Nine-Power Treaty.

TREATY OF BREST-LITOVSK (1918) Germany and Russia. Terminated hostilities between the Central Powers and Russia. Russia renounced all claim to Poland and the Baltic region and the Ukraine emerged as a distinct entity. Prisoners of war were exchanged and diplomatic relations established between Germany and the new Bolshevik regime.

WEBB-POMERENE ACT (1918) This law exempted foreign commercial activity from the economic monopoly restrictions imposed by the Sherman Antitrust Act (1890). See Edge Act (1919)

KING-CRANE COMMISSION (1919) This commission sought to investigate the circumstances and conditions existing in the defunct Ottoman Empire. It was conducted by Henry Churchill King (President of Oberlin College) and Charles R. Crane (Chicago industrialist). The commission visited Palestine, Syria, Lebanon and Anatolia to determine if the regions were ready for self-determination, or, alternatively, to determine if the populace favored specific nations as mandatory powers. The commission report was submitted 28 August 1919.

EDGE ACT (1919) This legislation is corollary to the Webb-Pomerene Act (1918) in that it exempted U.S. banks from antitrust rules when they operated to engage in foreign financial transactions. This act inadvertently circumvented an existing prohibition against branch banking in that said corporations could be set up anywhere, including other states in the U.S.

MISSOURI v. HOLLAND (1920) Supreme Court rules that a treaty, once ratified, becomes the supreme law of the land.

BERLIN TREATY (1921) Germany and U.S. Formal end of hostilities between Germany and U.S. Provided that the value of confiscated German property in U.S. would be applied against American claims and that Americans would be treated equally in any claims settlement. The treaty expressly disavowed an American commitment to any provisions of the Versailles agreement in the matter of political or military obligations.

FOUR-POWER TREATY (1921) France, Japan, U.K. and U.S. Agreement to respect one another's rights in the Pacific and refer future disputes to a joint conference. Also provided for mutual consultation and joint action in the event of a threat to the four signatories. Terminated the Anglo-Japanese Treaty (1902).

FIVE-POWER TREATY (1922) France, Italy, Japan, U.K. and U.S. Established ratios of naval strength based on the tonnage of capital ships (battleships and air-craft carriers), a ten-year ban on the construction of capital ships and the U.S. and U.K. to forego further fortifications in the Pacific, save Hawaii. Submarines, destroyers and cruisers were not subject to quantitative limitations until the London Naval Conference (1930) although qualitative limits were established for cruisers by this agreement.

NINE-POWER TREATY (1922) Belgium, China, France, Italy, Japan, Netherlands, Portugal, U.K. and U.S. The signatories agreed to respect the sovereignty, the independence and the territorial and administrative integrity of China. Further pledged to uphold the principles of the Open Door and to assist China in forming a stable government.

JAPAN-U.S. TREATY (1922) Resolves the Yap Island controversy. U.S. received cable, radio and residential rights on the island equal to that of Japan. U.S. recognizes Japanese sovereignty over Yap Island.

BUCARELI AGREEMENT (1923) Mexico and U.S. Claims commissions established, U.S. agreed to accept Mexico's claim to subsoil minerals (Article 27 of 1917 Mexican Constitution) and recognize the government of Alvaro Obregon.

ROGER'S ACT (1924) This legislation amalgamated the diplomatic and consular services into a unified service. Permanent officers below the rank of minister were designated foreign service officers and subject to both diplomatic and consular assignments. The act further created an open, competitive examination with promotion based on merit. See Moses-Linthicum Act (1931)

GENEVA PROTOCOL (1925) A diplomatic consequence of an American suggestion offered to the Geneva Conference for the Supervision of the International Traffic in Arms (1925). The pact bans the use of lethal gases, bacteriological and biological agents in war. It was ratified by all the major powers save the U.S. and Japan. Opposition in the U.S. Senate kept the measure from a vote until 1969. Debate over the applicability of the treaty to the use, by the United States, of herbicides and tear gas in South Vietnam delayed acceptance until 16 December 1974.

TREATY OF LOCARNO (1925) Belgium, Czechoslovakia, France, Germany, Italy, Poland and U.K. Guaranteed existing boundaries of Belgium, France and Germany, renounced the use of force save in self-defense or in fulfillment of League of Nations obligations and provided that disputes be submitted to arbitration. Mutual assistance pact against German aggression signed by France and Poland and France and Czechoslovakia. The Rhineland recognized as a demilitarized zone.

PACT OF PARIS (1928) Multilateral agreement that began as an executive agreement, viz., Kellogg-Briand Pact. It was signed by the nations of the world save Andorra, Argentina, Bolivia, El Salvador, Liechtenstein, Monaco, Morocco, San Marino and Uruguay. Signatories renounced resort to war as an instrument of national policy and declared that disputes would be settled by peaceful means alone. The treaty is perpetual and stipulates that a resort to war denies to a Power the benefits furnished by the treaty, and thus served as a legal foundation for the war crimes trials in Germany and Japan after WW II.

CLARK MEMORANDUM (1928) This policy statement by Under Secretary of State J. Reuben Clark, written in 1928 and publicly released in 1930, was designed to improve relations betwixt the

United States and the nations of Latin America. To the extent, the memorandum explicitly renounces the use of military force to intervene in Latin American nations it repudiates the Roosevelt Corollary (1904).

ESTRADA DOCTRINE (1930) Genero Estrada (Foreign Minister, Mexico) insisted that the Tobar Doctrine of recognition (1907) be modified to apply to de facto governments no matter how they came to power. See the Convention on the Rights and Duties of States (1933).

LONDON NAVAL TREATY (1930) France, Italy, Japan, U.K. and U.S. Quantitative limits placed on all categories of warships and qualitative limits established for destroyers and submarines. New qualitative limits established for battleships and cruisers and replacement of capital ships under the Five Power Treaty (1922) postponed for five years.

MOSES-LINTHICUM ACT (1931) This legislation sought to redress inequities incident to the administration of the Foreign Service. It provided for an impartial promotion process as well as an increase in salaries and allowances.

ROOSEVELT-LITVINOV AGREEMENT (1933) U.S. and U.S.S.R. In return for a resumption of diplomatic relations, the U.S.S.R. agreed to protect the religious liberty of Americans in Russia, to prohibit and refuse aid to organizations dedicated to the overthrow of the U.S. government and to pay at least $75 million as compensation for existing debts.

CONVENTION ON RIGHTS AND DUTIES OF STATES (1933) Pan-American Union. This agreement formally embraced the principle of nonintervention as a tenet of international conduct in the Americas. The so-called Montevideo Pledge extended the Estrada Doctrine (1930) to assert that no nation had the right to intervene in the internal or external affairs of another.

U.S. v. CURTIS-WRIGHT EXPORT CORPORATION (1936) Supreme Court rules that U.S. government has sweeping powers over foreign affairs which derive, not from the Constitution, but from the nation's sovereignty. Congress has broad latitude to delegate foreign affairs responsibilities to the president.

U.S. v. BELMONT (1937) Supreme Court rules that executive agreements enjoy the same force of law as treaties submitted and approved by the Senate.

DECLARATION OF LIMA (1938) Eighth International Conference of American States. Supported common action by American states to meet a common danger and provided that the foreign ministers of all would convene upon the call of any one of them.

NAZI-SOVIET NON-AGGRESSION PACT (1939) Germany and U.S.S.R. Although each nation retained the right to declare war on the other, they agreed to foreswear joining a third power at war with the other. Secret protocols defined spheres of influence: the Baltic States, save Lithuania, were Russian; Poland was divided along the Narew-Vistula line; Lithuania was German and Russia was accorded predominance in Bessarabia.

DECLARATION OF PANAMA (1939) First Conference of the Foreign Ministers of the American Republics. Proclaimed the existence of a so-called safety belt around the Western Hemisphere south of Canada between 300 and 1000 miles in width. Combatants were enjoined to refrain from warlike actions within that area.

NO TRANSFER RESOLUTION (1940) Joint Resolution of Congress. The U.S. would not acquiesce in any transfer of geographic regions in the Western hemisphere from one non-American power to another. If such a situation occurred the U.S. would, in addition to other measures, immediately consult with the other American nations.

ACT OF HAVANA (1940) Second Conference of the Foreign Ministers of the American Republics. Colonies of European powers may be occupied, and administered, by American republics if in danger of falling into hostile hands. Individual American nations might occupy such colonies on a temporary basis subject to review by the entire body.

DESTROYER-BASES DEAL (1940) U.K. and U.S. Executive agreement whereby U.S. exchanged fifty WW I destroyers previously considered surplus for sites for bases in Newfoundland and Bermuda for ninety-nine years and rent-free leases for ninety-nine years on six additional sites. U.K. gave formal pledge never to sink or surrender the Royal Navy.

TRIPARTITE PACT (1940) Germany, Italy and Japan. Japan recognized German and Italian dominance in Europe and they similarly accepted Japanese dominance in East Asia. They agreed to come to one another's aid if attacked by any nation not then engaged in war in either Europe or China. The treaty did not affect the relations between any of the signatories and the U.S.S.R.

SOVIET-JAPANESE NEUTRALITY PACT (1941) Japan and U.S.S.R. Signatories would maintain peaceful relations and respect each other's territory. If either became involved in a war on the part of any one of several other powers then other would remain neutral throughout the duration of the conflict. (Abrogated by U.S.S.R. on 6 August 1945)

BIOGRAPHICAL SKETCHES

BETHMANN-HOLLWEG, Theobald von (1856-1921) A successful Prussian civil servant when named Chancellor (1906) he was inclined toward the contemplative and frequently hesitated to act. He failed to please any of various factions within the German government and resigned under pressure but with relief (1917).

BORAH, William E. (1865-1940) Lawyer and politician, he was elected to the Senate (1907) as a Progressive Republican and served until his death. A member of the Foreign Relations Committee (1913-1940), he was also Chairman of the committee (1925-1933). A firm nationalist, he opposed all peacetime alliances and intervention in foreign wars.

GREW, Joseph C. (1880-1965) Career diplomat, he was prominent in the effort to establish diplomacy as a career in the U.S. Selected as Ambassador to Japan (1932-1941) he displayed the skill, patience and tact of diplomacy at its best. Moreover, "in the midst of the fantasy and hatred of war, he presented a realistic and objective view of the Japanese that prepared the U.S. for peace and reconciliation."

GREY, Edward (1862-1933) A successful English politician, he nonetheless disliked the profession and preferred bird watching, a passion he shared with his friend Theodore Roosevelt. As Foreign Secretary (1905-916), he resisted German attempts to disrupt the Anglo-French Entente and during WW I took a line calculated to keep Anglophobic sentiments in the U.S. from reaching impossible limits.

HORNBECK, Stanley K. (1883-1966) Chief of the Division of Far Eastern Affairs (1928-1937), he maintained a generally sympathetic attitude toward China and proposed a strong stand against Japanese expansion in East Asia. As political adviser to Secretary of State Cordell Hull (1937-1944), and the most senior of the State Department's experts on East Asia, he was a supporter of unlimited aid to Chiang Kai-shek (Chiang Chung-cheng).

LITVINOFF, Maxim Maksimovich (1876-1951) Born in Russian Poland, he joined the Social Democratic party in 1898 and adhered to the Bolshevik faction when the party split (1903). As Commissar for Foreign Affairs (1930), he advocated cooperation with Germany and Japan until 1933 and then became an advocate of collective security with the West. Dismissed as Foreign Secretary in 1939 as an obstacle to rapprochement with Germany, he became Ambassador to the U.S. (1941-43) and Deputy Commissar for Foreign Affairs (1943-1946).

LUDLOW, Lewis L. (1873-1950) Journalist and politician, he was elected to the House of Representatives (1929-1949) after almost thirty years in the press gallery. As a journalist and legislator, he established no great claim to fame until his persistence in pressing the war referendum that bears his name.

PAGE, Walter Hines (1855-1918) Journalist and editor, he founded *THE WORLD'S WORK*, a journal devoted to politics and practical affairs, wherein often appeared the work of his friend Woodrow Wilson. Appointed Ambassador to the United Kingdom (1913-1918), he was an enthusiastic proponent of Anglo-American cooperation and thus disagreed with Wilson's policy of neutrality, although he followed instructions, albeit somewhat selectively.

ZIMMERMAN, Arthur (1864-1940) Career civil servant, he served as Counselor in German Foreign Office (1908-1911) and Undersecretary for Foreign Affairs (1911-1916). His appointment as Secretary of State for Foreign Affairs (1916) led Americans to believe more liberal elements were surfacing in the German government, but actually, this commoner was more Prussian than the most conservative aristocrat.

ANNOTATED BIBLIOGRAPHY

American diplomacy of the first half of the twentieth century reflects the United States' accession to the position of a world leader. Major foreign policy issues focus on U.S. willingness to assume that role and the degree to which the country exploited its status in the global community. This period is characterized by wartime involvement, beginning and ending with world wars that surround almost two decades of attempts to evade many of the chief international problems.

General

The period of America diplomacy beginning with the Great War deals with a United States that is a world power both economically and militarily. Scholars seek to explain the use of this significant and increasing influence and to assess the short- and long-range impact of decisions reached during these years.

Bailey, Thomas A. A DIPLOMATIC HISTORY OF THE AMERI-CAN PEOPLE (1904). Bailey analyzed what he viewed as the generally harmful effect that public opinion had exerted on American diplomacy.

Bemis, Samuel Flagg. A DIPLOMATIC HISTORY OF THE UNITED STATES (1936). According to Bemis, the United States made no serious mistakes in its diplomacy and committed few minor errors, from 1775 to 1898 but thereafter endured a long succession of deplorable diplomatic blunders.

Buckley, Thomas H and Edwin B. Strong. AMERICAN FOREIGN AND NATIONAL SECURITY POLICIES, 1914-1945 (1987). This volume examines U.S. foreign relations from 1941 to 1945 in light of their connection with American military power and strategy.

Carroll, John M. and George C. Herring. MODERN AMERICAN DIPLOMACY (1986). This collection of essays on twentieth century American diplomacy addresses the major phases and issues of the modern period. Topics explored in this volume include the U.S. intervention in World War I, the U.S. role at the Versailles Conference American diplomacy during the 1920s, U.S. foreign relations of the depression years, and the U.S. entry into World War II.

Cohen, Warren I. EMPIRE WITHOUT TEARS: America's Foreign Relations 1921-1933 (1987). Cohen maintains that U.S. involvement in world affairs during the 1920s was actually rather extensive and seeks to describe the diplomacy of the period from that perspective.

Combs, Jerald A. AMERICAN DIPLOMATIC HISTORY: Two centuries of changing interpretations (1986). Combs offers a general overview of American foreign policy from 1775 to the present and outlines the major viewpoints which have been presented by American diplomatic historians.

Gardner, Lloyd C. A COVENANT WITH POWER: America and World Order from Wilson to Reagan (1984). Gardner examines the various ways in which U.S. presidents since Wilson have used power and their particular records in reconciling the application of power with democratic ideology.

Graebner, Norman A. AMERICA AS A WORLD POWER: A Realist Appraisal from Wilson to Reagan (1984). Graebner maintains that the United States sacrifices world influence by elevating ideals and principles above diplomacy.

Johnson, Robert. THE PEACE PROGRESSIVES AND AMERICAN FOREIGN RELATIONS (1995). Peace Progressives, according to Johnson, were a loose coalition of senators who combined anti-imperialism economic diplomacy, and antimilitarism to produce a dissenting position opposing not only Wilsonianism but also corporatism as well as business internationalism in the 1920s

Jones, Kenneth Paul, ed. U.S. DIPLOMATS IN EUROPE, 1919-1914 (1981-1983). This collection of essays investigates the actions and attitudes of individual U.S. diplomats in Europe from the Wilson through the Roosevelt administrations and explores their impact on foreign relations.

Lake, David A. POWER PROTECTION, AND FREE TRADE: International Sources of U.S. Commercial Strategy, 1987-1939 (1988). This work examines the structure of international trade and U.S. international economic strategy form the last quarter of the nineteenth century until World War II. The author uses the findings of this study to support his prognosis that the present multilateral opportunistic structure of international trade is likely to endure despite declining U.S. hegemony.

Link, Arthur S., ed. WOODROW WILSON AND A REVOLUTIONARY WORLD, 1913-1921 (1982). This series of essays deals with Wilsonian foreign policy toward the Russian and Mexican revolutions, the (re)birth of Poland, world order and world peace.

Rosenberg, Emily S. SPREADING THE AMERICAN DREAM: American Economic and Cultural Expansion, 1890-1945 (1982). Rosenberg coins the term *liberal-developmentism* to describe the impact of the American dream and U.S. attempts to apply it to other parts of the world.

Schulzinger, Robert D. AMERICAN DIPLOMACY IN THE
TWENTIETH CENTURY (1990). This work provides a valuable introduction to the major phases of American diplomacy in
the twentieth century. The first chapter is particularly useful in
describing the distinguishing characteristics of foreign policy in
the modern age and in orienting the reader to the unique features
of the American version.

World War I

Scholarship concerning American entry into the Great War argues various motivations. Some contend that protection of trade was the
precipitating factor. Others cite national prestige, the domestic
economy, or the protection of neutral rights as preeminent issues
affecting the U.S. decision to engage in the conflict.

Bailey, Thomas and Paul B Ryan. THE *LUSITANIA* AFFAIR: An Epi-
sode in Modern Warfare and Diplomacy (1975). This work investigates Germany's sinking of the passenger ship *Lusitania,* one of
Britain's largest and fastest commercial steamers. Bailey and Ryan
assess the impact of this event on the U.S. domestic debate regarding the war in Europe and on the seas.

Burk, Kathleen. BRITAIN, AMERICA AND THE SINEWS OF
WAR, 1914-1918 (1985). Burk traces British relations with American
private industry throughout World War I, focusing on the increasing American influence in European politics that resulted from
this partnership. She concludes that despite the crucial position
in which the United States found itself at the end of the war, the
nation lacked two key qualities of great power status: the capacity
as well as the will to be a world leader.

Carroll, John M. and George C. Herring. MODERN AMERICAN
DIPLOMACY (1986). This collection of essays on twentieth century American diplomacy addresses the major phases and issues
of the modern period. Topic explored in this volume include the
U.S. intervention in world War I, the U.S, role at the Versailles
conferences, American diplomacy during the 1920's, U.S. foreign
relations of the depression years, and the United States entry into
world War II.

Coogan, John W. THE END OF NEUTRALITY: The United States,
Britain and maritime Rights, 1899-1915 (1981). Coogan contends
that American neutrality during World War I and its ultimate

breakdown cannot be fully explained apart from an understanding of the legal aspects of the blockade of Germany and the reaction of American to the consequent reduction of trade.

Ferrell, Robert H. WOODROW WILSON AND WORLD WAR I: 1917-1921 (1985). This work examines the success and failures of American foreign policy from U.S. entry into World War I through the American rejection of world leadership following the conferences at Versailles.

Gregory Ross. THE ORIGINS OF AMERICAN INTERVENTION IN THE FIRST WORLD WAR (1971). Ross investigates foreign policy during the period in which the U.S. emerged as the world's greatest economic power and examines the impact of that role on the American entry in to the First World War.

Jonas, Manfred. THE UNITED STATES AND GERMANY: A Diplomatic History (1984). Jonas investigates the history of U.S. and German relations in its geopolitical context, contending that greater continuity can be found in this approach to international relations.

The Interwar Years

Because United States entry into the Great War was facilitated by the assertion that this conflict would be the war to end all wars, the failure of both the peace settlement which was arranged at Versailles and the arms control agreements reached thereafter dominate research on American diplomacy in the interwar years. Woodrow Wilson's strenuous efforts to promote the League of Nations as a peacekeeping tool and the U.S. Senate's rejection of American participation in the organization are also highly debated events of the period as scholars seek to assign responsibility to various segments of the U.S. political scene for the American attempt to withdraw from international leadership. The practical outworking of the U.S. efforts to stabilize its relations with individual European nations and to establish and maintain reliable trade connections with its closest neighbors in the Western Hemisphere apart from involvement in global politics illustrates the problems inherent in the hands off approach to world events.

Peacemaking and Arms Control

Ambrosius, Lloyd E. WOODROW WILSON AND THE AMERICAN DIPLOMATIC TRADITION: The Treaty Fight in Perspective (1987). This volume departs from a Wilson-centered approach to the Versailles Treaty fight and rejects the isolationism vs. internationalism interpretation of Wilson's policies. Ambrosius substitutes the concepts of interdependence and pluralism for those terms, describing Wilsonian foreign policy as one of control, universalism and unilateralism.

Bailey, Thomas. WOODROW WILSON AND THE GREAT BETRAYAL (1945). Bailey criticized Wilson for his mistakes in dealing with the Senate and he believed that Henry Cabot Lodge more closely represented the sentiments of a majority of Americans.

Bailey, Thomas. WOODROW WILSON AND THE LOST PEACE (1955). While approving of Wilson's idealistic plans for the peace treaty with Germany, Bailey criticized Wilson for the blunders that compromised his principles at Versailles.

Buckley, Thomas H. THE UNITED STATES AND THE WASHINGTON CONFERENCE, 1921-1922 (1970). This work describes the issues and events of what Buckley considers the only successful arms limitation conference in modern history.

Cole, Bernard O. GUNBOATS AND THE MARINES: The United States Navy in China 1925-1928 (1983). Cole investigates the U.S. naval presence in Chinese waters and considers its role in the diplomacy of the United States.

Cable, James. GUNBOAT DIPLOMACY, 1919-1979: Political Applications of Limited Naval Force (1981). Cable examines the use of definitive (limited) naval force throughout the twentieth century and concludes that future application will be appropriate in only a small number of disputes.

Calhoun, Frederick S. POWER AND PRINCIPLE: Armed Intervention in Wilsonian Foreign Policy (1986). The author describes Wilson's use of force in foreign relations and explains its connection to Wilsonian efforts to circumscribe international behavior through the League of Nations.

Dingman, Roger. POWER IN THE PACIFIC: The Origins of Naval Arms Limitation, 1914-1922 (1976). Dingman investigates the period in which the international naval system moved from competitive expansion to neutral limitation. He concludes that although technological change, economics and shifting diplomatic realities played a role in the decision for limitation, it was domestic considerations that dominated this drift.

Foglesong, David. AMERICA'S SECRET WAR AGAINST BOL-
SHEVISM: U.S. Intervention in the Russian Civil War, 1917-1920
(1995). Foglesong believes that ideological antipathy to bolshevism
led Wilson in December 1917 to wage a secret war in Russia.

Hall, Christopher. BRITAIN, AMERICAN AND ARMS CONTROL
(1987). Hall studies naval diplomacy during the period in which the
U.S. emerged as a modern sea power and challenged the still preeminent thought declining supremacy of the British. This work
emphasizes the role of arms negotiations in the development of
U.S. naval policy.

Mee, Charles L., Jr. THE END OF ORDER: Versailles, 1919 (1980).
Mee focuses on the Treaty of Versailles as the source of the chaos
that emerged in the decades following 1919.

Relations with Europe

Bennett, Edward M. RECOGNITION OF RUSSIA: An American
Foreign Policy Dilemma (1970). Bennett examines the U.S. decision for non-recognition of Russia during the Wilsonian era and
describes the considerations bearing on the reversal of that position under Franklin D. Roosevelt.

Buckingham, Peter H. INTERNATIONAL NORMALCY: The Open
Door Peace with the Former Central Powers 1921-1929 (1983). This
work investigates the process of renewing commercial relation
with Germany, Austria, Hungary, and Turkey after World War I and
context of complex ideological issues.

Costigliola, Frank. AWKWARD DOMINION (1984). Costigliola
examines U.S. relations with Western Europe from the Treaty of
Versailles to the rise of Nazi Germany and concludes that most
leaders of the period lacked the kind of long-rang perspective
needed to handle the problems of the period. The result, he maintains, was a limited and awkward dominion by the United States
that actually aggravated the problem of instability.

Leffler, Melvyn P. THE ELUSIVE QUEST: America's Pursuit of European Stability and French Security 1919-1933 (1979). This study
depicts American interest in Europe following World War I as
characterized by a substantial interest in achieving stabilization
without military commitments and a domestic mood powerfully
opposed to entanglement.

Little, Douglas. MALEVOLENT NEUTRALITY: The United States, Great Britain and the Origins of the Spanish Civil War (1985). Little argues against the assumption that British and American neutrality in the Spanish Civil War derived from fear of provoking a broader European conflict. This study seeks to demonstrate that the roots of that neutrality are best found in ideological differences and investment disputes.

Pease, Neal. POLAND, THE UNITED STATES, AND THE STABILIZATION OF EUROPE 1919-1933 (1986). Pease investigates U.S. relations with Poland during the interwar years and concludes that despite the era of dollar diplomacy, the United States neither favored nor opposed Polish interests.

Rhodes, Benjamin D. THE ANGLO-AMERICAN WINTER WAR WITH RUSSIA (1988). This work analyses the U.S. and British intervention in Northern Russia against the Bolsheviks and concludes that the enterprise was ill advised.

Schmitz, David F. THE UNITED STATES AND FASCIST ITALY, 1922-1940 (1988). Schmitz investigates the U.S. decision to support Italy's right wing dictatorship during the interwar years and concludes that this endorsement figures critically into the Cold War foreign policy.

Unterberger, Betty Miller. THE UNITED STATES, REVOLUTIONARY RUSSIA, AND THE RISE OF CZECHOSLOVAKIA (1989). Woodrow Wilson's desire to implement the principle of national self-determination, Unterberger argues, shaped his policies towards the Russian revolution and Czechoslovakia independence.

White, Christine A. BRITISH AND AMERICAN COMMERCIAL RELATIONS WITH SOVIET RUSSIA, 1918-1924 (1992). White argues that Anglo-American trade and investment with the Soviet Union increased in spite of ideological animosity.

The Americas

Andrews, Gregg. SHOULDER TO SHOULDER?: The American Federation of Labor, the United States, and the Mexican Revolution, 1910-1924 (1991). Samuel Gompers, according to Andrews, played a crucial role in the establishment of moderate unionism and the emerging corporate order in the United States and Mexico.

Bemis, Samuel Flagg. THE LATIN AMERICAN POLICY OF THE UNITED STATES: an historical interpretation (1943). Bemis approved of American intervention in Latin America since he viewed instability there as a threat to the security of the United States. He disagreed with those who believed that the United States was motivated to act by economic interest.

Gilderhus, Mark T. PAN AMERICAN VISIONS: Woodrow Wilson in the Western Hemisphere 1913-1921 (1986). This work deals with Wilsonian attempts at racial integration in the Western Hemisphere and maintains that pan-Americanism was a key aspect of his failed policy toward Latin America.

Healy, David. GUNBOAT DIPLOMACY IN THE WILSON ERA (1976). Healy examines the role of the U.S. Navy in the Haitian intervention of 1915-1916 and assess the relationships among Haitian elite's, the Haitian masses, military diplomats, and U.S. foreign policy making officials to explain the course of the negotiations leading to the a Treaty of Friendship in 1915.

Hill, Larry D. EMISSARIES TO A REVOLUTION: Woodrow Wilson's Executive Agents in Mexico (1973). Hill describes the diplomatic role of eleven U.S. agents sent to Mexico by Wilson for the purpose of influencing the course of the Mexican revolution.

Joseph, Gilbert M. REVOLUTION FROM WITHOUT: Yucatan, Mexico, and the United States, 1880-1924 (1982). This work focuses on the process of revolution in the Yucatan during the early twentieth century, concluding that the failure to achieve a tight urban-rural alliance, the absence of a revolutionary tradition, and the dependency on foreign-dominated markets limited the options of Yucatan revolutionaries.

Krenn, Michael. U.S. POLICY TOWARD ECONOMIC NATIONALISM IN LATIN AMERICA, 1917-1929 (1990). This volume examines what Krenn identifies as the vital years in U.S. and Latin American affairs to determine the sources of U.S. policies and discover the origins of the problems that still characterize U.S. relations with its southern neighbors.

Lael, Richard L. ARROGANT DIPLOMACY: U.S. Policy toward Columbia, 1903-1922 (1987). Lael investigates the efforts of early twentieth century U.S. presidents to reconcile national economic and strategic interests on the one hand with the rights and sovereignty of Columbia and other Latin American counties on the other. He concludes that the presidents of that period were not particularly successful in resolving the issue and, that later presidents fared little better.

LaFeber, Walter. INEVITABLE REVOLUTIONS: The United States in Central America (1983). This work investigates the history of U.S. relations with Central American countries from their inception through the Reagan administration. LaFeber's explanation of American diplomacy in the region emphasizes the role of the tight integration of this area into the U.S. economic-political system.

Langley, Lester D. THE BANANA WARS: An Inner History of American Empire, 1900-1934 (1983). Langley investigates America's empire in the Caribbean during the early ears of the twentieth century and suggests that certain vestiges of that old relationship confound positive progress between the United States and its neighbors today.

Langley, Lester D. THE UNITED STATES AND THE CARIBBEAN, 1900-1970 (1980). Langley presents a chronological and episodic account of U.S. relations with Caribbean nations from the advent of American influence during the Spanish-American war through the demise of the U.S. Empire in the Caribbean. The author maintains that the paradox which characterized early relations continues today: The United State's desire for democracy and progress on one hand and its treatment of its Caribbean neighbors as inferior on the other. Langley contends that these conflicting objectives constitute the determinative element in relations.

Munro, Dana G. THE UNITED STATES AND THE CARIBBEAN REPUBLICS, 1921-1933 (1974). Munro investigates State Department documents concerning U.S.-Caribbean relations during the interwar years to construct a narrative account of the shift from a policy of active intervention to a policy of noninterference.

O'Brien, Thomas. THE REVOLUTIONARY MISSION: American Enterprise in Latin America, 1900-1945 (1996). O'Brien analyzes the response of Latin Americans to American corporate culture and how this interaction influences Latin American societies and shaped their relationship with the United States. He believes that this relationship prefigured the global response to American culture during the rest of the twentieth century.

Salisbury, Richard V. ANTI-IMPERIALISM AND U.S. COMPETITION IN CENTRAL AMERICA, 1920-1929 (1989). Salisbury examines the isthmian crisis of the 1920s for similarities to and differences from the situation in the 1980s. He concludes that although many factors are common to both, the Catholic Church,

Central American militaries, and political parties played determinative and unique roles in the recent crisis.

Steward, Dick. TRADE AND HEMISPHERE: The Good Neighbor Policy and Reciprocal Trade (1975). This work examines the clash of the United States search for foreign markets with the ideals of equality, self-determination and mutual gain.

Wood, Bryce. THE DISMANTLING OF THE GOOD NEIGHBOR POLICY (1985). Wood investigates the period in which the United States pursued a policy of noninterference and nonintervention and concludes that the departure from this policy lost the United States credibility and an honorable reputation among its neighbors.

The Road to War

Discussions of the U.S. entry into World War II center on assessing the process whereby U.S. public opinion was moved from favoring isolationism to affirming intervention. Some argue that Franklin Roosevelt's internationalist leanings moved him to engage in a concerted effort to guide the American people into war. Others maintain that this was largely motivated by the desire to guarantee his own political longevity. Still others cite such motivations as the commitment to assure free trade, the desire to protect Britain, or the intention of protecting European Jews.

Anderson, Irvine H., Jr. THE STANDARD VACUUM OIL COMPANY AND UNITED STATES EAST ASIAN POLICY, 1933-1941 (1975). Anderson investigates the role of this oil company in the formulation and execution of U.S. East Asian Policy before 1941. The author concludes that as tensions in East Asia increased, Stanvac's role moved from that of instigator to implementer of U.S. policy.

Bailey, Thomas Andrew and Paul B. Ryan. HITLER VS. ROOSEVELT: The Undeclared Naval War (1979). The authors examine the undeclared naval war between the Untied States and Germany during 1939-1941 and maintain that the feud was at least in part a factor of a personal clash between Hitler and Roosevelt.

Bennett, Edward M. FRANKLIN D. ROOSEVELT AND THE SEARCH FOR SECURITY (1985). Bennett Studies U.S.-Soviet relations during the 1930s and concludes that misperceptions prevented effective cooperation during these years.

Brune, Lester H. THE ORIGINS OF AMERICAN NATIONAL SECURITY POLICY: Sea Power, Air Power and Foreign Policy 1900-1941 (1981). Brune provides a history of U.S. Sea and Air Power during the first half of the twentieth century. He concludes that American separation of force and diplomacy led to bureaucratic competition, the development of a separate foreign policy view by the military, the heavy use of sea concepts in early aviation strategy, and difficulties in centralizing national security options on the eve of World War II.

Cole, Wayne S. ROOSEVELT AND THE ISOLATIONISTS, 1932-1945 (1983). Cole recounts the U.S. shift from traditional isolationism to extensive, multilateral involvement in world affairs.

Heardon, Patrick J. ROOSEVELT CONFRONTS HITLER: America's Entry into World War II (1987). Heardon studies U.S. entry into World War II and concludes that economic considerations as well as ideological commitments formed the basis of Roosevelt's decision to pursue war in Europe. The book contends that it was concern about Nazi domination of critical economic zones rather than the Jewish problem or fear of Nazi world conquest that constituted the primary impetus for U.S. involvement.

Heinrichs, Waldo. THRESHOLD OF WAR: Franklin D. Roosevelt and American Entry into World War II (1988). This work focuses on the events form March 1941 until the attack on Pearl Harbor. The author contends that FDR was active and purposeful in the formulation of U.S. foreign policy.

Lipstadt, Deborah E. BEYOND BELIEF: The American Press and the Coming of the Holocaust 1933-1945 (1986). Lipstadt investigates U.S. press coverage of Nazi Germany from the mid 1930s until the end of World War II and concludes that the media was responsible to a large degree for American skepticism about and ignorance of the extent of the tragedy.

Marks, Frederick W., III. WIND OVER SAND: The diplomacy of Franklin Roosevelt (1988). Marks depicts FDR as leading a double life in politics, presenting a democratic presidential style to the public while pursuing hidden strategies. The author seeks to find discernible patterns in FDR's policies.

McCann, Frank D., Jr. THE BRAZILIAN-AMERICAN ALLIANCE, 1937-1945 (1973). McCann describes the impact of U.S. economic and military aid on Brazil's entry into World War II on the side of the Allies and the long-range impact of the decision on Brazilian autonomy.

Neu, Charles E. THE TROUBLED ENCOUNTER: The United States and Japan (1975). New synthesizes the commercial, cultural, and political aspects of twentieth century U.S. and Japanese relations.

Wyman, David S. PAPER WALLS: America and the Refugee Crisis 1938-1941 (1968). Wyman investigates the forces in American society that formed what he believes to be early but inadequate U.S. response to the problem of German Anti-Semitism.

GLOBALISM AND TRAGEDY

1942-1960

The United States entered 1941 as a neutral, albeit not impartial, observer of global affairs, and emerged as the self-ordained leader of the free world. With the surrender of the Axis powers, the United States lay claim to global leadership by reason of its superior virtue and overweening power. The needs of a war-torn world and the expansion of American power were inextricably intertwined as Americans went abroad in pursuit of benevolent perfectionism. Of course, any opposition to this unilateral altruism was ascribed to the powers of totalitarian darkness. The human community was seemingly afforded a stark choice: Pax Americana or economic ruin. Unfortunately, for the survivors of global conflict, the Soviet Union offered an equally unpalatable selection: Soviet domination or a nuclear holocaust. This acrimonious duel between the U.S. and the U.S.S.R. soon found itself into the collective consciousness as the Cold War.

The response of the Truman administration to the postwar world was constrained by the two party system and the limitations inherent in a tripartite system of government. Thus, Dwight D. Eisenhower's decisive victory in 1952 seemed to afford him an opportunity to initiate fundamental changes in the course of American diplomacy. Yet, although the rhetoric changed, the basic assumptions underlying the American approach continued to be those outlined in National Security Paper #68. The United States would resist any Soviet expansion of its sphere of influence by appropriate means. This program to contain the spread of Russian influence would presumably continue until the government of the U.S.S.R. unilaterally altered its behavior.

In the summer of 1953, some within the western alliance believed the new Soviet leadership was amenable to negotiation. President Eisenhower, however, summarily rejected the idea. Still, if Soviet expansion could not be contained by negotiation, another procedure needs must be developed. The threat of nuclear war served to end the Korean affair, but massive retaliation was not a viable option with respect to armed internal subversion. Thus, Eisenhower proposed to deal with such threats by recourse to covert intelligence operations. In consequence, the United States obtruded into the internal affairs of Iran and Guatemala and prepared a massive undertaking aimed at the new communist regime in Cuba. Dwight Eisenhower mayhap pushed the edge of the envelope of presidential restraint, but he functioned within traditional parameters. Unfortunately, the capability to perform could produce a willingness to act in a more vigorous manner in the hands of one less constrained.

CHRONOLOGY

1942
Jan 15 Pan-American Union (Rio de Janeiro)
Jan 25 Diplomatic relations suspended (Thailand)
Jan 25 State of War (Thailand and U.S.)
Apr 24 Diplomatic relations (New Zealand)
Nov 19 Diplomatic relations (Lebanon)
Nov 30 Diplomatic relations (Syria)

1943
Jan 14 Casablanca Conference (ends 24 January)
Jan 24 Unconditional surrender doctrine
May 12 Trident Conference (ends 25 May)
May 29 Algiers Conference (ends 3 June)
Aug 11 Quebec Conference (ends 24 August)
Sept 21 Fulbright Resolution (House of Representatives)
Sept 29 Italy surrenders
Oct 13 State of War—Germany and Italy
Oct 18 Moscow Conference (ends 1 November)
Oct 30 Four-Power Declaration on General Security
Nov 5 Connally Resolution (Senate)
Nov 9 United Nations Relief and Rehabilitation Administration
Nov 22 Cairo Conference (ends 6 December)
Nov 28 Teheran Conference (ends 1 December)

1944
Jul 1 Bretton Woods Conference (ends 22 July)

Aug 21 Dumbarton Oaks Conference I (ends 28 September)
Sept 11 Quebec Conference (ends 16 September)
Sept 29 Dumbarton Oaks Conference II (ends 7 October)
Oct 9 Moscow Conference (ends 18 December)
Dec 1 Edward R. Stettinius (Secretary of State)

1945

Jan 31 Malta Conference (ends 2 February)
Feb 4 Yalta Conference (ends 11 February)
Feb 21 Inter-American Conference on the Problems of War and Peace—Mexico City (ends 8 March)
Mar 22 Arab League established
Apr 17 Lend-Lease—Egypt (unperfected)
Apr 25 San Francisco Conference (ends 26 June)
May 7 Germany surrenders
Jun 5 Occupation zones established for Germany and Berlin (European Advisory Commission)
Jul 3 James F. Byrnes (Secretary of State)
Jul 17 Potsdam Conference (ends 2 August)
Jul 26 Potsdam Declaration
Jul 28 United Nations Charter
Aug 6 U.S.S.R. terminates non-aggression pact with Japan
Aug 8 State of War—Japan and U.S.S.R.
Aug 8 London Charter (France, U.K. and U.S.S.R.)
Aug 14 Japan surrenders
Aug 21 Lend-Lease aid terminated
Sept 2 Ho Chi Minh proclaims independence of Vietnam
Nov 20 Nuremberg War Crimes Trials (ends 1 Oct 1946)
Dec 27 International Monetary Fund

1946

Jan 5 Diplomatic relations resume (Thailand)
Jan 17 Edward R. Stettinius, Jr. (Ambassador to United Nations)
Feb 22 *The Long Telegram* (George F. Kennan)
Mar 4 Spanish people asked to reject Franco regime (France, U.K. and U.S.)
Mar 5 Iron Curtain Address (W. S. Churchill)
Mar 16 Acheson-Lilenthal Plan (atomic energy)
Jun 3 Tokyo War Crimes Trials (ends 12 Nov 1948)
Jun 14 Baruch Plan (atomic energy)
Jul 4 Diplomatic relations (Philippines)

Jul 29 Paris Peace Conference (ends 15 October)
Jul 30 Bevin-Byrnes Bizonal Fusion Agreement (Germany)
Aug 2 Connally World Court Amendment (Senate)
Sept 30 Diplomatic relations (Yemen Arab Republic)
Nov * Diplomatic relations suspended (Albania)
Dec 2 U.K. and U.S. create unified German occupation zone (Bizonia)
Dec 11 General Assembly prohibits Spanish participation in UN activities and urges members to sever diplomatic relations (rescinded 4 Nov 1950)

1947
* * Charles A. Eaton (House Foreign Affairs Committee)
 * * Arthur H. Vandenburg (Senate Foreign Relations Committee)
Jan 14 Warren R. Austin (Ambassador to United Nations)
Jan 21 George C. Marshall (Secretary of State)
Feb 10 Treaties of Paris
Mar 4 Treaty of Dunkirk (France and U.K.)
Mar 12 Truman Doctrine proclaimed
Jun 5 George Marshall delivers speech Harvard University suggesting aid program for Western Europe
Jul 1 Diplomatic relations (India)
Jul 26 National Security Act (U.S. Congress)
Sept 2 Rio Pact
Sept 25 Diplomatic relations resume (Romania)
Oct 30 General Agreement on Tariffs and Trade (GATT)
Nov 8 Diplomatic relations resume (Bulgaria)

1948
Feb 26 Diplomatic relations (Pakistan)
Mar 3 Diplomatic relations (Burma)
Mar 17 Brussels Pact (Belgium, France, Luxembourg, The Netherlands and U.K.)
Mar 20 U.S.S.R. withdraws from Allied Control Council (Germany)
Mar 30 International Conference of American States— Bogota (ends 2 May)
Apr 30 Organization of American States
May 3 Diplomatic relations (Nepal)
May 14 U.S. recognizes the state of Israel
May 15 State of War—Egypt, Israel, Jordan and Syria (ends 20 July 1949)
Jun 1 France, U.K. and U.S. unify German occupation zones

Jun 24 Berlin Blockade (ends 12 May 1949)
Jul 1 U.S.S.R. withdraws from Berlin Kommandatura
Aug 3 Diplomatic relations (Ceylon)
Aug 15 Republic of Korea
Sept 9 Democratic People's Republic of Korea
Dec 9 Genocide Treaty (UN)

1949
* * Sol Bloom (House Foreign Affairs Committee)
* * John Kee (House Foreign Affairs Committee)
* * Tom Connally (Senate Foreign Relations Committee)
Jan 21 Dean G. Acheson (Secretary of State)
Jan 20 Point Four Speech (President H. Truman)
Jan 25 Council for Mutual Economic Assistance (COMECON)
Mar 28 Diplomatic relations (Israel)
Apr 4 North Atlantic Treaty
May 8 Federal Republic of Germany established
Aug 2 U.S. closes embassy in Beijing, China
Oct 1 People's Republic of China established
Oct 7 German Democratic Republic established
Dec 8 Nationalist (China) government withdraws to Taiwan
Dec 22 Eugenie Moore Anderson—Denmark (first woman ambassador)
Dec 30 Diplomatic relations (Indonesia)

1950
Feb 19 Diplomatic relations suspended (Bulgaria)
Feb 24 Diplomatic relations (Jordan)
Apr 14 National Security Council Paper #68
May 25 Tripartite Declaration (France, U.K. and U.S.)
Jun 25 Democratic People's Republic of Korea invades Republic of Korea
Jun 25 President H. Truman approves limited air and naval operations (Korea)
Jun 27 President H. Truman approves unrestricted air and naval operations (Korea)
Jun 27 United Nations imposes military sanctions against Democratic People's Republic of Korea (Security Council)
Jul 11 Diplomatic relations (Cambodia)
Oct 7 UN Resolution 376 (General Assembly)
Oct 15 Wake Island Conference (D. MacArthur and H. Truman)

Oct 22 Diplomatic relations (Republic of Vietnam)
Oct 29 Diplomatic relations (Laos)
Nov 2 People's Republic of China acknowledges presence of Chinese troops in Korean peninsula

1951
* * James P. Richards (House Foreign Affairs Committee)
Jan 5 Defense Agreement (Portugal and U.S.)
Apr 11 Douglas MacArthur relieved of command
Apr 18 European Coal and Steel Community (Belgium, Federal Republic of Germany, France, Italy, Luxembourg and The Netherlands)
Jul 10 Korean armistice negotiations (end 23 Aug)
Aug 30 Security Treaty (Philippines and U.S.)
Sept 1 ANZUS Treaty
Sept 8 Peace treaty (Japan and U.S.)
Sept 8 Security Treaty (Japan and U.S.)
Oct 1 Eugenia Anderson signs treaty with Denmark (first U.S. treaty signed by woman)
Oct 25 Korean armistice negotiations (Panmunjom)
Nov 12 UN forces cease offensive operations in Korea

1952
Feb 28 Bases agreement (Japan and U.S.)
Mar 6 Diplomatic relations (Libya)
Mar 26 Bonn Conventions (Federal Republic of Germany, France, U.K. and U.S.)
Jun 2 *Youngstown Sheet and Tube Company v. Sawyer* (Supreme Court)

1953
* * Robert B. Chiperfield (House Foreign Affairs Committee)
 * * Alexander Wiley (Senate Foreign Relations Committee)
Jan 21 John Foster Dulles (Secretary of State)
Jan 26 Henry Cabot Lodge, Jr. (Ambassador to United Nations)
Mar 5 Joseph Stalin's death reported (U.S.S.R.)
Mar 23 Robert Cutler (National Security Advisor)
Apr 20 Exchange of sick/wounded POWs (ends 3 May)
Jul 27 Korean Armistice agreement
Aug 5 POW exchange (ends 24 September)
Aug 19 Anglo-American sponsored coup in Iran (Operation AJAX)
Sept 26 Defense agreement (Spain and U.S.)
Oct 1 Mutual defense agreement (Republic of Korea and U.S.)

Oct 9 Francis E. Willis—Switzerland (first woman career ambassador)

Oct 16 Jessie D. Locker—Liberia (first African American Ambassador)

Dec 4 Bermuda Conference (France, U.K. and U.S.)

Dec 8 Atoms for Peace address (President D. Eisenhower)

1954

Jan 25 Berlin Summit (France, U.K., U.S. and U.S.S.R.)

Feb 26 Bricker Amendment rejected (Senate)

Mar 1 International Conference of American States— Caracas (ends 28 March)

Mar 13 Declaration of Caracas

Apr 26 Geneva Conference on Indochina (ends 21 July)

May 18 Wriston Report submitted to Secretary of State

Jun 18 U.S. sponsored coup in Guatemala (Operation SUCCESS)

Jul 10 Food for Peace Program (Congress)

Jul 21 Indochina Accords (Geneva)

Sept 8 Southeast Asia Treaty

Dec 2 Defense Treaty (Republic of China and U.S.)

1955

* * James P. Richard (House Foreign Affairs Committee)

* * Walter F. George (Senate Foreign Relations Committee)

Jan 28 Formosa Resolution (Joint Resolution of Congress)

Apr 2 Dillon Anderson (National Security Advisor)

May 14 Warsaw Pact

May 15 Austrian State Treaty (Austria, France, U.K., U.S. and U.S.S.R.)

Jul 18 Geneva Summit (France, U.K., U.S. and U.S.S.R.)

Nov 21 Middle East Treaty Organization (Iran, Iraq, Pakistan, Turkey and U.K.)

1956

Mar 12 Diplomatic relations (Sudan)

Jun 6 Diplomatic relations (Tunisia)

Jul 22 Summit of the Americas—Panama (ends 29 July)

Jul 26 Egypt nationalizes Universal Suez Canal Company

Oct 23 Hungarian uprising (Budapest)

Oct 26 International Atomic Energy Agency

Oct 29 Suez Crisis (ends 6 November)

Oct 29 Israeli forces invade Gaza Strip and Sinai Peninsula

Oct 30 Soviet forces withdraw from Budapest
Oct 31 British and French aircraft bomb Egypt
Nov 6 British and French troops land in Egypt
Nov 4 Soviet forces re-enter Budapest
Nov 5 UN Force to supervise Egyptian cease-fire (General Assembly)
Nov 6 France, U.K. and Israel cease hostilities

1957
* * Thomas S. Gordon (House Foreign Affairs Committee)
 * * Theodore F. Green (Senate Foreign Relations Committee)
Jan 5 Eisenhower Doctrine proclaimed (Joint resolution of Congress
on 8 March)
Jan 7 Robert Cutler (National Security Advisor)
Feb 9 Pelagic Sealing Convention (Multilateral)
Mar 25 Treaty of Rome (European Economic Community)
Apr 7 Suez Canal reopens
Jun 10 *Reid v. Covert* (Supreme Court)
Sept 4 Diplomatic relations (Malaysia)
Oct 4 U.S.S.R. launches earth-orbit satellite (Sputnik)

1958
Feb 1 United Arab Republic created (Egypt and Syria)
Mar 7 Clifton R. Wharton — Romania (first African American chief of
mission to a European nation)
Mar 14 U.S. suspends arms shipments to Cuban government
Mar 31 U.S.S.R. suspends nuclear weapons testing
Jun 24 Gordon Gray (National Security Advisor)
Jul 15 U.S. forces land Lebanon (ends 19 October)
Nov 7 U.S. suspends nuclear weapons testing

1959
* * Thomas E. Morgan (House Foreign Affairs Committee)
 * * J. William Fulbright (Senate Foreign Relations Committee)
Jan 1 Forces loyal Fidel Castro seize Havana, Cuba
Apr 22 Christian A. Herter (Secretary of State)
Jul 24 Kitchen Debate (N. Khruschev and R. Nixon)
Jul 30 Diplomatic relations (Guinea)
Aug 19 Central Treaty Organization (Iran, Pakistan, Turkey and U.K.)
Sept 25 Camp David Summit (U.S. and U.S.S.R.)
Dec 1 Antarctic Treaty

1960
Jan 4 European Free Trade Association
Jan 19 Security Treaty (Japan and U.S.)
Mar 14 Diplomatic relations resume (Bulgaria)
May 1 Francis Gary Powers shot down whilst flying espionage mission over U.S.S.R. (U-2 Incident)
May 8 Diplomatic relations (Cuba and U.S.S.R.)
May 11 President D. Eisenhower acknowledges aerial surveillance of U.S.S.R.
May 16 Paris Summit (France, U.K., U.S. and U.S.S.R.)
Jun 9 Diplomatic relations (Cameroon)
Jul 5 Diplomatic relations (Zaire)
Aug 6 Cuban government nationalizes foreign property
Aug 22 Diplomatic relations (Togo)
Sept 8 James J. Wadsworth (Ambassador to United Nations)
Sept 19 Diplomatic relations (Cyprus)
Oct 4 Diplomatic relations (Nigeria)
Oct 5 Diplomatic relations (Malagasy Republic)
Oct 19 U.S. imposes economic embargo (Cuba)
Oct 31 Diplomatic relations (Senegal)
Nov 2 Guatemalan Civil War begins (ends 29 Dec 1996)
Nov 14 Organization of Petroleum Exporting Countries
Nov 20 Diplomatic relations (Ivory Coast)
Nov 23 Diplomatic relations (Niger)
Nov 26 Diplomatic relations (Dahomey)
Nov 28 Diplomatic relations (Mauritania)
Dec 6 Diplomatic relations (Upper Volta)
Dec 14 UN Resolution 1514

TREATIES, AGREEMENTS, SUPREME COURT CASES AND ACTS OF CONGRESS

CASABLANCA CONFERENCE (1943) U.K. and U.S. In addition to various military decisions, the Allied Powers agreed to wage war until the Axis Powers surrendered unconditionally.
QUEBEC CONFERENCE (1943) China, U.K. and U.S. Secret executive agreement between Churchill and Roosevelt in which they pledged never to use atomic bombs against each other, against any third party without mutual consent, nor communicate any infor-

mation to third parties without mutual consent. Abrogated in 1948 and made public on 5 April 1954.

FULBRIGHT/CONNALLY RESOLUTION (1943) J. William Fulbright introduced a resolution in the House of Representatives favoring U.S. membership in an effective postwar international organization. Tom Connally introduced a similar measure in the Senate. Both measures passed.

MOSCOW CONFERENCE (1943) U.K., U.S. and U.S.S.R. The conferees signed the Four Power Declaration on General Security, and established commissions to study postwar operations in the Axis nations. Agreement was also obtained upon a Declaration on German atrocities providing for the punishment of the perpetrators of such atrocities.

FOUR-POWER DECLARATION ON GENERAL SECURITY (1943) China, U.K., U.S. and U.S.S.R. Proposed the establishment of an international organization to insure world peace, an avoidance of the use of force except for securing peace and a pledge of cooperation toward postwar arms regulation.

CAIRO CONFERENCE (1943) China, U.K. and U.S. Pledged to fight until Japan's unconditional surrender and announced that Japan would be relieved of all territories seized or occupied since 1914, especially the islands originally under mandate to the League of Nations. It was further noted that Korea in due course would become independent. During the second phase of the conference (after Teheran) Churchill and Roosevelt attempted to persuade the Turkish government to abandon its neutral stance.

TEHERAN CONFERENCE (1943) U.K., U.S., and U.S.S.R. First meeting of Roosevelt and Stalin, the conference established for the first time a personal relationship among the so-called Big Three. It was here that President Roosevelt enunciated his *Four Policemen concept* that China, UK, U.S.S.R. and U.S. should police the postwar world to prevent or combat aggression. This concept was later incorporated into the United Nations Organization through the permanent membership of those nations, plus France, on the Security Council.

BRETTON WOODS CONFERENCE (1944) Also called the United Nations Monetary and Financial Conference, this gathering included representatives of 44 nations. This group recommended the creation of the International Monetary Fund and the International Bank for Reconstruction and Development (World Bank).

DUMBARTON OAKS CONFERENCE (1944) Representatives from 39 nations produced a tentative draft for the United Nations Organization.

QUEBEC CONFERENCE (1944) U.K. and U.S. Established the location of the British and American zones in postwar Germany, thus laying the groundwork for the later Soviet and French zones. The Morgenthau Plan for punishing Germany by reducing it to an agrarian economy was adopted but dropped a month later. Its influence and some of its provisions later surfaced in a Joint Chiefs of Staff recommendation (JCS 1067) which served as the basic occupation policy document in the immediate postwar years.

MALTA CONFERENCE (1945) U.K. and U.S. Provided that France would be accorded an occupation zone in Germany, rejected recognition of the Soviet-dominated government in Poland and agreed on a veto by the permanent members of the Security Council.

YALTA CONFERENCE (1945) U.K., U.S. and U.S.S.R. Establishment of a government in Yugoslavia under Tito, but with a broader base. Pro-Communist Lubin government (Poland) to be reorganized along more democratic lines with elections in the near future. Russo-Polish border to be moved west to the Curzon Line with Poland to receive additional territory from Germany. Declaration on Liberated Europe pledging all parties to work for the establishment of representative governments with free elections in those nations liberated from the Axis. Details of the Security Council veto established and Ukraine S.S.R. and the Byelorussia S.S.R. to receive votes in the General Assembly. Reparations Commission established to determine the amount to be exacted from Germany. Repatriation of civilians and P.O.W.'s liberated by Allied armies to their homelands. U.S.S.R. agrees to enter the war against Japan in return for: cession of Kurile Islands, lower Sakhalin, leaseholds in Port Arthur and Darien, control of the main Manchurian railroads and recognition of Outer Mongolia's independence from China. (See Sino-Soviet Treaty of Alliance, 1945) Germany to be divided into four zones (France, U.K., U.S. and U.S.S.R.).

MEXICO CITY CONFERENCE (1945) Also called the Chapultepec Conference. It involved all of the nations of the Western Hemisphere, save Argentina. Approved the Act of Chapultepec, which asserted that an attack on one nation was an attack on all and provided for consultation to agree upon a response. See also Rio Pact (1947).

ARAB LEAGUE (1945) Algeria, Bahrain, Egypt, Iraq, Kuwait, Lebanon, Libya, Mauritania, Morocco, Oman, Qatar, Saudi Arabia, Somalia, Sudan, Syria, Tunisia, United Arab Emirates, Yemen Arab Republic and Yemen People's Democratic Republic. Originally focused on economic, cultural and social cooperation, but on 13 April 1950 an agreement was concluded which obligated the members to take all steps available, including the use of armed force if one of them was attacked.

POTSDAM CONFERENCE (1945) U.K., U.S. and U.S.S.R. Allowed U.S.S.R. to transfer ten percent of the industrial equipment from the Western zone as reparations and a further fifteen percent as compensation for food and raw materials shipped to the West from the Russian zone. U.K. and U.S. to obtain reparations from the Western zones and from German external assets. Austria not required to pay reparations but partitioned into four zones. Council of Foreign Ministers created to work on peace treaties with Germany and its allies. Allied control Council established to administer occupied Germany. Conditions to be offered Japan for its surrender embodied in the Potsdam Declaration. Reaffirmation of the principle of war crimes trials for those whose actions could not be geographically localized.

LONDON CHARTER (1945) France, U.K., U.S. and U.S.S.R. Provided the details for the establishment of a tribunal to deal with crimes against peace, crimes against humanity and war crimes that had no particular geographic locale. The Far East Military Tribunal, which held a similar brief, was established by order of General Douglas MacArthur, Supreme Commander-Allied Forces (19 Jan 1946).

SINO-SOVIET TREATY OF ALLIANCE (1945) China and U.S.S.R. Provides for no separate peace with Japan and defense against Japanese aggression as well as economic assistance after the war. Pledges of mutual respect for each nation's sovereignty, territorial integrity and non-intervention in each other's internal affairs. The Nationalists were recognized as the central government of China and moral and material assistance was to be afforded that government by the U.S.S.R. Outer Mongolia was declared independent and Dairen was to be a free port, Port Arthur was to be jointly administered and ownership of the Chinese Eastern and South Manchurian railways was to be shared.

INTERNATIONAL MONETARY FUND (1945) Although the organization came into being with ratification of the agreement, formal operations did begin until 1 March 1946. The fund became a specialized agency of the United Nations on 15 November 1946. The IMF was in consequence of a decision by the U.S. and other nations to replace the international economic warfare endemic in the pre-war years with an economic system of a cooperative nature.

BEVIN-BYRNES BIZONAL FUSION AGREEMENT (1946) U.K. and U.S. Unification of the British and American occupation zones in Germany with respect to economic/agricultural policy, food distribution, transportation and communication. Each of the signatories retained control over military and political affairs in its zone. France was later persuaded to merge its occupation zone with the British and American zones to create Trizonia (1948).

CONNALLY AMENDMENT (1946) In accepting the United Nations Charter (1945) the Senate endorsed U.S. participation in the World Court. This amendment placed U.S. domestic affairs firmly beyond the court's jurisdiction. On 7 Oct 1985, the U.S. announced it would not accept the Court's compulsory authority in areas other than domestic affairs.

TREATIES OF PARIS (1947) Peace treaties between the Allied Powers and Bulgaria, Finland, Hungary, Italy and Romania. Inasmuch as the U.S. did not declare war on Finland, it was not party to that pact, but was signatory to the rest.

TREATY OF DUNKIRK (1947) France and U.K. Treaty of friendship and mutual assistance in the event of a renewal of German aggression. Forerunner of the Brussels Pact (1948).

NATIONAL SECURITY ACT (1947) This legislation created the Central Intelligence Agency, the National Security Council and the National Security Resources Board. The Department of War became the Department of the Army and the Department of the Air Force was created. The departments of the Air Force, Army and Navy were placed under a cabinet-level civilian secretary. Those civilian secretaries lost their cabinet status when the Department of Defense, and its corresponding civilian head, was created in 1949.

RIO PACT (1947) The Inter-American Treaty of Reciprocal Assistance put into more permanent form the defensive arrangements envisaged by the Act of Chapultepec (1945). A regional organization as defined by Article 51 of the U.N. Charter. It provided for joint action against an attack of any American republic—even from another American state and thus served to further multi-lateralize the Monroe Doctrine. As the first regional pact, it served as model and precedent for the North Atlantic Treaty (1949).

GENERAL AGREEMENT ON TARIFFS AND TRADE (1947) This agreement was designed to provide a temporary framework for tariff negotiations pending the establishment of the International Trade Organization (ITO) under U.N. auspices. Opposition within the U.S. prevented acceptance of the ITO, which left GATT as the only available instrument that could seek agreement on rules for the conduct of international trade. GATT attempts to fill the vacuum through a series of ad hoc arrangements. See General Agreement on Tariffs and Trade (1994).

BRUSSELS PACT (1948) Belgium, France, Luxembourg, Netherlands and U.K. A fifty-year defensive pact in which the signatories bound themselves to aid one another against an attack by aggressor. It was a further expansion of the Treaty of Dunkirk (1947) and constituted a regional alliance based on Article 51 of the U.N. Charter.

GENOCIDE TREATY (1948) United Nations. The Convention on the Prevention and Punishment of Genocide defines that action as the intentional destruction of a national, ethnic, racial or religious group. This agreement was submitted to the United States Senate in 1949. It was approved, with reservations affirming the precedence of the Constitution and rejecting any compulsory jurisdiction by the World Court, on 19 February 1986.

NORTH ATLANTIC TREATY (1949) Belgium, Canada, Denmark, France, Iceland, Italy, Luxembourg, Netherlands, Norway, Portugal, U.K. and U.S. The signatories agreed that an attack against one constituted an assault on all, and that in such an eventuality each nation would take such action as it deemed necessary including armed force. Greece (1952), Turkey (1952) and the Federal Republic of Germany (1955) were later adherents, but France withdrew from the integrated military command (1966) and participates in NATO's military and related activities selectively. Greece withdrew its forces from the command structure from 1974 to 1980. Spain joined NATO in 1982, Czech Republic, Hungary and Poland, in 1999, Bulgaria, Estonia, Latvia, Lithuania, Romania, Slovakia and Slovenia in 2004.

TRIPARTITE DECLARATION (1950) France, U.K. and U.S. Stated opposition to the development of an arms race in the Middle East and declared that any attempt to violate frontiers or armistice lines by any state in the region would result in actions, within or outside the U.N., to prevent such violations

UN RESOLUTION 376 (1950) Provided that Korea should be stabilized and a unified, independent, and democratic government should be established in the peninsula. This resolution provided a loose mandate for the movement of forces of the United Nations Command across the 38th parallel.

ANZUS TREATY (1951) Australia, New Zealand and U.S. Provides for consultation when one of the signatories feels threatened, but does not allow for an immediate military response. Implicit in the agreement is the maintenance of the ability to resist collectively any armed attack.

EUROPEAN COAL AND STEEL COMMUNITY (1951) Belgium, Federal Republic of Germany, France, Italy, Luxembourg and The Netherlands. The objective was to pool the coal and steel resources of the member states with the intent to avoid another European war. The plan was developed by Jean Monnet and implemented by Robert Schuman. The ECSC is viewed as a precursor of the later European Economic Community (1957). The functions of the ECSC were assumed by the European Union on 23 July 2002.

JAPANESE PEACE TREATY (1951) Signed at San Francisco by fifty nations with the Soviet Union and the Communist-bloc nations abstaining. Ended the state of war, restored Japanese sovereignty in politico-economic sphere and gave Japan the right to maintain a military establishment sufficient for individual and collective self-defense. (Article 9 of the Japanese Constitution approved on 3 May 1947 prohibits the maintenance of armed forces, but was interpreted to allow the existence of self-defense forces.) Reparations were allowed, but left the details to bilateral agreements. Japan renounced all claims to its overseas possessions but the legal disposition of those regions was left to the future. (The Bonin and Volcano Islands were returned to Japan by the U.S. in 1968, the Amami and Tokara groups in the northern Ryukyus in 1953 and Okinawa and the other islands of the southern Ryukyus in 1972. The stationing or retention of foreign armed forces in Japanese territory was allowed under the terms of bilateral or multilateral agreements that might be concluded.

BONN CONVENTIONS (1952) Federal Republic of Germany, France, U.K. and U.S. Provided for German sovereignty over all matters save unification, the status of Berlin and the presence of foreign (NATO) troops.

YOUNGSTOWN SHEET AND TUBE COMPANY v. SAWYER (1952)
Supreme Court rules that the president's power to take action in
support of U.S. foreign policy objectives is limited.

BRICKER AMENDMENT (1954) A proposed constitutional amendment concerning the legal status of international agreements
within the U.S. *Missouri v. Holland* (1920) left unclear if treaties must
conform to the Constitution or whether they could change that
document. Senator John W. Bricker (OH) sponsored an amendment that would require any treaty or international agreement
to conform to the Constitution, restrict the impact of treaties on
powers reserved to the states and subject all executive agreements
to Senate approval. Intense presidential opposition led to the measure's defeat, but by only one vote. *Reid v. Covert* (1957) disposed of
this constitutional question.

DECLARATION OF CARACAS (1954) International Conference
of American States. "The domination or control of the political
institutions of an American state by the International Communist
Movement constitutes a threat to the sovereignty and independence of American states." Guatemala opposed passage of the declaration. Argentina and Mexico abstained from voting.

WRISTON REPORT (1954) Commission appointed by John F. Dulles
to recommend changes to create a more effective foreign service.
The recommendations were generally accepted, most especially
the necessity to recruit specialists over generalists and to provide
more opportunities for Foreign Service Officers within the continental United States.

INDOCHINA ACCORDS (1954) Cambodia, Democratic Republic of
Vietnam, France, Laos, People's Republic of China, State of Vietnam, U.K., U.S. and U.S.S.R. Ten documents comprise the results
of this conference: three military agreements, six unilateral declarations and a final declaration. The documents are just that, no
actual treaty bound all the participants, indeed no political treaties
were signed. The military agreements were between the French
and Vietminh High Command and dealt separately with Vietnam,
Cambodia and Laos. Troops were to be withdrawn from Laos and
Cambodia and Vietnam divided along the 17th parallel by a demilitarized zone. No new troops were to be sent into Vietnam, no new
bases established free movement through the demilitarized zone
for 300 days and no alliances with outside powers. French-Viet-
namese Armistice Commission and International Supervisory

Commission (Canada, India and Poland) established to enforce the restrictions and nation-wide elections to be held in two years. The State of Vietnam announced it reserved full freedom of action with respect to the national elections, while the U.S. promised to refrain from the threat of force in disturbing the armistice agreements. Laos became an independent monarchy and Cambodia's independence (9 Nov 1953) was further guaranteed.

SOUTHEAST ASIAN TREATY (1954) Australia, France, New Zealand, Philippines, Pakistan, Thailand, U.K. and U.S. Signatories bound themselves to develop their individual and collective capacity to resist armed attack or subversion while agreeing that an armed attack on one contributed to the danger of all. In the event of aggression or subversion, they agreed to act in accord with their own constitutional processes. It was not a firm military alliance in the sense of NATO but a consultive pact with some moral commitment. It provided for the defense of the South Pacific (excluding Hong Kong and Taiwan). An additional protocol designated Cambodia, Laos and the free territory under the jurisdiction of the State of Vietnam as part of the treaty area. (Cambodia rejected the protection of SEATO in 1956 and Laos did the same in 1962). Any application to India and Pakistan was excluded as a result of a reservation by Australia and the U.S. Organization dissolved in 1977, but defense treaty remains in force. See also Geneva Conference (1961).

FORMOSA RESOLUTION (1955) This resolution gave the president to "employ the Armed Forces of the United States as he deems necessary for the specific purpose of securing and protecting Formosa and the Pescadores against armed attack" until such time as "the President shall determine" the area is reasonably assured. The effect of Formosa Resolution is controversial. Some believe it strengthens the office of the president, others avow to the contrary. Meantime, it is averred that Congress relinquished its power to declare war and thereby rendered the balance betwixt the legislative and executive branches moot.

WARSAW PACT (1955) Albania, Bulgaria, Czechoslovakia, German-Democratic Republic, Hungary, Poland, Romania and U.S.S.R. Signatories agreed that an attack against one constituted an assault on all and that in such an eventuality each nation would come to the assistance of the state attacked with any means as it deems necessary, including armed force. Irrelevant in light of the dismantling of the Communist governments in Eastern Europe. Formally disbanded at Prague Summit (1 July 1991).

MIDDLE EAST TREATY ORGANIZATION (1955) Iran, Iraq, Pakistan, Turkey and U.K. Also called the Baghdad Pact. Originated as a treaty between Iraq and Turkey (24 Feb 1955) to which the U.K. (5 Apr 1955), Pakistan (23 Sept 1955) and Iran (3 Nov 1955) later acceded. The United States was linked to each member by executive agreements (28 July 1958). Iraq withdrew (24 March 1959), and the group reorganized as the Central Treaty Organization.

PELAGIC SEALING CONVENTION (1957) Canada, Japan, U.S. and U.S.S.R. The objective was to take effective measures towards achieving the maximum sustainable productivity of the fur seal resources of the North Pacific Ocean with due regard to their relation to the productivity of other living marine resources of the area. This agreement expired 14 October 1984.

TREATY OF ROME (1957) Belgium, France, Federal Republic of Germany, Italy, Luxembourg and The Netherlands. Established the European Economic Community to achieve freedom of market and competition within the member states and a common external tariff with the rest of the world. Denmark, Ireland and the U.K. joined the EEC in 1973, Greece in 1981 and Portugal and Spain in 1986. Austria, Finland and Sweden joined in 1995 and Cyprus, the Czech Republic, Estonia, Hungary, Latvia, Lithuania, Malta, Poland, Slovakia, and Slovenia in 2004. The EEC became the European Community (1992) and then the European Union (1995).

REID v. COVERT (1957) Supreme Court rules that when the U.S. government acts against citizens outside the country it can do so only in accord with all the limitations imposed by the Constitution. Thus, no agreement with another nation can confer on any branch of the government any power that is free from the restraints of the Constitution. See Bricker Amendment (1954)

CENTRAL TREATY ORGANIZATION (1959) Iran, Pakistan, Turkey and U.K. Formed from the wreckage of the Middle East Treaty Organization after Iraq withdrew. The United States was a participating non-member. Members were required to cooperate for security and defense but developed only a minimal organizational structure. The organization collapsed when Iran, Pakistan and Turkey withdrew (1979).

ANTARCTIC TREATY (1959) Argentina, Australia, Belgium, Chile, France, Japan, New Zealand, Norway, Union of South Africa, U.K.,

U.S. and U.S.S.R. Provided that Antarctica would be used exclusively for peaceful purposes and not the scene or object of international discord. Fortifications, military maneuvers, weapons testing (nuclear or otherwise) and the disposal of radioactive waste material are prohibited.

EUROPEAN FREE TRADE ASSOCIATION (1960) Austria, Denmark, Norway, Portugal, Sweden, Switzerland and U.K. Finland joined as an associate member in 1961 (full member in 1986), and Iceland joined in 1970. Denmark and U.K. joined the European Community (1973), as did Portugal (1986), Austria, Finland, and Sweden (1995). Iceland, Norway, Switzerland and Liechtenstein now comprise the EFTA.

ORGANIZATION OF PETROLEUM EXPORTING COUNTRIES (1960) Iran, Iraq, Kuwait, Saudi Arabia and Venezuela. Qatar joined (1961), followed by Indonesia and Libya (1962). The United Arab Emirates joined (1967) as did Algeria (1969) and Nigeria (1971). Gabon was a member (1975-1995), as was Ecuador (1973-1992). Designed to secure favorable prices for a finite commodity and to arrange for an increased role by the member states in the world's industrial market by the establishment of an infra-structure for future industrialization.

UN RESOLUTION 1514 (1960) Declaration on the Granting of Independence to Colonial Countries and Peoples. All peoples are entitled to self-determination and inadequacy of political, economic, social or educational preparedness was not acceptable as a pretext for delaying independence. Resolution adopted 89-0 with nine abstentions, of which the U.S. was one.

BIOGRAPHICAL SKETCHES

BRICKER, John W. (1893-1986) Lawyer and politician, he was elected Governor of Ohio (1939-45) and represented that state in the U.S. Senate (1946- 58). Generally viewed as a conservative isolationist, he was the Republican Vice-Presidential candidate (1944) and sponsor of a proposed constitutional amendment to restrict the treaty-making powers of the President.

FORRESTAL, James Vincent (1892-1949) After considerable success as an investment banker he joined the Roosevelt administration as Undersecretary (1940) and then Secretary of the Navy (1944-47). He became the first Secretary of Defense (1947-49) and was one of the shapers of American foreign policy during the early cold war years. Forrestal was concerned about Soviet Union's postwar intentions and convinced of its inveterate hostility to the U.S.

HARRIMAN, William A. (1891-1986) Preeminent elder statesman, this son of E. H. Harriman was not only successful in business in his own right but undertook a distinguished career of public service: Lend-Lease administrator to the U.K. (1941-42); Ambassador to U.S.S.R. (1943-46); Ambassador to the U.K. (1946); Secretary of Commerce (1946-48); Director, Mutual Security Agency (1951-53); Assistant Secretary of State, F. E. Affairs (1961-63); Under Secretary of State, Political Affairs (1963-65); and Chairman, U.S. delegation, Paris Peace Conference-Vietnam (1968-69). He negotiated the nuclear test ban treaty (1963). Although an early supporter of the policy of containment, he opposed its implementation, save for China and S.E. Asia.

KENNAN, George F. (1904-2005) A career Foreign Service Officer, he joined the service in 1926, becoming one of early specialists in Soviet affairs (Riga school), and after several wartime appointments (notably Portugal) he served as Director of the Policy Planning Staff of the State Department where the policy of containment originated. His *Foreign Affairs* article entitled *The Sources of Soviet Conduct* (1947) is considered one of the seminal sources of postwar American policy. Kennan later insisted it was misread and misused.

LEAHY, William D. (1875-1959) Naval officer, his early friendship with Franklin D. Roosevelt led to his selection as Ambassador to Vichy France (1941-42) and later as Chief of Staff to the President and Chairman of the Joint Chiefs of Staff (1942-49). He restrained military influence over civilian affairs while discouraging civilian control over strategy, operations and often foreign policy. A strong anti-communist, he retired as a result of his opposition to reduced military appropriations and foreign policy discontinuities in 1949.

McCARTHY, Joseph R. (1908-1957) Lawyer and politician, he represented Wisconsin in the U.S. Senate (1946-58) and in a 9 February 1950 speech in Wheeling, West Virginia, he claimed to have the names of 205 known Communists employed by the State Department. McCarthy was more the product than the cause of the second great *red scare* in America. Still, he symbolized more than any other person, the political extremism of the era. Censured by the Senate on 2 December 1954, his career was, for all practical effects, over.

However, the legacy of his tenure continued to affect the conduct of American diplomacy for decades.

MOSSADEGH, Mohammed (1880-1967) A student of political science, he received a law degree from the University of Lausanne (Switzerland) and backed Reza Khan's seizure of power in Iran (1921) but later broke with him (1925) and went into political retirement. Resumed his career when Reza Shah abdicated in favor of his son Reza Pahlavi (1941) and emerged as a dominant force in the Iranian parliament (Majlis). Named premier by the Majlis (29 April 1951), he moved increasingly to the political left until overthrown by a CIA-sponsored royalist uprising.

PERON, Juan (1895-1974) After graduation from the Argentine Military Academy (1915) he began 32 years of undistinguished military service until a coup overthrew the civilian government (1943). His perception of the sociopolitical circumstances of the country led to his election as President in 1946. Although he was overthrown (1955), his years in power were perceived as a golden age and the political movement he founded remained active. He returned to power in 1973 but died soon after. He was mayhap the most significant figure in 20th Century Argentine history.

WELLES, Benjamin Sumner (1892-1961) A career Foreign Service Officer (1915) who specialized in Latin America, he was appointed Assistant Secretary of State (1933-1937) and Undersecretary of State (1937-1943). Welles was a life-long friend of Franklin Roosevelt, but the latter's confidence in his professional competence was fully justified. Welles resigned in 1943 amid much controversy.

ANNOTATED BIBLIOGRAPHY

American diplomatic activity during the two decades between 1941 and 1961 pivots on two major issues: World War II and the advent of the Cold War. The unquestioned position of the United States as a world leader is characteristic of the period, and studies reflect the significance of U.S. foreign relations not only for the American people, but also for an increasingly global community.

General Works

Ambrose, Stephen E. RISE TO GLOBALISM: American Foreign Policy Since 1938 (1988). Ambrose traces the development of

American attitudes and practices in world affairs and the shifts of attention and policy from 1938 until the 1980s. He concludes that, despite increased dependency on other parts of the world, the United States of the 1980s was richer and more powerful than ever.

Carroll, John M. and George C. Herring. MODERN AMERICAN DIPLOMACY (1986). This collection of essays on twentieth century American diplomacy addresses the major phases and issues of the modern period, especially the U.S. entry into World War II and the advent of the Cold War.

Combs, Jerald A. AMERICAN DIPLOMATIC HISTORY: Two Centuries of Changing interpretations (1986). Combs offer a general overview of American foreign policy from 1775 to the present and outlines the major viewpoints which have been presented by American diplomatic historians. His chapters on World War II, the Truman Administration, and the Eisenhower years are particularly useful.

Gardner, Lloyd C. A COVENANT WITH POWER: America and World Order from Wilson to Reagan (1984). Gardner examines the various ways in which U.S. presidents since Wilson have used power and their particular records in reconciling the application of power with democratic ideology.

Graebner, Norman A. AMERICA AS A WORLD POWER: A Realist Appraisal from Wilson to Reagan (1984). Graebner maintains that the United States sacrifices world influence by elevating ideals and principles above diplomacy.

Graebner, Norman A., ed. THE NATIONAL SECURITY: Its Theory and Practice 1945-1960 (1986). This is a collection of essays by experts in the field of national security. Graebner's introduction summarizes the foreign policy issues and events that molded the concept.

Hunt, Michael H. IDEOLOGY AND U.S. FOREIGN POLICY (1987). Hunt examines the interplay between ideology on one hand and the formulation and execution of policies on the other through the history of American foreign relations. He concludes that a tendency to exclude ideology in policymaking has been a common and fundamental error.

Immerman, Richard H., ed. JOHN FOSTER DULLES AND THE DIPLOMACY OF THE COLD WAR (1990). This collection of essays by Dulles experts examines the former secretary of state's orientation to the major issues that characterized the Cold War period.

Kegley, Charles W., Jr. and Eugene R. Wittkopf. AMERICAN FOREIGN POLICY: Pattern and Process (1979). Dealing with American foreign policy in the post-World War II period, this work investigates its domestic and international context, describes institutions and roles, and contrasts continuity and change. The authors conclude that American diplomacy tends more toward pattern than process.

Kegley, Charles W., Jr. and Eugene R. Wittkopf. PERSPECTIVES ON AMERICAN FOREIGN POLICY: Selected Readings (1983). This is a companion volume to AMERICAN FOREIGN POLICY by the same author. It provides a useful introduction to the theoretical framework of American foreign policy.

Melanson, Richard A. and David Mayers, eds. REEVALUATING EISENHOWER (1987). Essays by specialists in the field of U.S. foreign relations in the 1950s reassess the traditional view of Eisenhower as an inactive or clumsy foreign affairs practitioner.

Paterson, Thomas G., ed. MAJOR PROBLEMS IN AMERICAN FOREIGN POLICY: Documents and Essays, Vol. II: Since 1914 (1984). Paterson divides the history of American foreign policy into broad categories and includes within each period essays by authorities and key documents.

Tananbaum, Duane. THE BRICKER AMENDMENT CONTROVERSY (1988). The author examines Eisenhower's performance during the struggle over the Bricker Amendment and concludes that his evidence supports the view that Eisenhower was active in steering his own policies and programs.

Treverton, Gregory F. COVERT ACTION: The Limits of Intervention in the Postwar World (1987). Treverton examines four decades of American covert action around the world and illustrates the central and unresolved problem of a democracy engaged in secret operations beyond the control of the electoral process.

Ungar, Sanford J., ed. ESTRANGEMENT: America and the World (1985). The authors in this collection of essays posit and seek to dissect America's post-World War II estrangement from the international community.

World War II

Studies investigating the American entry into World War II address the question of whether or not involvement was necessary, what Franklin Roosevelt's motives actually were in precipitating U.S. participation in the war, and to what extent the conduct of diplomacy during the war contributed to the ensuing Cold War.

Some authors contend that American involvement was unnecessary, that Hitler had no designs to extend Nazi control to the United States, and that Nazi subjugation of European powers would not have seriously affected American interests. Others argue that Germany posed a serious threat to America, particularly if the Nazi regime gained control of European resources and lines of communication.

As regards FDR's motives and pace in entering the war, historians debate whether Roosevelt sought to precipitate a *casus belli* with the Nazis, or simply waited for one to occur. Some maintain that FDR favored internationalism as a style of diplomacy, but was slowed by strong isolationist sentiment in the United States. Others hold that he himself hesitated to commit the United States to war and did so at the expense of improved preparations for what they characterize as an inevitable conflict.

Lastly, opinions differ concerning the necessity of including Asia in the struggle. One group of historians' holds that FDR actually sought confrontation with Germany and withheld information he received concerning the impending attack on Pearl Harbor in order to heighten its impact and precipitate a declaration of war against the Axis powers. Those who accept this explanation debate the wisdom of Asian involvement in any case, and particularly as a price for thwarting the Nazis. Some contend that the Pacific war contributed to the complexities of U.S. and Soviet relations that led to the Cold War.

General

Edward M. Bennett. FRANKLIN D. ROOSEVELT AND THE SEARCH FOR VICTORY: American-Soviet Relations, 1939-1945 (1990). Instead of attempting to achieve a peace based on the Atlantic charter, Bennett argues that Roosevelt should have concluded an agreement with Stalin on Eastern European boundaries in 1942.

Buckley, Thomas H. and Edwin B. Strong. AMERICAN FOREIGN AND NATIONAL SECURITY POLICIES, 1914-1945 (1987). This volume examines U.S. foreign relations from 1914-1945 in light of their connection with American military strategy and policies.

Buhite, Russell D. DECISIONS AT YALTA: An Appraisal of Summit Diplomacy (1986). This work examines summitry in general and the meeting at Yalta as an example of a summit conference that should not have taken place. The author concludes that summitry's useful applications are few.

Cole, Wayne S. ROOSEVELT AND THE ISOLATIONISTS, 1932-1945 (1983). Cole recounts the U.S. shift from traditional isolationism to extensive, multilateral involvement in world affairs.

Dallek, Robert. FRANKLIN D. ROOSEVELT AND AMERICAN FOREIGN POLICY 1932-1945 (1979). Dallek investigates FDR's foreign policy history and concludes that the president would not have been neither surprised by nor disappointed in the U.S. postwar role in international relations.

Godfried, Nathan. BRIDGING THE GAP BETWEEN RICH AND POOR (1987). This work examines American development policy in the Third World during the 1940s with particular attention to the Arab East. The author concludes that the capitalist class elite in the United States was critical in the decision to maintain a policy of traditional capitalist development in the Third World.

Hess, Gary R. THE UNITED STATES AT WAR, 1941-1945 (1986). The author provides the fundamental events of U.S. foreign policy during World War II and orients the reader to major viewpoints concerning that conflict.

Hilderbrand, Robert C. DUMBARTON OAKS: The Origins of the United Nations and the Search for Postwar Security (1990). Hilderbrand argues that at the Dumbarton Oaks Conference the Big Three did not create a truly internationalist organization, but rather a United Nations that allowed complete freedom of action for the strongest powers.

Kimball, Warren F. THE JUGGLER: Franklin D. Roosevelt as Wartime Statesman (1991). Roosevelt's policies during World War II, according to Kimball, moved in "a detectable and consistent direction" to create a liberal new world order overseen by the Big

Marks, Frederick W. III. WIND OVER SAND: The Diplomacy of Franklin Roosevelt (1988). Marks depicts FDR as leading a double life in politics, presenting a democratic presidential style to the public while pursuing hidden strategies. The author seeks to find discernible patterns in FDR's policies.

McCann, Frank D, Jr. THE BRAZILIAN-AMERICAN ALLIANCE, 1937-1945 (1973). McCann describes the impact of U.S. economic and military aid on Brazil's entry into World War II on the side of the Allies and the long-range impact of that decision on Brazilian autonomy.

Schaffer, Ronald. WINGS OF JUDGMENT: American Bombing in World War II (1985). Schaffer investigates the destructive power afforded those responsible for the U.S. air war in World War II, the reactions of decision-makers to that power, and the moral issues raised by such capabilities.

Smith, Bradley F. THE SHADOW WARRIORS: OSS and the Origins of the CIA (1983). Smith recounts the creation of the Office of Strategic Services and its role during World War II.

Stoler, Mark A. THE POLITICS OF THE SECOND FRONT (1977). Stoler examines American military planning and diplomacy in conducting a coalition war from 1941 to 1943.

Vatter, Harold G. THE U.S. ECONOMY IN WORLD WAR II (1985). Vatter subscribes to the hypothesis that World War II accelerated and defined the advent of the U.S. mixed economy and illustrates that process.

The War in Europe

Abzug, Robert H. INSIDE THE VICIOUS HEART: Americans and the Liberation of Nazi Concentration Camps (1985). This work investigates U.S. public reaction to the entry of allied troops into German prison camps and the confrontation with the reality of Nazi atrocities.

Beaulac, Willard L. FRANCO: Silent Ally in World War II (1986). Beaulac argues that Spain's policy of frustrating Germany's efforts to draw it into the war on the Axis side actually rendered the Iberian nation a *de facto* ally of the United States.

Beitzell, Robert. THE UNEASY ALLIANCE: America, Britain, and Russia, 1941-1943 (1972). Beitzel explores Allied negotiations of the early years of World War II and concludes that the major weakness of American foreign policy during the period was an unwillingness to face difficult realities.

Dobson, Alan P. U.S. WARTIME AID TO BRITAIN, 1940-1946 (1986). This work investigates the economic side of U.S. and British relations during the war and concludes that, despite the problems that came with collaboration, the venture constituted a successful diplomatic undertaking.

Hurstfield, Julian G. AMERICA AND THE FRENCH NATION, 1939-1945 (1986). Hursfield investigates Franco-American relations during World War II with special attention to the influence of public opinion on foreign policymaking.

Levering, Ralph B. AMERICAN OPINION AND THE RUSSIAN ALLIANCE, 1939-1945 (1976). Levering traces changing American attitudes toward Russia during World War II and concludes that the role of national leadership in the opinion-making process was enormous.

Louis, Wm. Roger. IMPERIALISM AT BAY, 1941-1945 (1986). Louis presents a thorough study of the questions of trusteeship, imperialism and the vital areas in which the United States and Britain negotiated the decolonization of the British empire.

Lipstadt, Deborah E. BEYOND BELIEF: The American Press and the Coming of the Holocaust, 1933-1945 (1986). Lipstadt investigates U.S. press coverage of Nazi Germany from the mid-1930s until the end of World War II and concludes that the media was responsible to a large extent for American skepticism and ignorance of the extent of the tragedy.

Lukas, Richard C. THE STRANGE ALLIES: The United States and Poland 1941-1945 (1978). Lukas demonstrates that there was considerably more sympathy than support in the United States for Poland during the war years and contends that Polish aspirations regarding the restoration of their country after the war became more a matter of Soviet aims than U.S. sentiment.

Thorne, Christopher. ALLIES OF A KIND: The United States, Britain and the War against Japan 1941-1945 (1978). This work examines the Anglo-American relationship as it developed through those allied conferences which dealt with policy vis-a-vis Japan.

Woods, Randall Bennett. A CHANGING OF THE GUARD: Anglo-American Relations, 1941-1946 (1990). Woods discusses the history of Anglo-American financial and commercial relations" during and immediately after World War II.

The War for Asia

Dower, John W. WAR WITHOUT MERCY: Race and Power in the
    Pacific War (1986). Dower investigates the role of racism in the
    conduct of World War II in Asia and projects it into cautions for
    the present competition in trade.
Michael Hogan. HIROSHIMA IN HISTORY AND MEMORY
    (1996). In this collection of essays, Hogan explores the various per-
    spectives on the use of atomic weaponry in 1945
Hoyt, Edwin P. JAPAN'S WAR: The Great Pacific Conflict (1986). This
    work examines Japan during World War II and maintains that,
    then and now, Japan pursued what it considered to be its destiny:
    leadership in Asia and perhaps the world.
Kurgman, Dan. DAY OF THE BOMB: Countdown to Hiroshima
    (1986). This book investigates the process that led to the use of the
    atomic bomb on Japan, particularly from the perspective of the
    American and Japanese leadership.
Neu, Charles E. THE TROUBLED ENCOUNTER: The United States
    and Japan (1975). Neu synthesizes the commercial, cultural and
    political aspects of twentieth century U.S. and Japanese relations.
Pelz, Stephen E. RACE TO PEARL HARBOR: The Failure of the
    Second London Naval Conference and the Onset of World War II
    (1974). This work stresses the role of the naval race in the U.S. entry
    in World War II.
Schaller, Michael. DOUGLAS MACARTHUR: Far Eastern General
    (1988). Schaller criticized MacArthur, who he views as a mere
    opportunist whose achievements were largely created by skillful
    public relations.
Shewmaker, Kenneth E. AMERICAN AND CHINESE COMMU-
    NISTS 1927-1945: A Persuading Encounter (1971). Shewmaker
    examines U.S. contact with the Chinese Communists from the
    early days of the movement to the conclusion of World War II.
    He concludes that neither a conspiracy thesis nor the image of the
    Chinese Communists as agrarian reformers is sufficient to explain
    that period of U.S. relations with the Chinese Communist Party.
Sbrega, John J. ANGLO-AMERICAN RELATIONS AND COLO-
    NIALISM IN EAST ASIA 1941-1945 (1983). Sbrega ascribes sub-
    stantial weight to idealism and moralism as factors complicating
    American relations with Britain during World War II.
Spector, Ronald H. EAGLE AGAINST THE SUN: The American War

with Japan (1985). Spector recounts the events of the war in Asia and concludes that the altered balance of power produced a more stable Asia.

The Cold War

Discussions of Cold War diplomacy seek to identify the roots of the U.S. and Soviet conflict and to analyze the elements that caused it to endure. Some researchers hold Roosevelt and the Anglo-American relationship responsible for the situation, citing FDR's lack of transparency and his closeness to Winston Churchill as factors that isolated Stalin. Others hold that it was Stalin, his objectives in Eastern Europe and his unpredictable behavior in Asia at the end of World War II that complicated and strained relations. Truman's interventionist policy, sometimes characterized as expansionistic, is criticized by some as a prime irritant to U.S. and Soviet relations, as is the Eisenhower-Dulles commitment to a deterrence strategy based on nuclear arms.

General

Brands, H. W. Jr. COLD WARRIORS: Eisenhower's Generation and American Foreign Policy (1988). Brands' rejects the hypothesis that either Eisenhower or Dulles conducted foreign policy single-handedly. He investigates the roles of nine subordinates to wham Eisenhower delegated authority.

Campbell, Thomas M. MASQUERADE PEACE: America's UN Policy, 1944-1945 (1973). Campbell links the United States' UN policy to the advent of the Cold War and describes Truman's use of the United Nations as a way of masquerading a peace behind which the U.S. struggle with Russia for world hegemony.

DeSantis, Hugh. THE DIPLOMACY OF SILENCE: The American Foreign Service, the Soviet Union and the Cold War 1933-1947 (1980). DeSantis investigates the different images of the Soviet Union held by Foreign Service officers of the postwar period and maintains that their role in the development of policy was prominent and merits closer study.

Donovan, John C. THE COLD WARRIORS: A Policy-Making Elite (1974). Donovan investigates the role of the foreign policymaking elite during the Cold War and concludes that such characteristics as exaggerated views of the Soviet threat, emphasis on the produc-

tivity of foreign markets, and blindness to serious domestic problems combined to reduce foreign policy alternatives.

Gaddis, John Lewis. THE LONG PEACE: Inquiries into the History of the Cold War (1987). Gaddis treats the subject of Russian-
American relations chronologically, beginning with factors in the
pre-World War II era.

Gaddis, John Lewis. STRATEGIES OF CONTAINMENT: A Critical Appraisal of Postwar American National Security Policy (1982).
Gaddis argues that there have been five successive geopolitical
codes to containment since World War II and investigates them to
determine possible patterns.

Gormly, James L. FROM POTSDAM TO THE COLD WAR: Big
Three Diplomacy, 1945-1947 (1990). Gormly analyzed the postwar
conferences where big Three foreign ministers drafted the peace
treaties for Bulgaria, Finland, Italy and Romania.

Harbutt, Fraser J. THE IRON CURTAIN: Churchill, America and
the Origins of the Cold War (1986). Harbutt contends that it was
Churchill's Iron Curtain speech that provoked the advent of the
Cold War.

Hixson, Walter. GEORGE F. KENNAN: Cold War Iconoclast (1989).
Kennan, according to Hixson, "sought not a realistic 'balance of
power,' but Soviet defeat and isolation and Western dominance."

LaFeber, Walter. AMERICA, RUSSIA AND THE COLD WAR 1945-
1984 (1985). LaFeber traces the U.S. and Soviet conflict back to the
late nineteenth century confrontation in North China and Manchuria, distinguishing between old and new world encounters and
contrasting the business-oriented United States with the bureaucratic Soviet Union.

Leffler, Melvyn P. A. PREPONDERANCE OF POWER: National
Security, the Truman Administration, and the Cold War (1992).
While Truman overestimated the Soviet threat to the United
States, Leffler argues that the president's Cold War initiatives were
nonetheless prudent and reasonable.

Leffler, Melvyn P. THE SPECTER OF COMMUNISM: The United
States and the Origins of the Cold War, 1917-1953 (1994). Leffler
believes that, for U.S. leaders, the specter of expanding communist
power abroad engendered real fears at home and helped to create
bipartisan support for the global containment policy.

Levering, Ralph B. THE COLD WAR 1945-1987 (1988). Beginning with
the Yalta Conference, Levering recounts the history of the Cold

War, including its eclipse by Detente and resurgence during the Reagan years. This work provides a brief, basic orientation to the Cold War its genesis, and its myths.

Messer, Robert L. THE END OF AN ALLIANCE: James F. Byrnes, Roosevelt, Truman and the Origins of the Cold War (1982). Messer describes the work and relationship of these two U.S. presidents, the influential secretary of state, and their combined impact on the Cold War.

Noer, Thomas J. COLD WAR AND BLACK LIBERATION: The United States and White Rule in Africa, 1948-1968 (1985). Noer examines two decades of U.S. relations with African nations and illustrates the complexities presented by a policy of pursuing the middle road between white supremacy and majority rule.

Pach, Chester J. Jr. ARMING THE FREE WORLD: The Origins of the United States Military Assistance Program, 1945-1950 (1991). U.S. arms aid, according to Pach, was given to pursue primarily political and psychological, rather than military, goals.

Paterson, Thomas G. MEETING THE COMMUNIST THREAT: Truman to Reagan (1988). This volume provides a general orientation to American foreign policy after 1945, particularly as it relates to the spread of communism.

Paterson, Thomas G. ON EVERY FRONT: The Making of the Cold War (1979). This book explains the roots and evolution of the Cold War from the perspective of American aims and values. It includes a description of the role played by U.S. public opinion, the desire and rationale for spheres of influence and the American value of firmness in negotiation.

Pollard, Robert. ECONOMIC SECURITY AND THE ORIGINS OF THE COLD WAR 1945-1950 (1985). Pollard posits that the extensive postwar U.S.-sponsored reform and reconstruction was motivated primarily by economic security considerations.

Rose, Lisle. AFTER YALTA: America and the Origins of the Cold War (1973). Rose contends that the militant anticommunist stance of the United States following 1946 was more a product of fear and confusion than of aggressive self-confidence.

Williamson, Samuel R., Jr., and Steven L. Rearden. THE ORIGINS OF U.S. NUCLEAR STRATEGY, 1945-1953 (1993). Williamson and Rearden put nuclear war planning into a political and diplomatic context.

Western European Relations

Anderson, Terry H. THE UNITED STATES, GREAT BRITAIN AND THE COLD WAR 1944-1947 (1981). This work examines the role of Great Britain in U.S. policies toward the Soviet Union from World War II until the Truman Doctrine. Anderson concludes that there were not only two powers (the United States and the Soviet Union) vying for control, but rather three.

Baylis, John. ANGLO-AMERICAN DEFENSE RELATIONS 1939-1984: The Special Relationship (1984). Baylis investigates the origins and characteristics of the American relationship with Britain from World War II to the present with particular attention to defense. The author forecasts the future of Anglo-American cooperation and suggests that new foci in American foreign policy, recent developments in the international system, and economic factors will alter certain aspects of the special relationship.

Darby, Phillip. THREE FACES OF IMPERIALISM: British and American Approaches to Asia and Africa 1870-1970 (1987). This book compares British and American domination in Africa and Asia during the past century. Darby concludes that the two areas were less important to the American and British policymakers than has previously been believed.

Dimbleby, David and David Reynolds. AN OCEAN APART (1988). This work examines U.S. and British relations during the twentieth century and suggests that despite a continued cultural affinity with the United States, Britain's future best interests will require growing political and economic attention to European allies.

Gimbel, John. SCIENCE, TECHNOLOGY, AND REPARATIONS: Exploitation and Plunder in Postwar Germany (1990). Gimbel asserts that the United States profited from the occupation of Germany by taking scientific and technological information that greatly benefited American industries

Hathaway, Robert M. AMBIGUOUS PARTNERSHIP: Britain and America 1944-1947 (1981). Hathaway maintains that Anglo-American relations from the close of World War II to the Truman Doctrine were principally affected by Britain's recognition that its economic position depended principally on the United States and by the conflicts that emerged from divergent views of world affairs.

Hoffman, Stanley and Charles Mater. THE MARSHALL PLAN: A Retrospective (1984). This collection of essays by specialists on the U.S. plan for European postwar recovery provides a concise, well-organized treatment of fundamental elements: origins, the European response, Marshall Plan economics, and long-range impact.

Hogan, Michael J. THE MARSHALL PLAN: America, Britain, and the Reconstruction of Western Europe, 1947-1952 (1987). Hogan investigates the Marshall Plan and concludes that it was one of the most successful peacetime foreign policies applied by the United States in the twentieth century.

Ireland, Timothy P. CREATING THE ENTANGLING ALLIANCE: The Origins of the North Atlantic Treaty Organization (1981). This book describes the evolution of NATO from inception to implementation. It also traces the gradual increase of U.S. involvement in European affairs as a result of its participation in the alliance.

Kaplan, Lawrence S. A COMMUNITY OF INTERESTS: NATO and the Military Assistance Program, 1948-1951 (1980). Kaplan contends that the greatest divisive element in NATO was the uneasy relationship between America and Europe and that the Military Assistance Program was the core of the problem.

Kaplan, Lawrence. NATO AND THE UNITED STATES: The Enduring Alliance (1988). Kaplan offers a concise, chronological presentation of the development of NATO, with attention to the influence of such issues as the role of the Korean War, the French rejection of the military treaty, Detente and arms control.

Kuklick, Bruce. AMERICAN POLICY AND THE DIVISION OF GERMANY: The Clash with Russia over Reparations (1972). Kuklick maintains that the post-World War II German issue played a substantive role in the advent of the Cold War and identifies the Potsdam reparations pact as the principal turning point in the postwar world.

Louis, Wm. Roger and Hedley Bull, eds. THE SPECIAL RELATIONSHIP: Anglo-American Relations Since 1945 (1986). Specialists analyze U.S. and British relations in the postwar era from the approaches of history, economic considerations, defense and the demands from other areas of the world community.

Miller, James Edward. THE UNITED STATES AND ITALY, 1940-1950 (1986). Miller investigates U.S. and Italian relations during this period and concludes that American motivations in Italy stemmed

from the desire to insure a world order founded on democratic
nations rather than to guarantee economic aims.

Nelson, Daniel J. A HISTORY OF U.S. MILITARY FORCES IN GER-
MANY (1987). This book investigates the impact of the American
troop presence in Germany on U.S. and West German relations.
Nelson believes that it behooves Americans to think as Germans
think regarding American troops on German soil.

Reid, Escott. TIME OF FEAR AND HOPE: The Making of the North
Atlantic Treaty 1947-1949 (1977). This book focuses on the forma-
tive years of the NATO alliance, providing detail on how and why
a group of nations with individual needs and aspirations negotiated and joined, together to guarantee commonly held values and
a specific way of life.

Ryan, Henry Butterfield. THE VISION OF ANGLO-AMERICA: The
U.S.-U.K. Alliance and the Emerging Cold War, 1943-1946 (1987).
This work examines British efforts to create an Anglo-American
bloc and the American resistance to it. The British perspective is
emphasized.

Shlam, Avi. THE UNITED STATES AND THE BERLIN BLOCK-
ADE 1948-1949 (1983). Shlam investigates the Berlin crisis as a
study in crisis decision-making and concludes that this case calls
into question the assumption that high, protracted stress in negotiations negatively affects the outcomes.

Wall, Irwin M. THE UNITED STATES AND THE MAKING OF
POSTWAR FRANCE, 1945-1954 (1991). Wall concludes that the
American attempt to build a suitable France in the postwar period
must be judged a failure.

Whitnak, Donald R. and Edgar L. Erickson. THE AMERICAN
OCCUPATION OF AUSTRIA (1985). This work examines the
planning and execution of the four power Allied occupation of
Austria from 1945 to 1955 and its impact on subsequent U.S. and
Austrian relations.

Eastern European Relations

Boll, Michael M. COLD WAR IN THE BALKANS: American Foreign Policy and the Emergence of Communist Bulgaria 1943-1947
(1984). Boll rejects the thesis that American non-policy in the
Balkans during this period precipitated the loss of the area to the

Soviet Union and builds the case that it was rather a question of American capabilities and priorities which best explains those events.

Korvig, Bennett. THE MYTH OF LIBERATION: East-Central Europe in U.S. Diplomacy and Politics Since 1941 (1973). This analysis of U.S. policies regarding East Central Europe deals with the period ranging from the signing of the Atlantic Charter to the invasion of Czechoslovakia.

Kovrig, Bennett. OF WALLS AND BRIDGES: The United States and Eastern Europe (1991). In this book, Kovrig seeks to trace the historical elements of continuity and flexibility in the pursuit of America's interests in Eastern Europe.

Lukas, Richard C. POLISH-AMERICAN RELATIONS IN THE WAKE OF WORLD WAR II (1982). Lukas examines the impact of the Yalta agreements on U.S. postwar relations with Poland and concludes that it would have been difficult to achieve greater influence on Polish political outcomes without sacrifices beyond those which the United States was able to make.

Lundestad, Geir. THE AMERICAN NONPOLICY TOWARDS EASTERN EUROPE 1943-1947 (1978). Lundestad maintains that U.S. policy from 1943 to 1947 focused on preserving key areas at the expense of regions of less substantial interest and describes how and why Eastern Europe came to be included among the latter.

The Near and Middle East

Anderson, Irvine H. ARAMCO, THE UNITED STATES AND SAUDI ARABIA: A Study of the Dynamics of Foreign Oil Policy 1933-1950 (1981). Anderson examines U.S. foreign oil policy in the Middle East and investigates the arrangements made by American companies, particularly ARAMCO, with oil producing nations. The author concludes that the U.S. policy in this region between 1943 and 1980 was a rational one.

Bill, James A. THE EAGLE AND THE LION: The Tragedy of American-Iranian Relations (1988). This author regards the 1953 American intervention in the Iranian domestic conflict as the turning point in U.S. and Iranian affairs and correlates increased U.S. influence with souring relations.

Cohen, Michael J. TRUMAN AND ISRAEL (1990). Cohen shows that Truman's recognition of Israel was undertaken primarily on the advise of Clark Clifford, who wanted to keep Jewish voters in the Democratic Party coalition in 1948.

Clymer, Kenton J. QUEST FOR FREEDOM: The United States and India's Independence (1995). Cohen shows that Truman's recognition of Israel was undertaken primarily on the advise of Clark Clifford, who wanted to keep Jewish voters in the Democratic Party coalition in 1948.

Freiberger, Steven Z. DAWN OVER SUEZ: The Rise of American Power in the Middle East, 1953-1957 (1992). Freiberger puts the Suez Crisis into the context of Anglo-American relations and he concludes that during this period the U.S. attempted to replace the British and block Soviet expansion in the region.

Hanh, Peter L. THE UNITED STATES, GREAT BRITAIN, AND EGYPT, 1945-1956: Strategy and Diplomacy in the Early Cold War (1991). Hanh concludes that the strategic demands of the Cold War left American officials unable to satisfy Egyptian national aspirations, which doomed their efforts to stabilize the Middle East.

Jones, Howard. A NEW KIND OF WAR (1989). This work examines the Truman Doctrine as a part of American global strategy, specifically its application in Greece. Jones examines the Greek operation as a prototype for America's Vietnam engagement and concludes that a distinguishing characteristic of the Greek situation was that the Greeks wanted American help.

Kuniholm, Bruce Robellet. THE ORIGINS OF THE COLD WAR IN THE NEAR EAST: Great Power Conflict and Diplomacy in Iran, Turkey and Greece (1980). Kuniholm describes the historical significance of Iran, Turkey and Greece in traditional balance of power issues and how these countries figured into the Cold War.

McMahon,Robert J. THE COLD WAR ON THE PERIPHERY: The United States, India, And Pakistan (1994). McMahon believes that American insecurity led to the foolish and unnecessary transformation of areas lacking the essential prerequisites for military-industrial power into Cold War pawns.

Merril,Dennis. BREAD AND BALLOT: The United States and India's Economic Develoment, 1947-1963 (1990). Merril sees U.S. policy towards India as shaped primarily by Cold War considerations.

Miller, David Aaron. SEARCH FOR SECURITY: Saudi Arabian Oil (1980). This volume provides background on U.S. foreign relations concerning Middle Eastern oil but focuses on the special relationship between the United States and Saudi Arabia.

Snetsinger, John. TRUMAN, THE JEWISH VOTE AND THE CRE-ATION OF ISRAEL (1974). This book gives an account of the effort of American Jews to enlist President Truman's support for the creation of a Jewish state. The author concludes that Truman's cooperation in that venture derived from short-range issues rather than long-range interests

Stoff, Michael B. OIL, WAR AND AMERICAN SECURITY: The Search for a National Policy on Foreign Oil 1941-1947 (1980). Stoff presents a history of U.S. and Middle East oil relations during World War II, especially its role as an area of competition and cooperation between the Americans and the British.

Stookey, Robert W. AMERICA AND THE ARAB STATES: An Uneasy Encounter (1975). Stookey provides an overview of the history of U.S. relations with Arab states and describes the primacy of the oil issue in the post-World War II era.

Wittner, Lawrence. AMERICAN INTERVENTION IN GREECE 1943-1949 (1982). This work examines U.S. involvement in Greece's leftist insurrection and concludes that American foreign policy ultimately eroded civil liberties and produced a rightist shift in Greece.

The Americas

Carr, Raymond. PUERTO RICO: A Colonial Experiment (1984). In this history of U.S. and Puerto Rican relations from the Hispano-American War through the 1980s, the author maintains that it was Puerto Rico's economy, not its relations with the United States, which posed the country's greatest problems.

Haines, Gerald K. THE AMERICANIZATION OF BRAZIL: A Study of U.S. Cold War Diplomacy in the Third World, 1945-1954 (1989). Brazil, Haines asserts, provides an appropriate Cold War case study of the attempt by the Truman and Eisenhower administrations "to deal with emerging Third World nationalism and the Third World's political and economic problems."

Immerman, Richard H. THE CIA IN GUATEMALA: The Foreign Policy of Intervention (1982). This study of the U.S. Cold War activity in Guatemala provides the background of early U.S. intervention into the affairs of Latin American countries in its attempt to prevent the spread of communism.

LaFeber, Walter. INEVITABLE REVOLUTIONS: The United States in Central America (1983). This work investigates the history of U.S. relations with Central American countries from their inception through the Reagan administration.

Langley, Lester D. THE UNITED STATES AND THE CARIBBEAN, 1900-1970 (1980). Langley presents a chronological and episodic account of U.S. relations with Caribbean nations from the advent of American influence in the Spanish-American war through the demise of the U.S. Empire in the Caribbean. The author maintains that the paradox that characterized early relations continues today: U.S. desire for democracy and progress on one hand and its treatment of its Caribbean neighbors as inferior on the other.

Leonard, Thomas M. CENTRAL AMERICA AND UNITED STATES POLICIES, 1820s-1980's: A Guide to Issues and References (1985). This book describes the Central American crisis as to its historical perspective, the role of the United States, and the problems of individual Central American nations. The author concludes that present day U.S. regional foreign policy and the objectives of revolutionaries are socio-economically incompatible.

Leonard, Thomas M. THE UNITED STATES AND CENTRAL AMERICA, 1944-1949: Perceptions of Political Dynamics (1984). Leonard describes the manner in which U.S. Central American policy was formulated during this period with particular attention to the perceptions held by U.S. officials and concludes that the United States remained largely an observer of regional political dynamics.

Morley, Morris H. IMPERIAL STATE AND REVOLUTION: The United States and Cuba, 1952-1986 (1987). Morley uses the imperial state model to interpret events and trends in U.S. and Cuban relations of the recent past and consequently emphasizes U.S. economic interests.

Paterson, Thomas. CONTESTING CASTRO: The United States and the Triumph of the Cuban Revolution (1994). Paterson analyzes the origins of the animosity in the Cuban-U.S. relationship since 1959.

Rabe, Stephen G. EISENHOWER AND LATIN AMERICA: The Foreign Policy of Anticommunism (1988). Rabe assumes the position that Eisenhower was a decisive player in foreign policy making and illustrates his thesis that Ike created a new approach toward Latin America. The author concludes that although Eisenhower's

Latin American policy was unsuccessful, its anticommunist motivation was consistent with U.S. policy around the world.

Smith, Wayne S. THE CLOSEST OF ENEMIES (1987). Smith charges that misrepresentation of facts and the absence of principles inhibited the effective functioning of the U.S. democratic system in U.S. and Cuban relations and maintains that recent foreign policy has lacked realistic expectations, has not been geared to achievable objectives, and has not been conducted on the basis of reciprocity

Welch, Richard E. RESPONSE TO REVOLUTION: The United States and the Cuban Revolution, 1959-1961 (1985). Welch investigates both the official U.S. reaction and the opinion of the U.S. public in regard to the Cuban revolution and concludes that their responses were remarkably similar and derived from shared assumptions about the role of Cuba in American security.

Wood, Bryce. THE DISMANTLING OF THE GOOD NEIGHBOR POLICY (1985). Wood investigates the period in which the United States pursued a policy of noninterference and nonintervention and concludes that the departure from this policy lost the United States credibility and an honorable reputation with its neighbors.

Asia

Anderson, David L. TRAPPED BY SUCCESS: The Eisenhower Administration and Vietnam, 1953-1961 (1991). The Eisenhower administration, according to Anderson, laid that foundation for the subsequent decisions to intervene, conditioned the American public to accept intervention, and greatly expanded the U.S. commitment to South Vietnam.

Billings-Yun, Melanie. DECISION AGAINST WAR: Eisenhower and Dien Bien Phu, 1954 (1988). This work investigates Eisenhower's performance in dealing with the French debacle at Dien Bien Phu and concludes that Ike actively handled a problem to which there were only wrong answers in a successful way against considerable odds

Borden, William S. THE PACIFIC ALLIANCE: United States Foreign Economic Policy and Japanese Trade Recovery, 1947-1955 (1984). This work investigates recovery, reconstruction, and stabilization during the postwar decade in Japan and Southeast Asia. The author concludes that military procurement played a large role in

Japanese recovery and inhibited the technological development of China.

Borg, Dorothy and Heinricks, Waldo, eds. UNCERTAIN YEARS: Chinese-American Relations, 1947-1950 (1980). This collection of essays analyses Sino-American relations from the perspective of U.S. policy, Chinese Nationalist policy, and the policy of the Chinese Communist Party.

Buhite, Russell D. SOVIET-AMERICAN RELATIONS IN ASIA, 1945-1954 (1981). This work examines the impact U.S. and Soviet relations in China, Japan, Korea, and Vietnam during the decade following World War II and places the events in those areas in the context of U.S. and Soviet relations in Western Europe.

Cohen, Warren I. AMERICA'S RESPONSE TO CHINA: An Interpretative History of Sino-American Relations (1980). Cohen describes U.S. and Chinese relations from the mid-nineteenth century onward.

Cullather, Nick. ILLUSIONS OF INFLUENCE: The Political Economy of United States-Philippines Relations, 1942-1960 (1994). Cullather reconsiders the traditional interpretation of Philippine-American relations and argues that U.S. security considerations allowed governments in Manila the leeway to pursue their own policy objectives.

Cumings, Bruce. THE ORIGINS OF THE KOREAN WAR (1981) Cummings work analyzes the causes and progress of the conflict in Korea.

Dobbs, Charles M. THE UNWANTED SYMBOL: American Foreign Policy, the Cold War, and Korea, 1945-1950 (1981). Dobbs traces four phases of American foreign policy throughout the crisis in Korea and concludes that the United States opposed legitimate nationalism and thereby played into the hands of the Soviet Union.

Foot, Rosemary. A SUBSTITUTE FOR VICTORY: The Politics of Peacemaking at The Korean Armistice Talks (1990). Foot blames the United States for the protracted peace negotiations and she suggests the desire to avoid "appeasement" as well as the pursuit of a diplomatic victory as two of several motivating factors.

Gallicchio, Marco S. THE COLD WAR BEGINS IN ASIA (1988). The author investigates U.S. policy in East Asia at the fall of the Japanese empire and describes the advent of the Cold War in that part of the world. Gallicchio maintains that the militarization of foreign policy and the slow development of a regional policy to protect American interests in Asia combined to complicate effective, peaceful containment of communism.

Gardner, Lloyd C. APPROACHING VIETNAM: From World War II through Deinbienphu (1988). Gardner investigates U.S. foreign policy concerning Vietnam from the Roosevelt through the Eisenhower administrations and focuses on the abstractions and contradictions of that policy which led to the use of force in Southeast Asia.

Grasso, June M. TRUMAN'S TWO-CHINA POLICY 1948-1950 (1987). Grasso maintains that it was Truman's secret two-China policy and his effort to keep it secret from all but a few select advisors which made him appear weak toward the expansion of communism. She concludes that he was consistent in his attempts to stop the Soviet advance in East Asia.

Hart, Robert A. THE ECCENTRIC TRADITION: American Diplomacy in the Far East (1976). Hart examines relations between the United States and Far Eastern countries from the late eighteenth century through the Vietnam War and suggests that the emotion, extravagance, and high expectations that have characterized U.S. policy in that area have significantly impeded productive relations.

Hess, Gary R. THE UNITED STATES' EMERGENCE AS A SOUTH-EAST ASIAN POWER, 1940-1950 (1987). Hess investigates the growth of U.S. concern for and influence in Southeast Asia, concluding that U.S. policy in the area was largely shaped by conditions in East Asia and Europe.

Kahin, George McTurnan. INTERVENTION: How America Became Involved in Vietnam (1986). Kahin pursues the theme of American attempts to control the political character of Vietnam in illustrating the path of U.S. involvement there.

Kaufman, Burton I. THE KOREAN WAR: Challenges in Crisis, Credibility, and Command (1986). In explaining the dynamics of the Korean War, this work attributes particular significance to the impact of the Red Scare crisis in the United States and to the need of the Truman administration to maintain credibility at home and abroad. Kaufman gives much weight to the fact that the United States had to accept terms of settlement that were less than those of total victory.

Lauren, Paul Gorden, ed. THE CHINA HANDS' LEGACY: Ethics and Diplomacy (1987). Lauren investigates the legacy of journalists and American Foreign Service officers of the World War II era who were accused of disloyalty to the United States. In addition to his own essay, the author includes observations by China Hands and experts on the period.

MacDonald, Callum A. KOREA: The War Before Vietnam (1986). Mac-Donald examines the war with Korea and concludes that it initiated a new era in U.S. relations with its major allies and was also a key factor in focusing foreign policy on the Far East.

McMahon, Robert J. COLONIALISM AND COLD WAR: The United States and the Struggle for Indonesian Independence, 1945-1949 (1981). This work deals with Indonesia's road to independence after World War II. McMahon concludes that although the United States played a major role in helping Indonesians secure independence from the Dutch, American strategy was aimed largely at the containment of communism and tended to underestimate the extent of Indonesian nationalism.

Matray, James I. THE RELUCTANT CRUSADE: American Foreign Policy in Korea, 1941-1950 (1985). Matray maintains that the Truman administration believed that U.S. aid to South Korea would eventually convince Democratic People's Republic of Korea of the superiority of the South's political and economic system and lead to reunification.

Mayers, David Allan. CRACKING THE MONOLITH: U.S. Policy Against the Sino-Soviet Alliance, 1949-1955 (1986). Mayers contends that U.S. policymakers were aware of the tensions between China and the Soviet Union even before the war in Korea but were unable to exploit those differences because of U.S. domestic constraints.

Rotter, Andrew J. THE PATH TO VIETNAM: Origins of the American Commitment to Southeast Asia (1987). Rotter investigates the roots of the American conflict in Vietnam and maintains that they are found in U.S. efforts to construct a global political economy in which Southeast Asia played a significant role.

Schonberger, Howard B. AFTERMATH OF WAR: Americans and the Remaking Of Japan, 1945-1953 (1989). The U.S., according to Schonberger, had only superficially accomplished its goals in Japan when the occupation ended in 1952.

Stueck, William Whitney, Jr. THE ROAD TO CONFRONTATION: American Policy toward China and Korea, 1947-1950 (1981). This volume traces the growing importance of Korea in the U.S. policy of containment.

Stueck, William. THE KOREAN WAR: An International History (1995). Stueck contends that the conflict in Korea served as a substitute for World War II, and allowed both Washington and Moscow to demonstrate their toughness to allies, enemies, the uncommitted, and themselves.

The Advent of Nuclear Issues

Botti, Timothy J. THE LONG WAIT (1987). Botti examines the creation of the U.S. and British nuclear alliance during the 1945-1958 period and characterizes the difficult road to nuclear partnership as concluding in an alliance based on mutual self-interest vis-a-vis the Soviet Union.

Helmreich, Jonathan E. GATHERING RARE ORES: The Diplomacy of Uranium Acquisition, 1943-1954 (1986). This work examines the problem of U.S. acquisition of uranium in the early years of the nuclear age from the standpoint of preemption and monopoly.

Herken, Gregg. COUNSELS OF WAR (1985). Herken investigates the history of the nuclear debate and contends that it needs to be refocused upon American intentions instead of speculation about Soviet actions.

Herken, Gregg. THE WINNING WEAPON: The Atomic Bomb in the Cold War, 1945-1950 (1980). Herken maintains that the U.S. effort to make its nuclear advantage central to its defense strategy proved fallacious in such confrontations as the Berlin crisis.

CONFRONTATION AND ACCOMMODATION

1961-2000

John F. Kennedy promised to start the country moving again and the nation applauded his enthusiasm. Yet, in the process of moving forward, Americans abandoned the pursuit of limited goals capable of fulfillment for unlimited objectives impossible to achieve. The world quickly learned that the historic American commitment to the ideal of liberty and service to the broader community possessed a malevolent side. Responsibility for the invasion of Cuba might rest with the preceding administration, but the crisis over Soviet missiles in Cuba bore the Kennedy imprimatur. The Cuban affair placed the fate of the world in the hands of two men, and the human community was not certain it could live with the consequences. The President and the Chairman found a solution that allowed them to step back from the brink of nuclear war. In the aftermath, some wondered if the world would be so lucky when time and circumstance changed the cast of characters.

More importantly, matters in South East Asia continued to deteriorate. After 1953, the whole of American policy in East Asia was designed to avoid the use of American forces. Unfortunately, the politics of deferral have their limits. John Kennedy might have withdrawn from the Vietnamese quagmire, but he did not. Therefore, his death left his successor with only one viable option, i.e., pursue the policy of his martyred successor. Therefore, in the fullness of time, the war in Vietnam became the lodestone of American foreign policy.

Meantime, the profound legacy of the Roosevelt administration was the assumption that national salvation emanated from the White House. The policies of the Johnson administration destroyed the faith of the American people in the president's mythological ability to deliver. Congress reasserted its traditional prerogatives, party loyalties dissolved, and the public mood turned cynical and conspiratorial. In consequence, his successor must not falter, lest the jackals leap to strip the presidential bones.

Richard M. Nixon, felt compelled to prosecute a foreign policy rich in milestones and breakthroughs whilst replete with deception, cynicism and realpolitik. Still, global stability during the years of the long armistice (1919-1939) was sustained by American economic power. The Great Depression caused that structure to rupture and led to the renewal of conflict. Richard Nixon and Henry Kissinger sought to prop up a new postwar structure, but the American economy and domestic support for their policies crumbled. Thus, the United States was presented with two diametrically opposed options.

It needs must design new policies for a thoroughly altered world, or disregard perceived reality and function as if the decades had not eroded that position atop the mountain the United States once occupied. Jimmy Carter viewed himself as president of a nation that was one among equals. However, the American people were uncomfortable with the idea of equality. They yearned for the days when the United States was Gulliver to a Lilliputian family of nations. President Carter sought to transcend such a nationalistic and combative posture, but a fractious world and the dictates of presidential politics brought the noble experiment to a close. President Ronald Reagan, therefore, proposed to steer the ship of state in new directions.

Unfortunately, the Republic soon discovered that no good deed goes unpunished, and the road to a warm place is paved with good intentions. Moreover, although individuals affect the course of history, the outcome is problematical and the cure is often worse than the disease. Americans found, to their chagrin, that the more things change, the more they remain the same.

Confrontational prudence made common cause with millenarian fanaticism in Iran, ideological simplicity helped send Central America reeling into the abyss, a return to containment heralded the devastation of Afghanistan, and a retreat from the nuclear precipice yielded the unexpected horrors of peace. Moreover, the nation discovered much to its chagrin that aggression was not a communist monopoly. President George H. Bush thought to continue the Reagan Revolution, only to find that one generation's solution is the next generation's problem. President William Clinton sought to circumvent that circumstance, only to find himself ensnared in a plethora of problems that surfaced in the wake of what was intended to be a new world order. Indeed, Americans rediscovered the truth of an observation as old as the Republic. Isolation is an inadequate response so long as the world remains a place where the unexpected goes bump in the night. Nonetheless, the first election of a new millennium brought to Washington an administration determined, at least in terms of rhetoric, to change the focus from problems foreign to dilemmas domestic. The new president averred he would unite a contentious nation, and abjure nation building.

CHRONOLOGY

1961
Jan 3 Diplomatic relations suspended (Cuba)
Jan 6 Diplomatic relations (Central African Republic)
Jan 9 Diplomatic relations (Chad)
Jan 13 Diplomatic relations (Gabon)
Jan 20 McGeorge Bundy (National Security Advisor)
Jan 21 Dean Rusk (Secretary of State)
Jan 22 Cuban membership in OAS suspended
Jan 23 Adlai E. Stevenson (Ambassador to United Nations)
Apr 17 Bay of Pigs Invasion (Cuba)
Jun 3 Vienna Summit (U.S. and U.S.S.R.)
Jun 9 Diplomatic relations (Sierra Leon)
Jul 18 Diplomatic relations (Mali)
Aug 31 U.S.S.R. resumes nuclear weapons testing
Aug 13 Construction of Berlin Wall
Aug 17 Alliance for Progress (Organization of American   States)
Sept 16 U.S. resumes nuclear weapons testing
Sept 22 Peace Corps Act (Congress)
Oct 18 Diplomatic relations (Kuwait)

1962
Jan 14 State of war—China and India (ends 21 November)
Feb 7 U.S. bans Cuban imports and re-export of U.S. products to Cuba from third countries.
Jul 21 Declaration on the neutrality of Laos (Second Geneva Conference on Indochina)
Aug 1 Hickenlooper Amendment (Congress)
Oct 2 U.S. ports closed to those nations allowing flagged ships to enter Cuban ports
Oct 3 Diplomatic relations (Tanzania)
Oct 14 U.S. verifies construction of missile sites in Cuba by U.S.S.R.
Oct 20 State of War—China and India (ends 4 June)
Oct 22 Cuban Missile Crisis (ends 28 October)

Oct 24 Naval blockade of Cuba (ends 21 Nov)
Dec 1 Diplomatic relations (Trinidad and Tobago)
Dec 17 Diplomatic relations (Algeria)

1963
Jan 14 Diplomatic relations (Uganda)
Feb 8 U.S. prohibits travel to Cuba and financial and   commercial transactions
Apr 19 Diplomatic relations (Rwanda)
May 25 Organization of African Unity
Jun 20 Hot Line Agreement (U.S. and U.S.S.R.)
Jul 8 Cuban assets in U.S. frozen
Aug 5 Limited Test Ban Treaty (U.K., U.S. and U.S.S.R.)
Nov 1 Ngo Dinh Diem assassinated (Saigon)
Nov 22 John F. Kennedy assassinated (Dallas, TX)

1964
Jan 17 Palestine Liberation Organization established
Jul 8 Diplomatic relations (Malawi)
Aug 2 Gulf of Tonkin Incident
Aug 5 U.S. forces bomb People's Republic of Vietnam
Aug 7 Gulf of Tonkin Resolution (Congress)
Oct 14 Nikita Khrushchev removed from office (U.S.S.R.)
Dec 2 President L. Johnson authorizes limited air operations (People's Republic of Vietnam)

1965
Mar 24 Diplomatic relations (Zambia)
Mar 24 Public protest against Vietnam War (University of Michigan)
Apr 25 U.S. forces land Dominican Republic (ends 27 September)
Jul 28 Arthur J. Goldberg (Ambassador to United Nations)
Aug 9 Diplomatic relations (Gambia)
Aug 24 State of War—India and Pakistan (ends 22 September)
Sept 7 Patricia Roberts Harris—Luxembourg (first African American woman ambassador)
Oct 3 Immigration quota system established in 1921 abandoned.
Oct 5 Diplomatic relations (Malta)
Nov 6 Freedom Flight Agreement (Cuba and U.S.)
Dec 25 President L. Johnson suspends bombing (People's   Republic of Vietnam)

1966
Mar 11 France withdraws from the military aspect of NATO
Apr 1 Walt W. Rostow (National Security Advisor)
Apr 9 Diplomatic relations (Maldives)
May 26 Diplomatic relations (Guyana)
Dec 8 Diplomatic relations (Singapore)

1967
Jan 27 Treaty for the Exploration and Use of Outer Space (U.K., U.S. and U.S.S.R.)
Jan 31 President L. Johnson resumes bombing (People's Republic of Vietnam)
Feb 14 Treaty of Tlatelolco
Apr 12 Summit of the Americas—Punta del Este (ends 14 April)
May 22 Egypt blockades Gulf of Aquaba
May 30 Nigerian Civil War (ends 26 October)
Jun 5 State of War—Egypt, Jordan, Syria and Israel (ends 11 June)
Jun 8 USS *Liberty* attacked by Israeli aircraft
Jun 23 Glassboro Summit (U.S. and U.S.S.R.)
Aug 8 Association of Southeast Asian Nations
Oct 25 Manila Conference (ends 26 October)
Nov 22 UN Resolution 242
Nov 27 Diplomatic relations (Barbados)

1968
Jan 23 USS *Pueblo* seized by People's Republic of Korea
Jan 30 Tet Offensive—Republic of Vietnam (ends 24 February)
Mar 31 President L. Johnson suspends air, sea and land   bombardment of a portion of the People's Republic of Vietnam
Mar 31 President L. Johnson announces he is not a candidate for re-election
Apr 3 President L. Johnson suspends air, sea and land   bombardment of a further portion of the People's Republic of Vietnam
Jun 12 Nuclear Weapons Nonproliferation Treaty (UN)
Jun 26 George W. Ball (Ambassador to United Nations)
Jul 29 Diplomatic relations (Mauritius)
Aug 20 U.S.S.R. forces invade Czechoslovakia
Aug 28 U.S. ambassador to Guatemala assassinated (John   Gordon Mein)
Oct 7 James R. Wiggins (Ambassador to United Nations)

Oct 31　President L. Johnson ends air, sea and land bombardment (People's Republic of Vietnam)
Nov 21　Diplomatic relations (Equatorial Guinea)
Dec 2　Henry A. Kissinger (National Security Advisor)

1969
Jan 22　William P. Rogers (Secretary of State)
Jan 23　Charles W. Yost (Ambassador to United Nations)
Jul 25　Nixon Doctrine proclaimed
Oct 15　Vietnam Moratorium (civil disobedience)

1970
May 1　Cambodian incursion (ends 29 June)
May 4　Kent State Massacre (Kent, Ohio)
May 15　Jackson State Massacre (Jackson, Mississippi)
Jun 30　Cooper-Church Amendment (Senate)

1971
Jan 6 Gulf of Tonkin Resolution repealed
Mar 1 George H. Bush (Ambassador to United Nations)
Mar 15　President R. Nixon lifts travel ban (People's Republic of China)
Apr 6　U.S. table tennis team invited to visit　People's Republic of China
Jun 9　Diplomatic relations (Lesotho)
Jun 9　Diplomatic relations (Swaziland)
Jun 13 *New York Times* begins publication of *Pentagon Papers*
Jun 22　Mansfield Amendment (Senate)
Jun 30　Pentagon Papers released by U.S. government
Jul 14　Diplomatic relations (Western Samoa)
Jul 15　President R. Nixon announces visit to People's Republic of China
Sept 3　Berlin Treaty (France, U.K., U.S. and U.S.S.R.)
Sept 14　Diplomatic relations (Botswana)
Sept 30　Hot-Line Modernization Agreement (U.S. and U.S.S.R.)
Oct 25　UN General Assembly recognizes the People's Republic of China
Dec 3　State of War—India and Pakistan (ends 17 December)

1972
Feb 17 Diplomatic relations (Bahrain)
Feb 17 President R. Nixon visits People's Republic of China (ends 28 February)
Feb 27 Shanghai Communique (People's Republic of China   and U.S.)
Feb 29 Diplomatic relations (Oman)
Mar 19 Diplomatic relations (Qatar)
Mar 20 Diplomatic relations (United Arab Emirates)
Apr 10 Convention on the prohibition of the development, production and stockpiling of bacteriological and toxin Weapons and on their destruction (UN)
May 10 U.S. resumes air bombardment People's Republic of Vietnam — Linebacker I (ends 23 October)
May 22 Moscow Summit (U.S. and U.S.S.R.)
May 25 Agreement on the Prevention of Incidents on and   over the High Seas (U.S. and U.S.S.R.)
May 26 Strategic Arms Limitation Treaty (U.S. and U.S.S.R.)
May 26 Anti-Ballistic Missile Treaty (U.S. and U.S.S.R.)
Jun 3 Berlin Agreement
Jun 17 Watergate burglary
Nov 6 Diplomatic relations (Tonga)
Dec 18 U.S. resumes air bombardment People's Republic of Vietnam — Linebacker II (ends 29 December)

1973
Jan 23 Cease-fire agreement (People's Republic of Vietnam and U.S.)
Jan 27 President R. Nixon halts all hostile acts by U.S. forces in Southeast Asia.
Jan 27 Paris Peace Agreement — People's Republic of Vietnam, Provisional Revolutionary Government of the Republic of South Vietnam (Vietcong), Republic of Vietnam and U.S.
Feb 15 Aerial Hi-Jacking Agreement — Cuba and U.S.
Feb 20 John A. Scali (Ambassador to United Nations)
Mar 1 U.S. ambassador to Sudan assassinated (Cleo A. Noel, Jr.)
Mar 2 Declaration of the International Conference on Vietnam
Mar 3 Convention on International Trade in Endangered   Species
Jun 14 Case-Church Amendment (Senate)
Jun 17 Washington Summit (U.S. and U.S.S.R.)
Jun 22 Prevention of Nuclear War Agreement (U.S. and U.S.S.R.)
Jul 3 Conference on Security and Cooperation in Europe

Sept 11 American-sponsored coup in Chile (Augusto Pinochet Ugarte)
Sept 22 Henry A. Kissinger (Secretary of State)
Oct 6 State of War—Egypt, Israel and Syria (ends 25 October)
Oct 21 OPEC Oil Embargo (ends 18 March 1974)
Oct 24 President R. Nixon vetoes War Powers Act (Veto overturned 7 November)

1974
Feb 7 Panama Canal Agreement (Panama and U.S.)
Apr 13 Diplomatic relations (Bangladesh)
May 18 India test-fires nuclear device
Jun 29 Moscow Summit (U.S. and U.S.S.R.)
Jul 3 Threshold Test Ban Treaty (U.S. and U.S.S.R.)
Jul 27 House of Representatives approves first article of impeachment (President R. Nixon)
Aug 8 President R. Nixon resigns
Aug 19 U.S. ambassador to Cyprus assassinated (Roger P. Davies)
Nov 24 Vladivostok Agreement on strategic armament (U.S. and U.S.S.R.)
Dec 20 Jackson-Vanik Amendment (Senate)
Dec 30 Hughes-Ryan Amendment (Congress)

1975
* * John Sparkman (Foreign Relations Committee)
Jan 25 Senate Select Committee to study Government Operations with Respect to Intelligence Activities (ends 26 April 1976)
Mar 19 Foreign Affairs Committee becomes International Relations Committee
Apr 29 Saigon surrenders to forces of the Democratic Republic of Vietnam
Apr 29 U.S. embassy in Saigon closes
May 12 *Mayaguez* Incident—Cambodia and U.S. (ends 14 May)
Jun 30 Daniel P. Moynihan (Ambassador to United Nations)
Aug 1 Conference on Security and Cooperation in Europe—Final Act (Helsinki Accords)
Sept 1 Sinai Agreement (Egypt and Israel)
Nov 3 Brent Scowcroft (National Security Advisor)
Nov 8 Diplomatic relations (Mozambique)
Dec 7 Indonesia invades East Timor (Timor Leste)
Dec 9 Harkin Amendment (Congress)

Dec 10 Clark Resolution (Senate)
Dec 16 Conference on International Economic Cooperation (ends 19 December)

1976
Mar 15 William W. Scranton (Ambassador to United Nations)
Apr 9 Syria invades Lebanon
May 28 Peaceful Nuclear Explosions Treaty (U.S. and U.S.S.R.)
Jun 16 U.S. Ambassador to Lebanon assassinated (Francis E. Meloy, Jr.)
Aug 18 Panmunjom Incident (Democratic People's Republic of Korea and U.S.)
Sept 14 National Emergencies Act (Congress)
Oct 21 Foreign Sovereign Immunities Act (Congress)

1977
* * Clement J. Zablocki (International Relations Committee)
Jan 20 Zbigniew Brzezinski (National Security Advisor)
Jan 23 Cyrus R. Vance (Secretary of State)
Jan 30 Andrew J. Young (Ambassador to United Nations)
Mar 18 U.S. lifts travel restrictions (Cuba)
Apr 27 Fishing and maritime boundaries (Cuba and U.S.)
May 18 Environmental Modification Convention (Multilateral)
Aug 8 State of War—Ethiopia and Somalia (ends 8 Mar 1978)
Sept 7 Panama Canal Treaties (Panama and U.S.)
Nov 19 Anwar al-Sadat visits Israel
Dec 28 International Emergency Economic Powers Act (Congress)

1978
Oct 16 Karol Wojtyla becomes Pope John Paul II
Oct 21 Camp David Accords (Egypt, Israel and U.S.)
Dec 2 Vietnam invades Cambodia (ends 21 Sept 1989)

1979
* * Frank Church (Foreign Relations Committee)
Jan 16 Mohammed Reza Pahlavi overthrown (Iran)
Jan 19 NATO announces deployment of IRBM (Pershing II)
Jan 31 Ayatollah Rudollah Khomeini returns to Iran
Feb 5 House International Relations Committee becomes Foreign Affairs Committee

Feb 14 U.S. Ambassador to Afghanistan assassinated (Adolph Dubs)
Feb 17 State of War—China and Vietnam (ends 5 March)
Feb 28 Diplomatic relations suspended (Republic of China, Taiwan)
Mar 7 Diplomatic relations (People's Republic of China)
Mar 26 Peace Treaty (Egypt and Israel)
Jun 18 Strategic Arms Limitation Treaty II (unperfected)
Jul 17 Somoza regime overthrown (Nicaragua)
Sept 23 Donald F. McHenry (Ambassador to United Nations)
Oct 22 Mohammed Reza Pahlavi enters New York hospital
Oct 23 El Salvador civil war (ends 16 January 1992)
Nov 4 U.S. embassy occupied (Teheran, Iran)
Nov 14 Iranian assets in U.S. frozen
Nov 21 U.S. embassy attacked (Islamabad, Pakistan)
Dec 2 U.S. embassy attacked (Tripoli, Libya)
Dec 26 U.S.S.R. invades Afghanistan

1980
Jan 4 U.S. embargo on grain shipments to U.S.S.R. (ends 24 April 1981)
Jan 24 Carter Doctrine proclaimed
Feb 27 U.S. Ambassador to Columbia taken hostage (released 27 April)
Apr 7 U.S. imposes economic embargo on Iran
Apr 21 Mariel, Cuba boatlift begins (ends 26 September)
Apr 24 Iranian hostage rescue mission aborted (Operation Blue Light)
Apr 28 Cyrus Vance resigns over Iranian hostage rescue attempt
May 8 Edmund S. Muskie (Secretary of State)
Jul 27 Mohammed Reza Phlavi dies
Sept 4 State of War—Iran and Iraq (ends 20 Aug 1988)
Oct 10 Convention on prohibitions or restrictions on the use of certain conventional weapons which may be deemed to be excessively injurious or to have indiscriminate effects (UN)

1981
* * Charles H. Percy (Foreign Relations Committee)
Jan 4 Richard V. Allen (National Security Advisor)
Jan 20 Remaining embassy hostages released (Iran)
Jan 20 Diplomatic relations (Kiribati)
Jan 22 Alexander M. Haig, Jr. (Secretary of State)
Feb 4 Jeane J. Kirkpatrick (Ambassador to United Nations)

Mar 30 Assassination attempt (President R. Reagan)
May 6 U.S. suspends diplomatic relations (Libya)
May 13 Assassination attempt (Pope John Paul II)
Jun 4 U.S. removes trade restrictions (People's Republic of China)
Aug 19 Armed confrontation—Gulf of Sidra (Libya and U.S.)
Sept 23 U.S. announces establishment of Radio Marti (first broadcast 20 May 1985)
Oct 6 Muhammad Anwar al-Sadat assassinated Cairo)
Nov 18 U.S. zero option proposal for European IRBM
Nov 23 President R. Regan authorizes creation of paramilitary force overthrow government of Nicaragua (National Security Decision Directive 17)
Nov 30 Intermediate-Range Nuclear Forces Limitation Talks—U.S. and U.S.S.R. (suspended 23 Nov 1983)
Dec 14 Israel annexes Golan Heights
Dec 13 Martial law proclaimed (Poland)
Dec 24 U.S. imposes economic sanctions on Poland (lifted 19 Feb 1987)

1982
Jan 4 William P. Clark, Jr. (National Security Advisor)
Mar 10 Kennedy-Hatfield Nuclear Freeze Resolution (Senate)
Mar 30 Jackson-Warner Nuclear Freeze Resolution (Senate)
Apr 2 State of War—Argentina and U.K. (ends 14 June)
Apr 9 Charter air links suspended (Cuba and U.S.)
Apr 19 U.S. imposes travel restrictions (Cuba)
Jun 6 Israel invades Lebanon (ends 24 May 2000)
Jun 12 Largest disarmament rally in U.S. history (NY City)
Jun 18 Pipeline controversy with U.S.S.R.
Jun 29 Strategic Arms Reduction Talks—U.S. and U.S.S.R. (suspended 8 Dec 1983)
Jul 5 Secretary of State Alexander M. Haig resigns
Jul 16 George P. Schultz (Secretary of State)
Aug 16 Communique (People's Republic of China and U.S.)
Aug 25 U.S. forces enter Lebanon (ends 10 September)
Sept 1 Palestine Liberation Front forces leave Beirut
Sept 14 Bashir Gemayel assassinated (Lebanon)
Sept 26 U.S. forces enter Lebanon (ends 26 Feb 1984)
Oct 1 U.S. grants limited independence to Federated States of Micronesia

Nov 10 Leonid Brezhnev dies (U.S.S.R.)
Nov 12 Yuri Andropov (General Secretary of Communist Party, U.S.S.R.)

1983
* * Dante B. Fascell (Foreign Affairs Committee)
* * Charles H. Percy (Foreign Relations Committee)
Jun 23 *Immigration and Naturalization Service v. Chadha* (Supreme Court)
Mar 23 Strategic Defense Initiative proposed
Mar 21 Benigno Aquiono assassinated (Manila)
Sept 1 Korean Airlines Flight 007 shot down by U.S.S.R. forces
Oct 23 Truck-bomb kills American Marines (Beirut)
Oct 25 U.S. forces land Grenada (ends 27 Oct)
Oct 27 Robert C. McFarlane (National Security Advisor)
Nov 14 American cruise missiles arrive in Europe
Nov 18 International Tropical Timber Agreement I

1984
Jan 11 National Bipartisan Commission on Central American Committee issues final report (Kissinger Commission)
Feb 9 Yuri Andropov dies (U.S.S.R.)
Feb 13 Konstantin U. Chernenko (General Secretary of Communist Party, U.S.S.R.)
Mar 8 Diplomatic relations resume (Vatican)
Oct 31 Indira Gandhi assassinated (New Delhi)
Dec 10 Convention against Torture (UN)
Dec 31 U.S. withdraws from United Nations Educational, Scientific and Cultural Organization (rejoins 1 Oct 2003)

1985
* * Richard G. Lugar (Foreign Relations Committee)
Mar 10 Konstantin U. Chernenko dies (U.S.S.R.)
Mar 11 Mikhail S. Gorbachev (General Secretary of Communist Party, U.S.S.R.)
Mar 12 Nuclear and Space Talks (U.S. and U.S.S.R.)
May 1 U.S. imposes economic sanctions on Nicaragua (ends 13 March 1990)
May 22 Vernon A. Walters (Ambassador to United Nations)

Jul 8 U.S. denounces Cuba, Iran, Libya, Nicaragua and Democratic People's Republic of Korea as outlaw states

Aug 7 Treaty of Rarotonga (South Pacific Nuclear-Free Treaty)

Aug 8 Pressler Amendment—Section 620E(e) Foreign Assistance Act

Sept 9 Limited economic sanctions imposed on Union of South Africa (ends 10 July 1991)

Sept 22 Plaza Accord (Federal Republic of Germany, France, Japan, U.K. and U.S.)

Oct 7 U.S. ends automatic compliance with decisions of International Court of Justice

Dec 4 John M. Poindexter (National Security Advisor)

1986

Jan 7 U.S. imposes economic sanctions (Libya)

Jan 31 John Claude Duvalier leaves Haiti for exile in France

Mar 24 Armed confrontation (Libya and U.S.)

Apr 14 Armed confrontation (Libya and U.S.)

Apr 26 Nuclear reactor fire (Chernobyl, U.S.S.R.)

Jun 27 International Court of Justice rules U.S. violated Nicaraguan sovereignty and directs payment of compensation for damages.

Aug 5 Wright-Reagan Plan (Nicaraguan Conflict)

Aug 7 Arias Plan (Nicaraguan Conflict)

Oct 2 Comprehensive Anti-Apartheid Act (Congress)

Oct 11 Reykjavik Summit (U.S. and U.S.S.R.)

Nov 3 Newspaper reports Iran and U.S. arms for hostages deal (*Al Shiraa*—Beruit, Lebanon)

Nov 3 Northern Mariana Islands becomes U.S. Commonwealth

Dec 2 Frank C. Carlucci (National Security Advisor)

Dec 16 Senate investigates Iran-Contra Affair

Dec 17 House investigates Iran-Contra Affair

1987

* * Claiborne Pell (Foreign Relations Committee)

Jan 29 Senate Intelligence Committee issues Iran- Contra Report

Feb 15 American Broadcasting Corporation begins broadcast mini-series *Amerika*

Apr 30 Meech Lake Accords (Canada)

May 5 Joint House-Senate Hearings Iran-Contra Affair

May 17 Armed confrontation (Iraq and U.S.)

May 19 U.S. agrees to re-flag Kuwaiti oil tankers

Jul 22 U.S. warships convoy re-flagged Kuwaiti tankers   in Arab/Persian Gulf
Sept 21 Armed confrontation (Iran and U.S.)
Sept 26 U.S. bans all imports (Iran)
Nov 18 Joint House-Senate Iran-Contra Report issued
Nov 23 Colin L. Powell (National Security Advisor)
Dec 8 Intermediate-Range Nuclear Forces Treaty

1988
Jan 2 Canada-U.S. Free Trade Agreement
Jan 7 Palestinian civil disobedience campaign in Gaza   and the West Bank begins (Intifadeh)
Feb 4 Grand juries in Tampa and Miami indict Manuel Antonio Noriega (Panama) on charges of aiding drug trafficking
Apr 14 U.S.S.R. withdraws troops (Afghanistan)
May 29 Moscow Summit (U.S. and U.S.S.R.)
Jun 2 Antarctica Mining Treaty
Jul 3 USS *Vincennes* destroys Iranian aircraft
Jul 3 Jordan surrenders West Bank territorial claims to the Palestine Liberation Front
Sept 13 Diplomatic relations (Mongolia)
Dec 14 Palestine Liberation Front recognizes State of Israel
Dec 21 Pan-American Flight 103 destroyed (Libyan government)
Dec 22 Cuba withdraws forces (Angola)

1989
Jan 4 Armed confrontation (Lybia and U.S.)
Jan 20 Brent Scowcroft (National Security Advisor)
Jan 25 James A. Baker III (Secretary of State)
Feb 14 Salman Rushie affair (Iran)
Feb 17 Arab Maghreb Union (Algeria, Libya, Mauritania,   Morocco, and Tunisia)
Mar 20 Thomas R. Pickering (Ambassador to United Nations)
Jun 3 Ayatollah Ruhollah Khomeini dies (Iran)
Jun 4 Tienanmen Square Massacre (China)
Nov 20 U.S. eases travel restrictions (Cuba)
Dec 2 Malta Summit (U.S. and U.S.S.R.)
Dec 20 U.S. forces land Panama (ends 21 Dec)

1990

Feb 11 Nelson Mandela released South African prison

Feb 26 U.S.S.R. withdraws forces (Czechoslovakia)

Mar 1 Lithuania declares independence from U.S.S.R.

Mar 11 U.S.S.R withdraws forces (Hungary)

Mar 11 Augusto Pinochet Ugarte vacates presidency of Chile

May 2 Federal Republic of Germany recognizes Oder/Neisse line as eastern border of Germany

May 4 Manuel Antonio Noriega (Panama) arraigned in U.S. on charges of aiding drug trafficking

May 22 Yemen Arab Republic (North Yemen) and People's Democratic Republic of Yemen (South Yemen) merge into Republic of Yemen

May 29 Boris Yeltsin elected president of the Russian Federation

Jun 1 Threshold Test Ban Treaty (U.S. and U.S.S.R.)

Jul 18 U.S. withdraws recognition of Cambodian rebel coalition

Aug 2 Iraq invades Kuwait

Aug 2 U.S. imposes economic sanctions on Iraq

Aug 3 U.S. and U.S.S.R. condemn Iraqi invasion

Aug 4 European Union imposes economic sanctions on Iraq

Aug 6 UN Security Council imposes economic sanctions on Iraq (Resolution 661)

Aug 8 U.S. forces land in Saudi Arabia (Operation DESERT SHIELD)

Aug 8 Iraq annexes Kuwait as 19th Province

Aug 9 UN Security Council declares Iraqi annexation of Kuwait null and void (Resolution 662)

Aug 10 Arab League authorizes deployment of troops to Saudi Arabia

Aug 12 U.S. Navy ordered to enforce UN economic sanctions against Iraq

Aug 18 UN Security Council demands release of all foreign nationals under Iraqi control (Resolution 664)

Aug 25 UN Security Council calls upon all member nations to respect economic sanctions imposed on Iraq (Resolution 665)

Aug 26 U.S.S.R. renounces the use of force to ensure compliance with UN resolutions pertaining to Iraq

Aug 27 OPEC agrees to increase production

Aug 30 Diplomatic relations (Namibia)

Sept 12 Treaty on the Final Settlement with respect to Germany

Sep t 25 UN Security Council authorizes air blockade of Iraq (Resolution 670)

Oct 1 House of Representatives supports actions by President G. H. Bush against Iraq

Oct 2 Senate supports actions by President G. H. Bush against Iraq

Nov 19 Conventional Forces in Europe (NATO and Warsaw Pact)

Nov 29 UN Security Council accepts Resolution 678

Dec 8 Diplomatic relations suspended (Iraq)

Dec 13 Diplomatic relations suspended (Kuwait)

1991

Jan 12 Congress authorizes use U.S. forces to support Security Council Resolution 678

Jan 16 Armed confrontation—U.S. and Iraq

Mar 1 Diplomatic relations resume (Kuwait)

Mar 2 UN Security Council approves Resolution 686

Mar 26 Argentina, Brazil, Paraguay and Uruguay establish free trade zone (Treaty of Asuncion)

Apr 3 UN Security Council approves Resolution 687

Apr 6 Iraq accepts ceasefire terms

Jun 12 Boris Yeltsen (President, Russian Republic)

Jul 31 Strategic Arms Reduction Treaty (U.S. and U.S.S.R.)

Aug 2 Senate authorizes the use all necessary means rid Iraq of weapons of mass destruction

Aug 19 *Coup d'etat*—U.S.S.R. (ends 21 August)

Aug 20 Estonia declares independence of U.S.S.R.

Aug 21 Latvia declares independence of U.S.S.R.

Aug 21 Lithuania reaffirms 1990 declaration of independence

Sept 7 Slovenia and Croatia declare independence from Yugoslavia

Sept 30 *Coup d'etat*—Haiti (ends 14 Oct 1994)

Oct 4 Treaty of Madrid

Oct 30 Middle East Peace Conference—Madrid (ends 4 November)

Nov 5 U.S. imposes economic sanctions on Haiti

Dec 10 Middle East Peace Conference—Madrid (ends 18 December)

Dec 21 Eleven republics of the U.S.S.R. become the Commonwealth of Independent States

Dec 25 M. Gorbachev resigns as president of U.S.S.R.

Dec 21 Diplomatic relations resume (Albania)

1992

Apr 9 Diplomatic relations resume (Estonia)

Apr 17 Diplomatic relations resume (Latvia)

Apr 14 Diplomatic relations resume (Lithuania)

Apr 25 Aid package Socialist Republic of Vietnam (first direct assistance since Vietnam War)

May 9 Framework Convention on Climate Change (UN)

May 12 Edward J. Perkins (Ambassador to United Nations)

May 21 U.S. announces will not recognize union of Serbia and Montenegro (Federal Republic of Yugoslavia) as successor to the previous Federal Republic of Yugoslavia

Jun 4 Diplomatic relations (Ukraine)

Jun 28 Council for Mutual Economic Assistance (COMECON) disbands

Aug 26 Diplomatic relations (Moldova)

Aug 3 Nuclear test moratorium (Senate)

Sept 4 Aviation Treaty (Netherlands & U.S.)

Sept 9 Diplomatic relations (Belarus)

Sept 9 Diplomatic relations (Georgia)

Sept 9 Diplomatic relations (Uzbekistan)

Sept 15 Diplomatic relations (Kazakhstan)

Sept 16 Diplomatic relations (Azerbaijan)

Sept 17 Diplomatic relations (Kyrgyzstan)

Sept 25 Diplomatic relations (Turkmenistan)

Oct 15 Cuban Democracy Act (Congress)

Oct 19 Diplomatic relations (Tajikistan)

Nov 24 U.S. withdraws Subic Bay Naval Base (Philippines)

Dec 8 Lawrence S. Eagleburger (Secretary of State)

Dec 14 U.S. lifts trade embargo (Socialist Republic of Vietnam)

Dec 17 North American Free Trade Agreement (Canada, Mexico and U.S.)

1993

* * Lee H. Hamilton (Foreign Affairs Committee)

Jan 13 Treaty of Paris (Convention on the prohibition of the development, production, stockpiling and use of chemical weapons and their destruction)

Jan 20 Warren M. Christopher (Secretary of State)

Jan 20 W. Anthony Lake (National Security Advisor)

Jan 27 Madeleine K. Albright (Ambassador to United Nations)

May 26 Diplomatic relations (Slovenia)

May 31 Diplomatic relations (Armenia)

Jun 23 Diplomatic relations (Bosnia-Herzegovina)

Jun 28 Diplomatic relations (Croatia)

Sept 13 Declaration of Principles on Interim Self- Government (Israel-Palestine Liberation Organization)

Nov 20 South African Democratic Transition Support Act (Congress)

Dec 31 Diplomatic relations (Eritrea)

1994
Jan 14 Final report on Iran-Contra affair finds G. H. Bush and R. Reagan not guilty of criminal acts

Jan 26 International Tropical Timber Agreement II

Feb 3 U.S. ends trade embargo (Socialist Republic of Vietnam)

Feb 28 First combat action undertaken by NATO forces (Bosnia)

Apr 6 Genocide in Rwanda (ends 16 July)

Apr 15 General Agreement on Tariffs and Trade

Apr 30 Radio Free Asia created

Jul 1 Yassar Arafat steps onto Palestinian soil for first time in 27 years (Gaza)

Jul 5 Palestine National Authority

Jul 8 Kim Il Sung dies (People's Republic of North Korea)

Jul 14 Diplomatic relations (Angola)

Jul 25 Washington Declaration (Israel and Jordan)

Jul 31 UN Security Council authorizes multi-national force to over-throw military regime in Haiti (first UN approved invasion of country in the Western Hemisphere)

Sept 9 Immigration agreement (Cuba and U.S.)

Oct 14 Jean-Bertrand Aristide returns to Haiti

Dec 9 Summit of the Americas — Miami (ends 11 December)

1995
* * Jesse A. Helms (Foreign Relations Committee)

* * Benjamin A. Gilman (International Relations Committee)

* * House Foreign Affairs Committee becomes International Relations Committee

Apr 11 U.S. imposes limited trade sanctions on Taiwan (first use of economic sanctions to save endangered wildlife)

Oct 5 U.S. allows non-governmental organizations to fund Cuban projects and provides that non- governmental organizations may receive funds from the Agency for International Development

Dec 14 Dayton Peace Accords

1996
Feb 24 Cuban Air Force destroys aircraft belonging to Cuban *emigre* organization
Mar 8 War games conducted by China threaten the territorial sovereignty of Taiwan (end 25 March)
Mar 10 U.S. naval forces dispatched to area adjacent to Taiwan
Mar 12 Cuban Liberty and Democratic Solidarity Act (Congress)
Apr 11 Treaty of Pelindaba (UN)
Jul 29 Diplomatic relations (Macedonia)
Aug 21 War Crimes Act (Congress)
Sept 24 UN Comprehensive Test Ban Treaty (unperfected)
Dec 6 Diplomatic relations (Palau)

1997
Jan 23 Madeleine K. Albright (Secretary of State)
Feb 18 Bill Richardson (Ambassador to United Nations)
Mar 14 Samuel R. Berger (National Security Advisor)
May 14 Diplomatic relations (Socialist Republic of Vietnam)
May 20 Economic sanctions imposed on Burma (executive order)
Jul 1 China resumes sovereignty over Hong Kong
Sept 18 UN Convention on the prohibition of the use, stockpiling, production and transfer of anti-   personnel mines and on their destruction (unperfected)
Nov 3 Economic sanctions imposed on Sudan (executive order)
Dec 11 Kyoto Protocol (UN)

1998
Apr 15 Pol Pot dies (Cambodia)
May 6 State of War—Ethiopia and Eritrea (ends 12 December 2000)
May 11 India test-fires nuclear device (again on 13 May)
May 21 India announces moratorium on nuclear testing
May 28 Pakistan test-fires nuclear device
May 28 U.S. imposes economic sanctions on India and Pakistan (Partially lifted 14 July, removed 6 November)
Jun 12 Pakistan announces moratorium on nuclear testing
Aug 7 U.S. embassies attacked (Kenya and Tanzania)
Aug 31 Democratic People's Republic of Korea launches three-stage ballistic missile
Oct 8 House of Representatives votes to hold impeachment hearings (President W. Clinton)

Oct 21 Arms Control and Disarmament Agency and United States Information Agency abolished

Oct 28 International Religious Freedom Act (Congress)

Dec 19 House of Representatives approves two articles of impeachment (President W. Clinton)

1999

Feb 12 President W. Clinton acquitted of impeachment charges

Mar 24 U.S. participates in joint intervention to restore order in Serbian province of Kosovo (ends 20 June)

May 7 U.S. aircraft bomb Chinese embassy (Belgrade, Yugoslavia)

Sept 4 East Timor (Timor-Leste) votes for independence   from Indonesia

Nov 25 Elian Gonzalez enters U.S. (returns Cuba 28 Jun 2000)

Dec 14 U.S. cedes Panama Canal to Panama.

2000

Jan 1 U.S. relinquishes final control of Panama Canal

May 24 House of Representatives approves permanent trade relations with China (Senate accedes 19 September)

Jul 13 Bilateral trade agreement (Vietnam and U.S.)

Nov 16 President W. Clinton visits Vietnam (ends 19 November)

Dec 31 UN International Criminal Court for War Criminals Treaty (unperfected)

TREATIES, AGREEMENTS, SUPREME COURT CASES AND ACTS OF CONGRESS

ALLIANCE FOR PROGRESS (1961) Meeting at Punta del Este, Uruguay, of 19 American states (Cuba excepted) whereby they agreed to carry through social reforms that would permit a fair distribution of the fruits of economic and social progress. U.S. pledged $20 billion (mainly from public funds) over a ten-year period to underwrite the program.

DECLARATION ON THE NEUTRALITY OF LAOS (1962) A fourteen nation conference called in an effort to defuse fighting in Laos following a series of coups and countercoups (1961). The declaration separated Laos from SEATO guarantees, prohibited foreign military bases, provided for a coalition government, pledged the withdrawal of any foreign forces and established an International

Control Commission (Canada, India and Poland) to supervise the
settlement.

HICKENLOOPER AMENDMENT (1962) This rider to the Foreign
Assistance Act of 1962 required the suspension of aid to those
nations that expropriate American property without just compensation. It was not specifically anti-Cuban legislation. Indeed, it
was prompted by an expropriation in Brazil. A similar, less rigorous
measure was part of the Mutual Security Act of 1954. That provision expired in 1961.

ORGANIZATION OF AFRICAN UNITY (1963) Algeria, Benin,
Botswana, Burundi, Cameroon, Cape Verde, Central African
Republic, Chad, Comoro Islands, Congo, Egypt, Equatorial
Guinea, Ethiopia, Gabon, Gambia, Ghana, Guinea, Guinea-Bis-
sau, Ivory Coast, Kenya, Lesotho, Liberia, Libya, Malagasy Repub-
lic, Malawi, Mali, Mauritania, Mauritius, Morocco, Mozambique,
Niger, Nigeria, Rwanda, Sao Tome and Principe, Senegal, Sierra
Leone, Somalia, Sudan, Swaziland, Tanzania, Togo, Tunisia, Uganda,
Upper Volta, Zaire and Zambia. This organization was designed to
promote the unity and solidarity of the African states.

LIMITED NUCLEAR TEST BAN TREATY (1963) U.K., U.S. and
U.S.S.R. Bans nuclear testing in the atmosphere and elsewhere save
underground. Many other nations adhered to this pact, but France
and the People's Republic of China are not among them.

GULF OF TONKIN RESOLUTION (1964) In the fashion of the
Formosa Resolution (1955), Congress authorized the president
to undertake "all necessary measures to repel attacks against U.S.
forces and all steps necessary for the defense of U.S. allies in Southeast Asia." Presidents Johnson and Nixon used this resolution to
justify military action in Southeast Asia. The Senate repealed the
measure in 1971.

IMMIGRATION ACT (1965) Quota system for immigration established by 1921 legislation is replaced by overall limits, to wit,
120,000 from nations of the Western Hemisphere and 170,000
from the rest of the world. In practice, 20,000 are allowed from
most nations on a first-come basis.

FREEDOM FLIGHT AGREEMENT (1965) Cuba and U.S. This executive agreement provided for daily airline flights from Havana to
Miami. Suspended by Cuba in 1981

TREATY FOR THE EXPLORATION AND USE OF OUTER
SPACE (1967) U.K., U.S., and U.S.S.R. Article Four bans nuclear
warheads in space.

TREATY OF TLATELOLCO (1967) This agreement establishes a nuclear free zone in Latin America. Protocol I applies to those nations outside the zone who control territory within the area and Protocol II obliges signatories to respect the non-nuclear status of those nations in the nuclear-free zone and obliges them to refrain from threatening the use of nuclear weapons. U.S. approved Protocol I on 26 March 1977 and Protocol II on 1 April 1968.

ASSOCIATION OF SOUTHEAST ASIAN NATIONS (1967) Indonesia, Malaysia, Philippines, Singapore and Thailand. Established to provide a framework for regional cooperation. Brunei joined in 1984, followed by Vietnam (1995), Laos (1997), Myanmar (1997) and Cambodia (1997).

UN RESOLUTION 242 (1967) Emphasized the inadmissibility of acquiring territory by war and called for a peace settlement in the Middle East based on: 1. withdrawal of Israeli armed forces from territories occupied in 1967 War; 2. recognition of the right of every state in the area to live in peace within secure and recognized boundaries free from threats and acts of force; 3. free navigation through international waterways; 4. a just settlement to the refugee problem; and 5. a guarantee of the territorial integrity of every state in the region.

NUCLEAR WEAPONS NON-PROLIFERATION TREATY (1968) Approved by the United Nations General Assembly and opened for ratification. Bound the signatory states possessing nuclear stockpiles to refrain from supplying such weapons to non-nuclear states and obligated non-nuclear states to refrain from the production of nuclear weapons. France, the People's Republic of China, India and Israel refused to sign the agreement. France and China later signed (1992). Democratic People's Republic of Korea withdrew 10 January 2003, the first nation to do so.

COOPER-CHURCH AMENDMENT (1971) Senators John Sherman Cooper (KY) and Frank Church (ID) sponsored an amendment to a foreign military sales bill to prohibit the funding of U.S. military activities in Cambodia. It was the first restriction on U.S. involvement in Southeast Asia enacted by a congressional body. The measure did not survive a House and Senate conference committee. It was revived, attached to a supplemental foreign aid authorization, and became law on 12 January 1971.

BERLIN TREATY (1971) France, U.K., U.S. and U.S.S.R. Guaranteed unimpeded access to West Berlin, with France, U.K. and U.S. agreeing that their sectors were not part of the Federal Republic of Germany and would not be governed by that state. See Berlin Agreement (1972)

MANSFIELD AMENDMENT (1971) Senator Michael Mansfield (MT) introduced an amendment to a Selective Service draft extension bill requesting that all U.S. forces withdraw from Indochina within nine months of the bill's passage subject to the release of American POW's. When the House of Representatives concurred on 4 August it was the first time Congress formally requested an end to an war in which the nation was still actively engaged.

SHANGHAI COMMUNIQUE (1972) Joint statement issued by President R. Nixon and Chairman Mao Tse-tung (Mao Zedong) at the conclusion of President Nixon's unprecedented trip to the People's Republic of China. The communique summarized the deliberations and stated the positions of the two governments on a variety of issues. The most controversial portion was an acknowledgement by the U.S. that Taiwan was part of China and that American forces would ultimately be withdrawn from the island. The communique served as the basis for China-U.S. relations until full diplomatic ties were established in 1978.

CONVENTION ON THE PROHIBITION OF THE DEVELOPMENT, PRODUCTION AND STOCKPILING OF BACTERIOLOGICAL AND TOXIN WEAPONS AND ON THEIR DESTRUCTION (1972) The terms of this United Nations sponsored agreement require all parties to refrain from developing, producing, stockpiling, or acquiring biological agents or toxins "of types and in quantities that have no justification for prophylactic, protective, and other peaceful purposes." Signatories also renounce weapons and means of delivery. Existing stockpiles were to be destroyed within nine months of the convention's entry into force. A mechanism was established to review all matters relative to a ban and the operation of same.

HIGH SEAS AGREEMENT (1972) U.S. and U.S.S.R. Each nation agreed to notify the other of naval maneuvers and to preserve a safe distance while underway. The agreement also bars simulated attacks by warships or aircraft of one nation against the other.

STRATEGIC ARMS LIMITATION TREATY (1972) U.S. and U.S.S.R. Established limits on the number of long-range offensive missiles deployed by either state for a five-year period. Senate approval achieved on 30 September 1972. As a prelude to a new agreement, new limitations were established in 1974 with the Vladivostok Agreements.

ANTI-BALLISTIC MISSILE TREATY (1972) U.S. and U.S.S.R. Limited each nation to two antiballistic missile complexes, one of which could protect each nation's capital. Each complex was limited to 100 missiles.

BERLIN AGREEMENT (1972) Comprehensive statement that combined the Berlin Treaty (1971) with a separate accord between the Federal Republic of Germany and the Democratic Republic of Germany.

PARIS PEACE AGREEMENT (1973) People's Republic of Vietnam, Provisional Revolutionary Government of the Republic of South Vietnam (Vietcong), Republic of Vietnam and U.S. Cease-fire proclaimed, American forces withdrawn, American bases dismantled, U.S. mines cleared from harbors and rivers of DRV, POW's returned, North Vietnamese forces could remain in ROV but not be reinforced and U.S. could replace military equipment in ROV but not add to existing stocks. Arrangements were made for an election in the ROV under the supervision of the International Commission of Control and Supervision (Canada, Hungary, Indonesia and Poland). Article 21 provided for American financial aid to assist the rebuilding of both the ROV and the DRV.

HI-JACKING AGREEMENT (1973) Cuba and U.S. A five-year executive agreement that was not retroactive. It provided for extradition or maximum prosecution of persons guilty of crimes in connection with the hi-jacking of airplanes or ships. Legitimate political refugees involved in minor offenses were not affected and all passengers, crews, planes, vessels and money were to be returned. U.S. further agreed to suppress conspiracies to attack Cuba and attacks on Cuba by American-based emigre groups.

CASE-CHURCH AMENDMENT (1973) Senators Clifford P. Case (NJ) and Frank Church (ID) sponsored an amendment to prohibit funding for U.S. forces in Southeast Asia after 31 Dec 1972. Although revised to require withdrawal of all U.S. combat forces within four months of an agreement to return U.S. POW's it was defeated on 16 May 1972. A subsequent amendment in 1973 barred spending on U.S. military activities in Indochina absent congressional approval. President R. Nixon signed a compromise measure (30 June 1973) to halt funding for combat activities after 15 August 1973. A version of the Case-Church amendment requiring congressional consent before military operations in Southeast Asia could be resumed was enacted as part of a State Department authorization measure on 18 Oct 1973

DECLARATION OF THE INTERNATIONAL CONFERENCE ON VIETNAM (1973) Canada, Democratic Republic of Vietnam, France, Hungary, Indonesia, People's Republic of China, Poland, Provisional Revolutionary Government of the Republic of South Vietnam (Vietcong), Republic of Vietnam, U.K., U.S. and U.S.S.R. Commits the signatories to uphold the Paris Peace Agreement on Vietnam and endorses the activities of the International Commission of Control and Supervision to supervise the terms of the cease-fire.

WAR POWERS RESOLUTION (1973) Controversial, possibly unconstitutional legislation to limit the presidential commitment of U.S. forces abroad. The law requires prior consultation with Congress, a written report within 48 hours of the introduction of forces into a potentially hostile environment and a 60-day time limit unless Congress authorizes an extension. Congress may withdraw U.S. forces by approving a joint resolution. Presidents Ford and Carter ignored the act whilst President Reagan rendered a partial acknowledgement. Congress approved a resolution expressly authorizing U.S. involvement in the Gulf War in 1991. See also *Immigration and Naturalization Service v. Chadha* (1983).

PANAMA CANAL AGREEMENT (1974) Agreement on those principles that would serve as the basis for the final settlement—including the eventual return of the canal to Panamanian control.

THRESHOLD TEST BAN TREATY (1974) U.S. and U.S.S.R. Limits the size of underground nuclear tests conducted by either nation. A dispute over verification procedures led to a lengthy delay. In 1976, both sides pledged to abide by treaty limits until ratification was achieved. See Threshold Test Ban Treaty (1990)

JACKSON-VANIK AMENDMENT (1974) Senator Henry M. Jackson (WA) and Representative Charles A. Vanik (OH) introduced legislation limiting the granting of most-favored-nation status or commercial trade credits to those Communist nations restricting emigration of their citizens. The Nixon administration opposed the measure but was forced to accept compromise legislation in 1975. The U.S.S.R. was not so amenable, and promptly repudiated a major trade agreement with the U.S. The question bedeviled Soviet-American relations until the disintegration of the U.S.S.R. The Supreme Soviet eased restrictions on travel and emigration (20 May 1991) and President G. H. Bush extended a waiver from the acts restrictions on 3 June 1991. President W. Clinton did the same for the Socialist Republic of Vietnam (10 Mar 1998).

HUGHES-RYAN AMENDMENT (1974) Senator Harold E. Hughes (IA) and Representative Leo J. Ryan (NY) sought to establish formal congressional oversight of covert actions by U.S. intelligence agencies. This amendment stipulated that the president must approve any covert action. Moreover, the president must inform relevant congressional committees of this action.

VLADIVOSTOK AGREEMENT (1974) U.S. and U.S.S.R. Called for development of a ten-year treaty (SALT II) that would be based on identical ceilings for strategic nuclear delivery vehicles and a limit on the number of warheads in the MIRV (multiple independent reentry vehicles) mode.

HELSINKI ACCORDS (1975) Agreement outlining measures to promote and strengthen improved relations between the members of NATO, the Warsaw Pact and various European states. The final act had four sections, to wit, confidence building measures, including human rights; economic, scientific, technical and environmental cooperation; cooperation in humanitarian efforts and educational and cultural exchanges; and follow-up conferences to review and expand on the accords.

HARKIN AMENDMENT (1975) Resolution introduced by Representative Thomas R. Harkin (IA) that required U.S. representatives to the Inter-American Development Bank and the African Development Fund to vote against loans to any nation consistently violating human rights unless said loan would directly benefit poor people in the nation. Similar provisions were subsequently affixed to bills governing U.S. participation in international financial institutions, especially the International Monetary Fund.

SINAI AGREEMENT (1975) Egypt and Israel. Under the accord, and subsequent agreements, Israel agreed to withdraw from the Suez Canal and to evacuate two Egyptian oil fields. Each nation agreed to refrain from the use of armed force in the area and to assist the UN emergency force (UNEF) to supervise the disengagement. Egypt agreed to allow nonmilitary Israeli cargoes to transit the Suez Canal and U.S. agreed to provide civilian technicians to man electronic early-warning systems in the Sinai. Egypt and U.S. agreed to make a serious effort to bring about collateral negotiations with Syria for disengagement on the Golan Heights. (Egypt signed on 23 Sept 1975 and Israel on 10 Oct 1975)

CLARK AMENDMENT (1975) Resolution introduced by Senator Richard Clark (IA) to bar U.S. support of armed groups opposing the government of Angola. It became law as part of legislation signed on 9 February 1976. It was the first time Congress halted a covert intelligence operation. It was revised to allow aid to Angolan groups subject to presidential discretion (1980) and repealed in 1985.

CONFERENCE ON INTERNATIONAL ECONOMIC COOPERATION (1975) Algeria, Argentina, Australia, Brazil, Cameroon, Canada, European Economic Community, Egypt, India, Indonesia, Iran, Iraq, Jamaica, Japan, Mexico, Nigeria, Pakistan, Peru, Saudi Arabia, Spain, Sweden, Switzerland, U.S., Venezuela, Yugoslavia, Zaire and Zambia. Organized to provide for an economic dialogue between developed and developing nations. Sometimes referred to as the North-South talks.

PEACEFUL NUCLEAR EXPLOSIONS TREATY (1976) U.S. and U.S.S.R. Limited the size of individual and group explosions for excavation purposes. It parallels the restrictions imposed on military testing by the Threshold Test Ban Treaty (1974). A dispute over verification procedures led to a lengthy protocol signed on 1 June 1990 that produced Senate approval on 25 September 1990.

NATIONAL EMERGENCIES ACT (1976) Public Law 94-412 (90 Stat 1255) All powers and authority possessed by the president in consequence of any declaration of national emergency shall terminate if Congress passes a concurrent resolution. No grant of emergency power shall exist for more than six months unless Congress agrees to a continuance.

FOREIGN SOVEREIGN IMMUNITIES ACT (1976) Outlines the procedure whereby jurisdiction is obtained over a foreign state or its instrumentalities. Amended in 1996 and 1999.

ENVIRONMENTAL MODIFICATION CONVENTION (1977) Agreement to prohibit environmental modification as a means of warfare.

PANAMA CANAL TREATIES (1977) Panama and U.S. The Panama Canal Treaty revoked Hay-Bunau-Varilla Treaty (1903). Complete control of canal reverted to Panama on 1 January 2000, joint U.S. and Panama defense of canal, allocated toll revenues and provided for U.S. loan and loan guarantees for the economic development of Panama. The Treaty concerning the Permanent Neutrality and Operation of the Panama Canal involves Panamanian pledges for the neutrality of the canal, non-discrimination among the users and provides for operation and maintenance of the waterway. U.S. allowed to intervene at any time, with force if need be, to guarantee normal transit, even in the face of a labor stoppage. Added protocol allows other nations to agree to the neutrality of the canal.

INTERNATIONAL EMERGENCY ECONOMIC POWERS ACT (1977) Public Law 95-223 Title II (91 Stat 1626) The President may regulate, restrict or prohibit economic activity involving U.S. citizens and any other nation. This legislation does not generally restrict humanitarian transfers, but does allow the prohibiting of same under certain circumstances. The president's authority is subject to a requirement to report to Congress every six months as to any actions authorized by this law.

CAMP DAVID ACCORDS (1978) Egypt, Israel and U.S. One agreement looked toward a solution to the various problems involving Israel, Jordan and the displaced Palestinians. Another compact called for an Israeli-Egyptian peace treaty to be signed within three months, with an Israeli withdrawal from Egyptian territory within three years.

SINO-U.S. COMMUNIQUE (1978) People's Republic of China and U.S. Established full diplomatic relations and the U.S. recognized that there is but one China and Taiwan is part of China. It was noted that the U.S. could continue to maintain cultural, commercial and other official relations with the people of Taiwan. A separate statement announced that the Mutual Defense Treaty with the Republic of China (Taiwan) would be terminated and that the U.S. would withdraw all military personnel from Taiwan within four months.

EGYPTIAN-ISRAELI PEACE TREATY (1979) Provided for Egyptian recognition of Israel and peace between the two nations in exchange for an Israeli withdrawal from the remaining portion of the Sinai in stages.

STRATEGIC ARMS LIMITATION TREATY II (1979) U.S. and U.S.S.R. Based on the Vladivostok Accord (1974) the agreement involved constraints on cruise missiles, limits on mobile ICBMs and qualitative constraints on ICBMs. President J. Carter requested a delay on Senate action in consequence of Soviet actions in Afghanistan. Despite the lack of action on the agreement, both nations announced they would respect the limitations established. That policy continued until a 26 May 1986 announcement by President R. Reagan to the contrary.

CONVENTION ON PROHIBITIONS OR RESTRICTIONS ON THE USE OF CERTAIN CONVENTIONAL WEAPONS WHICH MAY BE DEEMED TO BE EXCESSIVELY INJU-

RIOUS OR TO HAVE INDISCRIMINATE EFFECTS (1980) United Nations sponsored agreement to ban use of fragmentation weapons, mines and booby traps against civilians. The U.S. approved on 24 Sept 1995.

SINO-U.S. COMMUNIQUE (1982) People's Republic of China and U.S. P.R.C. promised to seek unification of Taiwan and mainland by peaceful means and the U.S. agreed to gradually reduce the level of arms sales to the Republic of China (Taiwan).

IMMIGRATION AND NATURALIZATION SERVICE v. CHADHA (1983) The Court ruled that with the exception of treaty approval and impeachment the only statutory impact Congress may exercise is in consequence of enacting legislation by a majority, obtaining presidential approval or overriding a presidential veto. This decision presumably affects the War Powers Act (1973), the Trade Act (1974), the Nuclear Proliferation Act (1978) and various actions by the executive branch in that it seemingly invalidates the so-called legislative veto. The court has not ruled further in this matter.

INTERNATIONAL TROPICAL TIMBER AGREEMENT (1983) This accord is designed to provide a venue for cooperative actions by the producing and consuming nations on all aspects of the tropical timber economy. The International Tropical Timber Organization was established on 1 April 1985. A successor agreement was signed 26 January 1994.

CONVENTION AGAINST TORTURE (1984) Defines torture and established UN committee to investigate alleged violations. U.S. Senate approved, with reservations, on 21 October 1994.

TREATY OF RAROTONGA (1985) This agreement establishes a South Pacific nuclear free zone. Those nations signatory agree that nuclear devices may not be acquired, manufactured or transferred to third parties. Nuclear devices under the control of other nations are prohibited. Visits by vessels containing nuclear devices as well as aircraft over-flights are at the discretion of the signatory nations. Testing of nuclear devices and storage of radioactive material is also forbidden. U.S. agreed to respect the treaty's provisions on 25 March 1996.

PRESSLER AMENDMENT (1985) Public law 99-83 Title IX, Section 902 (99 Stat 268) This provision was inserted at the request of Senator Larry Pressler (SD). It states that any military assistance furnished to Pakistan will be subject to conditions. The president must certify that Pakistan does not possesses a nuclear explosive device that such assistance will significantly reduce the risk it will possess such a device. Sanctions were invoked in 1990. The ban was modified to a degree by subsequent legislation (22 January 1996).

PLAZA ACCORD (1985) France, Japan, West Germany, U.K. and U.S. An agreement to decrease value of the U.S. dollar to make U.S. exports more competitive; resist domestic protectionist pressures and increasingly open markets to international trade. U.S. agrees to reduce budget deficit.

COMPREHENSIVE ANTI-APARTHEID ACT (1986) This legislation represented the most far-reaching sanctions legislation introduced by any of South Africa's trading partners. It imposed an extensive trade embargo as well as a ban on new U.S. loans or investments n South Africa. It passed the Senate on 15 August and the House on 12 September. It was promptly vetoed by President R. Reagan and passed over his veto by the Senate on 2 October 1986. The act allowed the lifting of some restrictions at the discretion of the president. A liberty taken by President G. H. Bush in 1991. See African Democratic Transition Act (1993)

CANADA-U.S. FREE TRADE AGREEMENT (1987) This agreement sought to eliminate all trade and investment barriers within ten years. Third party origin products were not covered save in specific circumstances. A joint commission was created to supervise implementation of the agreement. The agreement went into effect on 1 January 1989 and was folded into the North American Free Trade Agreement (1993).

INTERMEDIATE-RANGE NUCLEAR FORCES TREATY (1987) U.S. and U.S.S.R. Prohibits and requires the destruction of all missiles with a range between 300 and 3,400 miles. Provides for continuous mutual verification for 13 years.

ANTARCTICA MINING TREATY (1988) Argentina, Australia, Belgium, Chile, France, Japan, New Zealand, Norway, Union of South Africa, U.K., U.S. and U.S.S.R. Prohibits any exploration or development of Antarctica unless all members of a twenty-nation commission agree and strict control regulations are met. Three levels of approval are required, and any nation may veto a proposal. See also Treaty of Madrid (1991).

OMNIBUS TRADE AND COMPETITIVENESS ACT (1988) Considered the most inclusive foreign trade legislation since the Trade Reform Act of 1974. It liberalizes and restricts foreign trade by expanding the president's authority to negotiate bilateral/multilateral trade agreements as well as retaliate against those nations perceived as trading unfairly with the U.S.

THRESHOLD TEST BAN TREATY (1990) A lengthy protocol tightening verification protocols to the Threshold Test Ban Treaty signed in 1974. The Senate approved the amended agreement on 25 September 1990.

TREATY ON THE FINAL SETTLEMENT WITH RESPECT TO GERMANY (1990) Democratic Republic of Germany, Federal Republic of Germany, France, U.K., U.S. and U.S.S.R. Ended responsibility of Allied Powers for Germany. Granted full sovereignty to unified country. Provides for German membership in NATO and prohibits any possession of nuclear, chemical or biological weapons.

CONVENTIONAL FORCES IN EUROPE TREATY (1990) NATO and Warsaw Pact. Limits each alliance to a specific number of battle tanks and artillery pieces, armored combat vehicles, combat aircraft and attack helicopters. The subsequent collapse of the U.S.S.R. necessitated a subsequent agreement in light of new boundary lines, to wit the CFE Flank Document. This agreement was approved on 31 May 1996.

SECURITY COUNCIL RESOLUTION 678 (1990) Members of the United Nations were permitted to use all means necessary to enforce previous UN resolutions concerning Iraq if Iraq did not withdraw from Kuwait by 15 January 1991. For the first, time an international peacekeeping body voted to authorize the use of force to prevent aggression. The League of Nations only condemned the Italian invasion of Ethiopia, while UN endorsement of the American use of force in Korea was after the fact. Twelve nations voted for the resolution, Cuba and Yemen voted against, while China abstained.

SECURITY COUNCIL RESOLUTION 686 (1991) Iraq will stop all hostile actions, return all POW's and hostages, rescind its annexation of Kuwait, accept liability for war damages, return all seized Kuwaiti property and disclose the location of all mine fields. Cuba voted against, China, India and Yemen abstained.

SECURITY COUNCIL RESOLUTION 687 (1991) Imposed UN supervised destruction of all chemical, biological and ballistic weapons of mass destruction possessed by Iraq. Also requires Iraq to pay reparations for war damage to Kuwait and allies.

STRATEGIC ARMS REDUCTION TREATY (1991) Imposed actual cuts in nuclear stockpiles of thirty percent from existing levels. Tight guidelines on the development of new strategic delivery systems. The disintegration of U.S.S.R. precluded ratification. The U.S. concluded a successor agreement with Russia, Ukraine, Belarus and Kazakhstan on 23 May 1992.

TREATY OF MADRID (1991) Established a 50 year moratorium on mining activities and oil exploration in Antarctica. This agreement extends the terms of the Antarctica Mining Treaty (1988).

FRAMEWORK CONVENTION ON CLIMATE CHANGE (1992) This treaty set no mandatory limits on greenhouse gas emissions for individual nations and contained no enforcement provisions. However, it included provisions for updates (protocols) that would set mandatory emission limits. The principal update is the Kyoto Protocol (1997).

CUBAN DEMOCRACY ACT (1992) This legislation prohibits foreign-based subsidiaries of U.S. companies from trading with Cuba, travel to Cuba by U.S. citizens and currency transfers between Cuba and U.S. by private parties. Non-governmental organizations are allowed to transfer food and medicine to Cuba.

AVIATION AGREEMENT (1992) Netherlands and U.S. This agreement eliminates most of the restrictions on airline flights between the two nations. When approved by the U.S. Senate, it was the most liberal air agreement to date.

NORTH AMERICAN FREE TRADE AGREEMENT (1992) Canada, Mexico and U.S. This agreement sought to eliminate all trade and investment barriers within ten years. Third party origin products were not covered save in specific circumstances. Unlike the European Union, this agreement did not envisage political, social or monetary integration. The agreement went into effect on 1 January 1994 after a bitter congressional debate.

TREATY OF PARIS (1993) Part of the continuing effort to eliminate weapons of mass destruction that began with the Geneva Protocol (1925) and continued with the Bacteriological/Tox Treaty (1972). Those party to the convention will not develop, produce, acquire, stockpile, retain or use chemical weapons. Parties will not assist third parties to violate the agreement and will destroy all existing stockpiles. Implementation by U.S. delayed until Congressional action on 20 October 1998.

SOUTH AFRICAN DEMOCRATIC TRANSITION SUPPORT ACT (1993) The obvious intent of the government of South Africa to abandon apartheid persuaded Congress to lift the remaining economic sanctions imposed by the Comprehensive Anti-Apartheid Act (1986).

GENERAL AGREEMENT ON TARIFFS AND TRADE (1994) Under the terms of this multi-national agreement GATT was essentially dissolved and replaced by the World Trade Organization. The WTO would henceforth police commerce among nations. The House of Representatives accepted the agreement on 29 November 1994 and the Senate on 1 December 1994. The agreement took effect on 1 January 1995.

WASHINGTON DECLARATION (1994) This agreement ended a 46-year state of war between Israel and Jordan. A subsequent treaty (26 October 1994) resolved certain territorial disputes, water rights and security issues. The treaty also provided for full diplomatic relations.

DAYTON PEACE ACCORDS (1995) Bosnia and Herzegovina. The nation retained its international boundaries and a joint multi-ethnic and democratic government charged with conducting foreign, diplomatic, and fiscal policy was created. The Bosniak/Croat Federation of Bosnia and Herzegovina and the Bosnian Serb-led Republika Srpska (RS) were to oversee local government functions. The Office of the High Representative (OHR) was created to oversee the implementation of the civilian aspects of the agreement, while an international peacekeeping force monitored the military aspects.

CUBAN LIBERTY AND DEMOCRATIC SOLIDARITY ACT (1996) Familiarly known as the Helms-Burton Act, this legislation establishes penalties for foreign companies conducting commercial transactions in Cuba, permits U.S. citizens to sue foreign investors using American property nationalized by Cuba and denies entry into U.S. of said individuals. (President W. Clinton suspended enforcement of provisions permitting suits against foreign investors on 16 July 1996. The "right to sue provisions" were suspended on 3 January 1997 and again on 16 July 1997. A permanent waiver was extended to European Union members on 18 May 1998.

TREATY OF PELINDABA (1996) This agreement establishes an African nuclear free zone. Protocol I requires signatories to refrain from threatening the use of nuclear devices and Protocol II obliges signatories to refrain from testing nuclear devices within the zone. U.S. signed both protocols on 11 April 1996.

WAR CRIMES ACT (1996) This act prescribes criminal penalties if a U.S. citizen, whether military or no, violates the 1949 Geneva Convention on War Crimes. This statute applies not only to those who choose to act, but all who order, know about or fail to prevent a proscribed action. The degree to which the act applies to actions committed in those circumstances when a nation proclaims individuals are not subject to the protection of the Geneva Convention. Details are found at 18 USC 2441.

COMPREHENSIVE TEST BAN TREATY (1996) Parties undertake to refain from any nuclear weapon test explosion or any other nuclear explosion, and to prohibit and prevent any such explosions at any place under its jurisdiction or control. Parties further promise to cause, encourage, or in any way participate in the carrying our of any nuclear weapons test explosion or any other nuclear explosion. Failed to achieve approval by U.S. Senate on 13 October 1999.

KYOTO PROTOCOL (1997) This agreement is an amendment to the United Nations Framework Convention on Climate Change (1992). Signatories agreed to reduce of carbon dioxide emissions, and five other greenhouse gases. Signatories may engage in emissions trading if they maintain or increase emissions of these gases. The United States Senate refused to approve the protocol.

INTERNATIONAL RELIGIOUS FREEDOM ACT (1998) This act created the U.S. Commission on International Religious Freedom. The commission monitors the status of freedom of thought, conscience, and religion or belief abroad, as defined in the Universal Declaration of Human Rights and related international instruments. It provides independent policy recommendations to the President, Secretary of State, and Congress. Revised in 1999.

CONVENTION ON THE PROHIBITION OF THE USE, STOCK-PILING, PRODUCTION AND TRANSFER OF ANTI-PERSONNEL MINES AND ON THEIR DESTRUCTION (1997) Signatories will not violate the agreement nor encourage others to do so. All stockpiles to be destroyed in ten years.

INTERNATIONAL CRIMINAL COURT FOR WAR CRIMINALS TREATY (2000) This 1998 UN treaty created an international court to try suspects for war crimes, genocide and crimes against humanity. The U.S. adhered to the agreement in 2000, and rescinded that signature 6 May 2002.

BIOGRAPHICAL SKETCHES

ARAFAT, Yassar (1929-2004) Although born in Egypt, Arafat was sent to Jerusalem to live with an uncle after the death of his mother. He was active in movements opposed to the creation of a Jewish state in Palestine and returned to Egypt with the establishment of the state of Israel. Trained as a civil engineer at the University of Cairo (1956), he entered Palestinian politics as the founder of a group opposed to the existence of Israel (Al Fatah). He was elected chairman of the Palestine Liberation Organization in 1968 and served as the most visible representative of the aspirations of the Palestinian people. He shared a Nobel Peace Prize with Shimon Peres (Israeli Foreign Minister) in 1994 and was elected the first president of the Palestinian Council in 1996.

ARIAS, Oscar Sanchez (1941-) President of Costa Rica from 1986 to 1987. Although best known for his peace-making efforts in Nicaragua he was also praised for his capable management of the Costa Rican economy. He won the Nobel Peace Prize (1987) for his leadership in what was known as the Contadora Peace Process.

ARISTIDE, Jean-Bertrand (1953-) Ordained a Catholic priest and a member of the Salesian Order (1982), his political activities in his native Haiti led to his expulsion from the order (1988) and his resignation as a priest in 1994. Whilst a parish priest Aristide organized groups to protest the despotism of Jean Claude Duvalier. He continued as a political activist, surviving nine assassination attempts, and was elected President of Haiti in 1990. Forced into exile by a coup d'etat in 1991 he returned in triumph in 1994. He left office in 1996 and took a position with the Foundation for Democracy. He returned to office in 2001, only to be forced into exile in 2004.

BEGIN, Menachem (1913-1992) Born in Poland, he made his way to Palestine by way of the labor camps of Siberia and the Soviet-organized Polish Army. Became chief of a terrorist organization fighting for an independent Jewish state in Palestine (Irgun Zvai Leumi) that he converted into a political party following the establishment of Israel. Recognized opposition leader in the Knesset (1965) and formed a coalition bloc (Likud) which led him to become Prime Minister in 1977. Resigned as Prime Minister 15 September 1983.

BIN LADIN, Osama (1957-) Born in to a wealthy family with close ties to the Saudi royal family, he earned a degree in civil engineering (1979) and one in economics and public administration (1981) from King Abdulaziz University in Jeddah. With the Soviet invasion of Afghanistan (1979), Bin Laden devoted his considerable resources to supporting the Afghan resistance. When forces from non-Muslim nations entered, Saudi Arabia to resist the 1990 Iraqi invasion of Kuwait Bin Laden was outraged. Bin Laden left Saudi Arabia for the Sudan in 1991. There he began to build an organization he dubbed al-Qaeda (the foundation or the base). Bin Laden is officially wanted in connection with the 1998 bombings of the United States embassies Tanzania and Nairobi, Kenya.

GONZALEZ, Elian (1993-) Despite laws to the contrary, scores of individuals attempt to flee Cuba for sanctuary in the United States. A 1995 accord with Cuba allows those who make it to American soil to seek political asylum. Elian Gonzalez, accompanied his mother and twelve others in an attempt to reach Florida by boat in November 1999. Elian and two others, not including his mother, survived. Because he was rescued at sea, Elian was not eligible for asylum. Although his mother took Elian without his father's knowledge, a routine child custody case became a *cause celebre* for the Cuban-American community. Elian returned to Cuba on 28 June 2000.

GORBACHEV, Mikhail (1931-) A graduate of the Lomonosov State University with a degree in law (1955) and the Stravropol Agricultural Institute as an agronomist and economist (1967), Gorbachev found a career in the Communist Party bureaucracy. Elected to the Central Committee of the Communist Party of the Soviet Union (1971), he became General Secretary of the CPSU in 1985. Instituted a series of reform measures (*perestroika*) that contributed to the breakup of the Soviet Union. Gorbachev undertook a valiant, albeit unsuccessful, effort to preserve the U.S.S.R. He resigned from public life to head the International Foundation for Socio-Economic and Political Studies in 1991. He received the Nobel Peace Prize in 1990.

HO Chi Minh (1890-1969) Left Vietnam as youth and ultimately took up residence in France where he took the nom de guerre under which he became famous. A founding member of the French Communist party (1920) he went to the U.S.S.R. (1923) and became an active Communist agent throughout East Asia. Founded the Indochinese Communist party (1930) but did not return to Vietnam until 1941. Formed the League for the Independence of Vietnam (Vietminh) and fought first the Japanese and later the French. The Geneva Accords (1954) divided Vietnam and Ho became president of the Democratic People's Republic of Vietnam. A seemingly

fragile man, he dressed simply and lived austerely. Many throughout S.E. Asia revered him as a patriot and liberator.

HOLBROOKE, Richard (1941-) A career Foreign Service officer (1962-
1972), he left to become editor of *Foreign Policy* from 1972 to 1976.
He returned to government service as Assistant Secretary for East
Asian and Pacific Affairs (1977-1981). He was the chief U.S. negotiator of the Dayton Peace Accord that stabilized affairs in portions
(Croatia and Bosnia) of the former state of Yugoslavia. In 1998, he
was appointed Special Presidential Envoy for Kosovo.

HUSSEIN, Ibn Talal (1935-1998) As King of Jordan, he survived wars,
countless assassinations attempts and several coups to become the
longest ruling leader in the Middle East. Hussein ascended the
Hashemite throne at 17 and spent the next decade fighting to survive. Although initially pro-western in his orientation, the demands
of Jordan's Palestinian minority required Hussein to adhere to positions sympathetic to that one-third of the population. Undeniably
popular among Jordanians, his support of Saddam Hussein in the
aftermath of Iraqi's invasion/annexation of Kuwait left him vulner-
able elsewhere in the world.

HUSSEIN, Saddam at-Takriti (1937-) Considered, with the possible
exception of Slobodan Milosevic, to be the most evil national
leader in the last decade of the Twentieth Century. An exile in
Egypt by age twenty, Hussein attended the Cairo Law School
(1962-63) and continued his studies at the Baghdad Law School
when the Ba'th Socialist Party came to power in 1963. The Ba'thist
regime was, however, quickly overthrown and Hussein was imprisoned. He escaped and assumed a leadership position. He was the
power behind the scenes when the Ba'th party returned to power
in 1968. He became president in 1979 and systematically eliminated
all opposition. His invasion of Iran (1980) wreaked havoc on Iraq,
as did his invasion of Kuwait in 1990.

MEIR, Golda (1898-1978) Born in Russia, the family immigrated to the
U.S. (1904), she married Morris Meyerson (1917) and immigrated
to Palestine (1921). A signer of the Israeli Declaration of Independence (14 May 1948), she served as envoy to U.S.S.R. (1948-1949)
and Minister of Labor (1949-1956). Taking the Hebrew name Meir
(1956) she was Minister of Labor (1949-1956), Minister for Foreign
Affairs (1956-1969) and Prime Minister from 1969 to 1974.

MILOSEVIC, Slobodan (1941-2006) Despite a law degree from the
University of Belgrade (1964), Milosevic pursued a career in management and banking. He served as president of Serbia (1989-1997)

and was elected President of Yugoslavia in 1997. He was indicted for war crimes by the International Criminal Tribunal for the former Yugoslavia in 1999, but died before a verdict was rendered. Next to Saddam Hussein he is considered one of the greatest villains in the last decade of the Twentieth Century.

NASSER, Gamal Abdel (1918-1970) A graduate of the Royal Military Academy (1938), he had an undistinguished military career until the 1948 defeat of Egypt by Israel led to the overthrow of the reigning monarchy (1952). Acquired power in the aftermath of the coup and by 1956 was President of Egypt. In 1956, he persuaded the British to withdraw their forces. He nationalized Suez Canal and turned the subsequent military action by France, Israel and the U.K. into a political victory. He guided his nation to complete independence and gave his people a sense of dignity and pride.

PINOCHET UGARTE, Augusto (1915-) A graduate of the Chilean Military Academy, he became commander-in-chief of the armed forces in 1972. He led a coup d'etat against the regime of Salvador Allende in 1973. His commitment to the free-market theories of the Chicago School appealed to the Right, and the brutality of the coup made him an easy target for the Left. His failure to win a third plebiscite in 1988 produced free elections in 1989 that allowed opposition-leader Patricio Aylwin to assume the presidency.

SADAT, Muhammad Anwar al- (1918-1981) A graduate of the Abbasiyah Military Academy and a close associate of Nasser, he was a leading participant in the coup which overthrew King Faruk. (1952). He succeeded to the Presidency with Nasser's death and, despite predictions, consolidated his power and remained in office. Inter-mixed war and diplomacy (Yom Kippur and Israeli visit) to create conditions that led to the Camp David Accords. Shared a Nobel Peace Prize with Menachem Begin (1978) but was assassinated by religious fundamentalists (1981).

YELTSIN, Boris Nickolaevich (1931-) A civil engineering graduate of the Ural Kirov Technical College (1955), Yeltsin became the quintessential party apparatchik. A member of the Central Committee of the Communist Party of the Soviet Union he was elected President of the Russian Federation in 1991. A flamboyant individual he oversaw, sometimes successfully, the transitional chaos that characterized the collapse of the Soviet Union. Widely criticized, at home and abroad, Yeltsin remained a dominant force in Russian politics and on the international stage.

Annotated Bibliography

Scholarship on American diplomacy during the three decades after the election of John F. Kennedy continues to be dominated by the U.S. and Soviet rivalry and its influence on the United States' relations with other countries as well as its approaches to global issues.

Analyses of the U-2 espionage incident, the Bay of Pigs operation, and the Cuban missile crisis highlight the tension that characterized the early years of this period. The Cold War remains the defining feature of foreign affairs and with the containment policy becomes the governing element for much of the decision-making of the 1960s and early 1970s. The conclusion of American involvement in Vietnam is both cause and effect in the emerging detente strategy of the 1970s, and considerable research has been done on this initiative, its progress, and the individual most closely associated with it, Henry Kissinger.

Some authors have described the decade of the 1980s as a New Cold War. Their works cite the renewed U.S. assertiveness in the Third World and the heightened public critique of Soviet policies as support for this representation.

General

Abel, Elie. THE MISSILE CRISIS (1966). Abel provides a day-by-day chronicle of the events that constituted the Cuban missile crisis of October 1962.

Allison, Graham T. ESSENCE OF DECISION (1971). Allison examines the assumptions that produced the decisions reached in the Cuban missile crisis and explores several problem-solving models that emerge from this study.

Ambrose, Stephen E. RISE TO GLOBALISM: American Foreign Policy Since 1938 (1988). Ambrose traces the development of American attitudes and practices in world affairs and the shifts of attention and policy from 1938 until today. He concludes that, despite increased dependency on other parts of the world, the United States is richer and more powerful than ever.

Beschloss, Michael R. EISENHOWER, KHRUSHCHEV AND THE U-2 AFFAIR (1986). Beschloss examines the U-2 incident and its impact on U.S. and Soviet relations, giving particular attention to American domestic opinion the first highly publicized admission that the U.S. government engaged in espionage.

Beschloss, Michael R. and Strobe Talbott. AT THE HIGHEST LEVELS: The Inside Story of the End of the Cold War (1993). Beschloss and Talbott had extraordinary access to top officials in Washington and Moscow and provide an insider analysis of the critical 1989-1991 period.

Bell, Coral. THE DIPLOMACY OF DETENTE: The Kissinger Era (1977). Bell regards the detente strategy as one aimed at a triangular U.S., U.S.S.R. and PRC balance of power and investigates its application and impact in fringe areas throughout the world, particularly from 1969 to 1977.

Bialar, Seweryn and Michael Mandelbaum. THE GLOBAL RIVALS (1988). Bailar and Mandelbaum investigate U.S.-Soviet relations and suggests that the historical primacy of military rivalry has derived from the difficulty of reconciling political differences. The authors suggest that a refocusing on the troublesome political issues under the Gorbachev regime could produce lessening tensions.

Bradsher, Henry S. AFGHANISTAN AND THE SOVIET UNION (1985). This work provides a general account of the Soviet intervention in Afghanistan and its global consequences.

Brown, Seyom. THE CRISIS OF POWER (1979). Brown investigates foreign policy during the Kissinger years and concludes that Kissinger made a substantial contribution in adapting the United States to the growing complexities of world politics.

Carroll, John M. and George G. Herring. MODERN AMERICAN DIPLOMACY (1986). This collection of essays on twentieth century American diplomacy addresses the major phases and issues of the modern period.

Carter, Jimmy. KEEPING FAITH (1982). This volume provides Carter's account of his presidency, including his description and assessment of its major foreign policy issues.

Cate, Curtis. THE IDES OF AUGUST (1978). Cate documents the events that led to the August 1961, construction of the Berlin Wall. He contends that Khrushchev turned the crisis into a duel between himself and Kennedy that led to the missile crisis in Cuba.

Catudal, Honor. KENNEDY AND THE BERLIN WALL CRISIS (1980). Catudal uses the Berlin Wall crisis as a vehicle for describing and assessing the U.S. diplomatic decision-making process during the Kennedy administration.

Chayes, Abram. THE CUBAN MISSILE CRISIS (1974). This work examines the missile crisis in the context of international law.

Divine, Robert A., ed. THE CUBAN MISSILE CRISIS (1971). This collection of essays by foreign policy experts and several key figures involved in the crisis examines the issues from various perspectives.

Divine, Robert A. EISENHOWER AND THE COLD WAR (1981). Divine concentrates on selected foreign policy issues of Eisenhower's presidency and concludes that Ike was skillful at foreign policy and that his performance is badly underrated in much of the research related to this period.

Divine, Robert A. SINCE 1945: Politics and Diplomacy in Recent American History (1985). Divine examines the major phases and issues U.S. diplomacy after World War II.

Gaddis, John Lewis. STRATEGIES OF CONTAINMENT: A Critical Appraisal of Postwar American National Security Policy (1982). Gaddis argues that there have been five successive geopolitical codes to containment since World War II and investigates them to determine possible patterns.

Gardner, Lloyd C. A COVENANT WITH POWER: America and World Order from Wilson to Reagan (1984). Gardner examines the various ways in which U.S. presidents since Wilson have used power and their particular records in reconciling the application of power with democratic ideology.

Gavshon, Arthur. CRISIS IN AFRICA (1981). Gavshon examines Africa's role in the post-World War II East-West struggle using Angola and the Horn of Africa as specific case studies.

George, Alexander L., Philip J. Farley, and Alexander Dallin, eds. U.S.-SOVIET SECURITY COOPERATION: Achievements, Failures, Lessons (1988). These 22 case studies deal with instances in which the United States and the Soviet Union endeavored to cooperate to enhance security. The author's purpose is to determine conditions under which cooperation succeeds or fails.

Graebner, Norman A. AMERICA AS A WORLD POWER: A Realist Appraisal from Wilson to Reagan (1984). Graebaer maintains that the United States sacrifices world influence by elevating ideals and principles above diplomacy.

Gurtov, Melvin. THE UNITED STATES AGAINST THE THIRD WORLD (1974). Gurtov examines U.S. foreign policy during the

Eisenhower, Kennedy, Johnson, and Nixon administrations and concludes that the themes of antinationalism and interventionism characterized American diplomacy in the Third World throughout the three decades studied. The author proposes a noninterventionist strategy based on receptivity to radical change and tolerant of a variety of ideologies and economic philosophies.

Heath, Jim F. DECADE OF DISILLUSIONMENT (1975). This work recounts the domestic and foreign policy events of the Kennedy and Johnson years. The author regards American diplomacy of the period as vintage containment.

Hersh, Seymour. THE PRICE OF POWER: Kissinger in the Nixon White House (1983). Hersh contends that Nixon's misuse of power distinguished the foreign policy of his administration and extracted a high cost for those who were involved.

Hoffmann, Stanley. PRIMARY OR WORLD ORDER (1978). Hoffmann examines American foreign policy during the Nixon-Kissinger years and concludes that moderation in dealing with the international community needed to be the focus of future relations.

Hyland, William G., ed. THE REAGAN FOREIGN POLICY (1987). This collection of thirteen articles from the journal FOREIGN AFFAIRS contains the assessments of American foreign policy actors and experts involved in the Reagan administration. Among the topics addressed are containment, summitry, the Congress, Stars Wars, the economy, the Reykjavik discussions, and U.S. defense strategy.

Isaacson, Walter. KISSINGER: A BIOGRAPHY (1992). Kissinger, according to Isaacson, bequeathed to his successors a strategy for dealing with the U.S.S.R. that blended containment as well as cooperation and that over the next two decades allowed the internal contradictions of the Soviet Union to play out.

Jackson, Henry F. FROM THE CONGO TO SOWETO (1982). Jackson presents a history of American diplomacy in Africa from 1960 until the early 1980s. He maintains that effective future U.S. policy must reconcile itself to what he considers the irresistible forces of change in Africa as well as other Third World regions.

Jeffrey-Jones, Rhodi. CHANGING DIFFERENCES: Women and the Shaping of American Foreign Policy, 1917-1994 (1995). Women, according to Jeffrey-Jones, will continue to increase their influence over American foreign policy and that this will be beneficial because of their more peaceful nature.

Kalb, Madelaine G. THE CONGO CABLES (1982). The author investigates the relationship of the Cold War to emerging Africa during the Eisenhower and Kennedy administrations.

Kegley, Charles W., Jr. and Eugene R. Wittkopf. AMERICAN FOREIGN POLICY: Pattern and Process (1979). Dealing with American foreign policy in the post-World War II period, this work investigates its domestic and international context, describes institutions and roles, and contrasts continuity and change. The authors conclude that American diplomacy tends more toward pattern than process.

Kegley, Charles W., Jr. and Eugene R. Wittkopf. PERSPECTIVES ON AMERICAN FOREIGN POLICY: Selected Readings (1983). This companion volume to AMERICAN FOREIGN POLICY by the same authors contains essays by experts and actors of the system. It provides a useful introduction to the theoretical framework of American foreign policy.

Kunz, Diane. BUTTER AND GUNS: America's Cold War Economic Diplomacy (1997). The United States successfully pursued a policy that gave equal attention to the domestic and military economy. Kunz argues that economic diplomacy determined the outcome of the Cold War.

LaFeber, Walter. AMERICA, RUSSIA, AND THE COLD WAR, 1945-1984 (1985). LaFeber traces the U.S. and Soviet conflict back to the late nineteenth century confrontation in North China and Manchuria, distinguishing between old and new world encounters and contrasting the business-oriented United States with the bureaucratic Soviet Union.

Lake, David A. POWER, PROTECTION, AND FREE TRADE. International Sources of U.S. Commercial Strategy, 1887-1939 (1988). This work examines the structure of international trade and U.S. international economic strategy from the last quarter of the nineteenth century until World War II. The author uses the findings of this study to support his prognosis that the present multilateral opportunistic structure is likely to endure despite declining U.S. hegemony.

Lagueur, Walter and Brad Roberts, eds. AMERICA IN THE WORLD 1962-1987: A Strategic and Political Reader (1987). Foreign policy experts and actors deal with a variety of topics including national strategy, Western security, the role of the U.S. Senate, arms control, international economies, and policy changes and processes.

Levering, Ralph B. THE COLD WAR, 1945-1987 (1988). Beginning with the Yalta Conference, Levering recounts the history of the Cold War including its eclipse by detente and resurgence during the Reagan years.

McCormick, Thomas J. AMERICA'S HALF-CENTURY: United States Foreign Policy in the Cold War (1989). McCormick applies a world systems analysis in this study of U.S. Cold War foreign policy.

Muravchik, Joshua. THE UNCERTAIN CRUSADE (1986). Muravchik contends that the Carter policy of forcing human rights issues into the arena of international debate was consistent with democratic government. He maintains, however, that Carter's uneven application of the principle complicated acceptance of his views.

Nelson, Daniel N. and Roger B. Anderson. SOVIET-AMERICAN RELATIONS: Understanding Differences, Avoiding Conflicts (1988). Contributors describe various aspects of daily life in the Soviet Union and suggest means of avoiding conflict through enhanced understanding. Nelson concludes that tensions can only be lessened if both parties diminish their involvement in the Third World, increase dialogue, and abandon aims of dominance in Western Europe.

Nelson, Keith L. THE MAKING OF DETENTE: Soviet-American Relations in the Shadow Of Vietnam (1995). Nelson believes that the Vietnam conflict played the key role in influencing Nixon's decisions regarding detente with the Soviets.

Newsom, David D. DIPLOMACY AND THE AMERICAN DEMOCRACY (1988). This volume deals with the impact of the U.S. democratic process in shaping American foreign policy. The author includes such issues as the role of the media, the U.S. Congress, the Third World, human rights, terrorism, economic assistance, and the expectations of American citizens.

Nogee, Joseph L. and John Spanier. PEACE IMPOSSIBLE—WAR UNLIKELY (1988). Nogee and Spanier examine U.S. and U.S.S.R. Cold War relations and conclude that, barring fundamental changes in the Soviet regime, conflict will endure. They contend that the existence of nuclear weapons will keep the rivalry from leading to war.

Noer, Thomas J. COLD WAR AND BLACK LIBERATION: The United States and White Rule in Africa, 1948-1968. (1985). Noer examines two decades of U.S. relations with African nations and illustrates the complexities presented by a policy of pursuing the middle road between white supremacy and majority rule.

Oye, Kenneth A., et al., eds. EAGLE DEFIANT (1983). This collection of essays assesses the first two years of the Reagan Administration and assumes that Reagan's foreign policy aimed at returning the United States to a position of preeminence.

Paterson, Thomas G., ed. KENNEDY'S QUEST FOR VICTORY (1989). This collection of essays investigates and descries the mixed foreign policy legacy of the Kennedy administration. The editor concludes that Kennedy and his advisors did not fundamentally reassess foreign policy assumptions, despite rhetoric to the contrary.

Paterson, Thomas G. ON EVERY FRONT: The Making of the Cold War (1979). This book explains the roots and evolution of the Cold War from the perspective of American aims and values. It includes a description of the role played by U.S. public opinion, the desire and rationale for spheres of influence, and the American value of firmness in negotiation.

Paterson, Thomas G., ed. MAJOR PROBLEMS IN AMERICAN FOREIGN POLICY: Documents and Essays, Vol. II: Since 1914 (1984). Paterson divides the history of American foreign policy into broad categories and includes key documents and essays by authorities.

Paterson, Thomas G. MEETING THE COMMUNIST THREAT: Truman to Reagan (1988). This volume provides a general orientation to American foreign policy after 1945, particularly as it relates to the spread of communism.

Pipes, Richard. U.S. and SOVIET RELATIONS IN THE ERA OF DETENTE (1981.). Pipes contrasts American and Soviet attitudes toward war and peace and suggests that the differences in their approaches to these two diplomatic issues leads to U.S. misinterpretation of Soviet intentions. Pipes maintains that Russian history demonstrates that Russians view times of peace as opportunities to prepare for inevitable future wars. He criticizes U.S. Detente strategy as overly compromising.

Prados, John. PRESIDENT'S SECRET WAR (1986). Prados analyses covert operations from their advent during World War II through Iranscam and concludes that intelligence reform is needed.

Report of the Study Commission on U.S. Policy toward Southern Africa. SOUTH AFRICA: Time Running Out (1981). This volume examines the conditions in South Africa that bear on the apartheid issue. The final section evaluates U.S. policy considerations and options especially in regard to social and economic pressures in Africa.

Richelson, Jeffrey. AMERICAN ESPIONAGE AND THE SOVIET TARGET (1987). Richelson describes American espionage of the Soviet Union since 1945 and suggests that the aims and use of U.S. intelligence gathering should not focus only on war preparations but also on gathering data that assists in ensuring stability and peace.

Schell, Jonathan. THE TIME OF ILLUSION (1976). The author attempts to reconcile many of the seemingly contradictory acts of the Nixon Administration by examining events from the standpoint of governmental credibility and need to maintain it at home and abroad.

Schick, Jack M. THE BERLIN CRISIS 1958-1962 (1971). Schick investigates the events surrounding the crisis and suggests that similar conflicts will occur as long as the Soviets perceive West Germany as a threat to their national security.

Schraeder, Peter. UNITED STATES FOREIGN POLICY TOWARDS AFRICA: Incrementalism, Crisis, and Change (1994). In this study of U.S. relations with Ethiopia, Somalia, South Africa, and Zaire, Schraeder contends that Africa has been a low priority for Washington in the post-1945 period.

Smith, Gaddis. MORALITY, REASON, AND POWER: American Diplomacy in the Carter Years (1986). Smith describes the major foreign policy issues of the Carter Administration and concludes that it was a whirlpool of disagreement over the fundamental nature of national and world security. He cites inexperience, a lack of connections in the nation's capital, and simple bad luck as the major deficiencies that produced the unsatisfactory outcomes of Carter's initiatives.

Spencer, Donald S. THE CARTER IMPLOSION (1988). Spencer maintains that the fundamental weakness of the Carter Administration was amateurism, characterized by an anti intellectual approach to statecraft and undue reliance on faith, good intentions, and vision. He concludes that corrective measures against the ascendancy of candidates who lack competence for effective statesmanship lie in reforms of the constitutional system and the nation's press.

Stevenson, Richard W. THE RISE AND FALL OF DETENTE (1985). The author examines the period of relaxation in U.S. and Soviet tensions from 1953 to 1984 and investigates the role of detente in the quest for world peace.

Szulc, Tad. THE ILLUSION OF PEACE (1978). Szulc analyzes Nixon's 1969-1974 record and concludes that despite the president's continual verbal emphasis on peace as the determinative foreign policy theme, his diplomacy was characterized by immorality and brutality.

Treverton, Gregory F. COVERT ACTION: The Limits of Intervention in the Postwar World (1987). Treverton examines four decades of American covert action around the world and illustrates the central and unresolved problem of a democracy engaged in secret operations beyond the control of the electoral process.

Ungar, Sanford J., ed. ESTRANGEMENT: America and the World (1985). This collection of essays examines America's post-World War II estrangement from the international community.

Wise, David and Thomas B. Ross. THE U-2 AFFAIR (1962). The authors present the events associated with the capture of U-2 pilot Francis Gary Powers and his spy plane by the Soviets and the subsequent upheaval in U.S. domestic and international affairs. Wise and Ross offer an analysis of the crisis, its significance, and its limitations.

Vietnam

The American involvement in Vietnam dominated the study of U.S. foreign affairs during the decade between 1965 and 1975. Because of the extended nature of the conflict, the opinion of scholarship changed and grew with the new developments and corresponding altered policies concerning U.S. and Vietnamese relations.

Many historians during the Johnson administration affirmed the president's policy of the containment of communism in Southeast Asia. Assenting views, however, argued that Southeast Asia lay outside those areas that were critical to U.S. national interests and maintained that drawing the line in Vietnam constituted an unreasonable strategy. As the war intensified and modern technology provided the public with the tragic visual images of the war, scholarly critique became increasingly moralistic. Some writers contended that containment offered inadequate justification for military intervention and posited that the U.S. Government's motivation derived less from ideological issues than from the desire to expand American economic power throughout the globe. Some writers carried the debate to greater extremes, condemning the war as a heinous crime that they characterized as the product of a fundamentally flawed American political system. Subsequent presentations of the conflict address the foregoing views, endeavoring to explain the debacle as a series of erroneous decisions but without undue reliance on hyperbolic descriptions. These works are as much a product of the large body of research available on the conflict as they are influenced by the inevitable developments in international relations that emerged during the several decades of the U.S. involvement in Vietnam.

Bain, Chester A. VIETNAM: THE ROOTS OF CONFLICT (1967). Bain undertakes a review of Vietnamese history from its earliest beginnings to support his contention that the Vietnamese in 1967 were struggling to escape domination by expansionist communists in Asia.

Brands, H. W. THE WAGES OF GLOBALISM: Lyndon Johnson and the Limits of American Power (1995). Brands' book is a sympathetic survey of Johnson's foreign policies.

Butlinger, Joseph. VIETNAM: The Unforgettable Tragedy (1977). Butlinger analyses the American involvement in Vietnam and concludes that, if workable foreign policies are to be achieved, Americans need to be more alert to international political matters, less quick to interfere in civil wars, and more insistent on adhering to facts in diplomatic issues

DeBenedetti, Charles, with Charles Chatfield. AN AMERICAN ORDEAL: The Antiwar Movement of the Vietnam Era (1990). The authors conclude that while the antiwar movement did not force the U.S. to quit the war, nevertheless its political significance was that it persistently identified that choice as the essential issue of American foreign policy and national identity.

Chomsky, Noam. RETHINKING CAMELOT: JFK, the Vietnam War, and U.S. Political Culture (1993). Chomsky argues that Kennedy had no plan or intention to withdraw [from Vietnam] without victory.

Fishel, Wesley R. ed. VIETNAM: ANATOMY OF A CONFLICT (1968) This volume includes 81 essays addressing the political, economic, and social aspects of Vietnam and the American involvement there.

Gardner, Lloyd C. PAY ANY PRICE: Lyndon Johnson and the Wars for Vietnam (1995). Gardner sees a fearful and fateful symmetry between Johnson's war in Vietnam and his Great Society programs in the U.S.

Gelb, Leslie H. and Richard K. Betts. THE IRONY OF VIETNAM (1979). The authors contend that although American foreign policy in Vietnam failed, the domestic decision-raking system actually worked. They also maintain that the issues of the Vietnam conflict that produced these two contradictory outcomes were not unique.

Goodman, Allan E. THE LOST PEACE (1978). Goodman recounts the events associated with U.S. efforts to achieve a negotiated settlement to the conflict in Vietnam. He contends that the ultimate impossibility of a peaceful conclusion to the war derived from Hanoi's commitment to the liberation of South Vietnam as a prerequisite for unification.

Gregg, Robert W. and Charles W. Kegley, Jr. AFTER VIETNAM: The Future of American Foreign Policy (1971). Foreign policy specialists contributed to this 1971 effort to look beyond the Vietnam conflict and focus on the future role of the United States in global affairs.

Hallin, Daniel C. THE UNCENSORED WAR: The Media and Vietnam (1986). Hallin investigates the role of the media in American political life in general and on public opinion regarding the Vietnam War in particular. The author contends that the media's part in the divisiveness of U.S. public opinion regarding Vietnam was less significant than is generally believed, basing his argument on studies which diminish the overall impact of the media on U.S. audiences.

Herring, George C. AMERICA'S LONGEST WAR (1986). Herring contends that the policy behind the American intervention in Vietnam was fundamentally flawed, and that the war could not be won in a way acceptable to the U.S. public.

Hilsman, Roger. TO MOVE A NATION (1967). This volume examines foreign policy during the Kennedy administration and concludes that at the advent of the Johnson era, a political rather than military approach to resolving the convict in Vietnam would have been the best choice.

Holsti, Ole R. and James N. Rosenau. AMERICAN LEADERSHIP IN WORLD AFFAIRS: Vietnam and the Breakdown of Consensus. (1984). This work is a study of the attitudes and beliefs of U.S. policy makers in 1976 and 1980 concerning Vietnam. The authors maintain that the deep divisions among political leaders concerning Vietnam continued to dominate policy into the 1980s and inhibited the ability to forge an effective foreign policy consensus.

Isaacs, Arnold R. WITHOUT HONOR: Defeat in Vietnam and Cambodia (1983). Isaacs adopts a critical view of both American and South Vietnamese wartime policies, especially during the last years of the Vietnam convict, and concludes that although the U.S. choice to withdraw was unavoidable, it was also an act of betrayal vis-à-vis millions of Vietnamese.

Johnson, Lyndon Baines. THE VANTAGE POINT: Perspectives on the Presidency 1963-1969 (1971). This volume contains the report of LBJ concerning decisions made about Vietnam and other aspects of his presidency.

Kahin, George McTurnan. INTERVENTION: How America Became Involved in Vietnam (1986). Kahin pursues the theme of American attempts to control the political character of Vietnam as a vehicle for illustrating the path of U.S. involvement there.

Karnow, Stanley. VIETNAM: A History (1983). This extensive work investigates the history of Vietnam and the course of the American conflict there. Karnow's book emerged from the television documentary project, VIETNAM: A TELEVISION HISTORY.

Kolko, Gabriel. ROOTS OF AMERICAN FOREIGN POLICY: An Analysis of Power and Purpose (1969). This work examines the affect of U.S. power abroad, especially in Vietnam, and regards its application as morally wrong. Kolko maintains that the American social order that gave rise to the foreign policy of 1969 was inherently defective and lacking in careful diagnosis.

Lewy, Gunter. AMERICAN IN VIETNAM (1978). This volume traces the American involvement in Vietnam from its roots to its conclusion, emphasizing especially the process of Vietnamization and the impact of atrocities on America's ability to prosecute the war.

Morgenthau, Hans J. VIETNAM AND THE UNITED STATES (1965). Morgenthau contends that while American power abroad constituted an essential tool of foreign policy, U.S. military power in Vietnam alone could not be equated with this key element. He opposed continued involvement and critiqued 1965 contemporary policy makers for what he called their misunderstanding of communism and of the containment policy.

Nixon, Richard. NO MORE VIETNAMS (1985). This volume provides Nixon's perspective on what he regards as the American defeat in Vietnam.

Pike, Douglas. VIET CONG: The Organization and Techniques of the National Liberation Front of South Vietnam (1966). Pike's study of the Vietcong in South Vietnam challenged the U.S. Government assertion that the armed communists in the South could be easily subverted. Despite his findings, the author warned against U.S. abandonment of the Vietnamese.

Podhoretz, Norman. WHY WE WERE IN VIETNAM (1982). This volume analyzes the reasons behind American entry into the war in Vietnam, the commitment to stay, and the decision to leave. Podhoretz concludes that the motivation for being there was indeed to save South Vietnam from communism, but that this rationale lost significance as the war progressed.

Porter, Gareth. A PEACE DENIED (1975). Porter examines United States and Vietnamese efforts at achieving a political settlement to the war and concludes that it was the U.S. policy of rejecting solutions that included the North Vietnamese in the power structure in tile south that confounded negotiations.

Prados, John. THE HIDDEN HISTORY OF THE VIETNAM WAR (1995). Prados challenges what he views as many of the commonly held myths surrounding the conflict in Vietnam.

Rostow, W. W. THE DIFFUSION OF POWER: An Essay in Recent History (1972). In several chapters, Rostow examines the American involvement in Vietnam. The author contends that Vietnam was critical to the balance of power in Asia and believed that Nixon should have continued to apply U.S. resources to tip the advantage away from the Communists.

Rotter, Andrew J. THE PATH TO VIETNAM: Origins of the American Commitment to Southeast Asia (1987). Rotter investigates the roots of the American conflict in Vietnam and maintains that they are found in U.S. efforts to construct a global political economy in which Southeast Asia played a significant role.

Schulzinger, Robert A. A TIME FOR WAR: The United States and Vietnam, 1941-1975 (1997). Schulzinger argues that a sense that time was running out in Vietnam led American officials to exaggerate its strategic significance. He also states that the Vietnam conflict was irrelevant regarding the outcome of the Cold War.

Shapley, Deborah. PROMISE AND POWER: The Life and Times of Robert Mcnamara (1993). McNamara, Shapley concludes, was a man defined by secretiveness, his boundless ambition to do good, [and] his habit of manipulative schemes built around simple, almost religiously held beliefs.

Sheehan, Neil, ed. THE PENTAGON PAPERS (1971). Sheehan synthesizes the New York Times publication of papers related to the Pentagon study of American participation in the Vietnam War with the documents concerning the court case that resulted from NYT's possession and publication of the materials. Through commentary and analyses, the author constructs a history of the war.

Summers, Harry. ON STRATEGY (1982). Summers contends that misunderstandings of military theory and strategy led to a faulty concept among Vietnam era Americans concerning the nature of war and its and role in the diplomatic process. The author suggests that this in turn led to U.S. defeat in Vietnam.

Trager, Frank N. WHY VIET NAM (1966). Trager argued for continued American commitment in Vietnam, citing the need to end Communist interference in South Vietnam in order to provide the environment in which that country could develop into a modern state.

Turner, Kathleen J. LYNDON JOHNSON'S DUAL WAR: Vietnam and the Press (1985). This work investigates the way in which LBJ interacted with the media and how it molded his communication concerning the war in Vietnam.

Westmoreland, William C. A SOLDIER REPORTS (1976). The author was Vietnam field commander from 1964 to 1968 and Army Chief of Staff the following four years. This volume contains his analysis of the war.

Young, Marilyn B. THE VIETNAM WARS, 1945-1990 (1991). Young explores the ongoing process of intervention to explain how the U.S. became mired in Vietnam.

Zagoria, Donald S. VIETNAM TRIANGLE (1967). Zagoria examined the relationship among Moscow, Peking, and Hanoi during the U.S. involvement in Vietnam and concluded that a resolution to the conflict in Southeast Asia would open doors to reconciliation between Washington and Peking.

Latin America

Studies of United States relations with its Latin American neighbors during this period focus on the United States' preoccupation with the spread of communism into the American hemisphere and the mutual economic Impact of relations between countries. Works dealing with the early years concern themselves with American interventionist activities such as the Bay of Pigs operation and evaluate the legacy of such efforts

The Cuban missile crisis of the early 1960s constitutes a further emphasis of scholarship in this area, although it is treated largely as a U.S. and Soviet Issue. Works from recent years address the role of the United States in the continuing instability of many Latin American countries and the inherent conflict produced by U.S. support of dictatorial regimes.

Arnson, Cynthia. EL SALVADOR: A Revolution Confronts the United States (1982). Arnson investigated U.S. and Salvadoran relations from the 1950s through the Reagan Administration for models in resolving conflicts and concluded that negotiated settlements should be used in resolving hostilities between guerrilla factions and existing governments. The author applied her theory to a similar situation in Rhodesia

Baily, Samuel L. THE UNITED STATES AND THE DEVELOPMENT OF SOUTH AMERICA, 1945-1975 (1976). Baily argues that U.S. policy towards South America during the three decades following World War II were characterized by a high degree of continuity. He contends however, that the basic assumptions underlying U.S. policy and those of South American countries are different and must be addressed if future relations are to be effective and humane.

Blaster, Cole. THE HOVERING GIANT (1985). Cole examines the history of U.S. response to revolutionary change in Latin America from 1910 to 1985. He identifies recurring patterns of U.S. official behavior which he believes strongly affect the ability to achieve desired goals.

Brune, Lester H. THE MISSILE CRISIS OF OCTOBER 1962 (1985). This work describes the issues involved in the 1962 missile crisis and provides an extensive bibliography on the topic

Burns, E. Bradford. AT WAR IN NICARAGUA (1987). Burns examines the Reagan Administration's record in dealing with Nicaragua and suggests that the issues involved offered the United States an opportunity to develop a new policy toward the Third World

Carr, Raymond. PUERTO RICO: A Colonial Experiment (1984). In this history of U.S. and Puerto Rican relations from the Spanish-American War through the 1980s, the author maintains that Puerto Rico's economy not its relations with the United States, have posed the country's most difficult problems.

Coleman, Kenneth M. and George C. Herring, eds. THE CENTRAL AMERICAN CRISIS: Sources of Conflict and the Failure of U.S. Policy (1985). This collection of essays by specialists in the field investigates the internal and external sources of Latin American conflict. The editor-authors propose a new Central American policy, social democratic in viewpoint and reliant on accommodation between rich and poor.

Diederich, Bernard. SOMOZA (1981). Diederich recounts the history of U.S. and Nicaraguan affairs, especially during the years of the Somoza dynasty, and examines the impact of the relationship on Central America in the 1980s.

Erb, Richard D. and Stanley R. Ross, eds. UNITED STATES RELATIONS WITH MEXICO (1981). This collection of essays by scholars and government officials examines the contemporary issues that constituted U.S.-Mexican affairs at the beginning of the 1980s.

Gettleman, Marvin E. et al., eds. EL SALVADOR: Central America and the New Cold War (1981). This collection of essays provides a broad and varied analysis of the role of Central America in the Cold War.

Gleijeses, Piero. THE DOMINICAN CRISIS (1975). The author provides a detailed explanation of the 1965 U.S. intervention in the Dominican Republic in response to a popular rebel uprising that threatened to topple the Dominican government. It was the first overt American intervention in the Western Hemisphere since FOR proclaimed the Good Neighbor Policy, and Gleijeses examines the impact of the action.

Higgins, Trumbull. THE PERFECT FAILURE (1987). This book examines the fiasco of the U.S. attempt to land troops on south coast of Cuba and concludes that is serves well as an example of how not to conduct covert operations.

LaFeber, Walter. INEVITABLE REVOLUTIONS: The United States in Central America (1983). This work investigates the history of

U.S. relations with Central American countries from their inception through the Reagan administration.

Langley, Lester D. CENTRAL AMERICA: The Real Stakes (1985). Langley analyses American foreign policy in Central America from the standpoint of Central American culture and concludes that military restraint and support for decent democratic regimes are the best means of expressing U.S. interests for the political development of these countries.

Langley, Lester D. THE UNITED STATES AND THE CARIBBEAN, 1900-1970 (1980). Langley presents a chronological and episodic account of U.S. relations with Caribbean nations from the advent of American influence during the Hispano-American war through the demise of the U.S. Empire in the Caribbean. The author maintains that the paradox that characterized early relations continues today, to wit the American desire for democracy and progress on one hand and its treatment of its Caribbean neighbors as inferior on the other.

Leonard, Thomas M. CENTRAL AMERICA AND UNITED STATES POLICIES, 1820s 1980s: A Guide to Issues and References (1985). This book describes the Central American crisis as to its historical perspective the role of the U.S., and the problems of individual Central American nations. The author concludes that present day U.S. regional foreign policy and the objectives of revolutionaries are not compatible.

Morley, Morris H. IMPERIAL STATE AND REVOLUTION: The United States and Cuba, 1952-1986 (1987). Morley uses the imperial state model to interpret events and trends in U.S. and Cuban relations of the recent past and consequently emphasizes U.S. economic interests.

Newsom, David D. THE SOVIET BRIGADE IN CUBA: A Study in Political Diplomacy (1987). Newsom investigates this 1979 incident and uses it to illustrate his contention that U.S. intelligence agencies sometimes work at cross-purposes. Domestic politics and their impact on this issue are addressed, as is the influence on SALT II.

Pastor, Robert A. CONDEMNED TO REPETITION: The United States and Nicaragua (1987). Pastor examines U.S. and Nicaraguan relations with particular emphasis on the period from the succession crisis of the late 1970s through the Reagan administration. The author discusses some of the lessons to be leaned from the history of that relationship and suggests alternatives that might have produced outcomes that were more acceptable.

Pastor, Robert A. and Jorge G. Castaveda. LIMITS TO FRIENDSHIP (1988). These authors examine economic, cultural, and political aspects of the U.S. and Mexican relationship and conclude that fundamental changes are needed. Pastor and Castaveda suggest specific and pragmatic changes in both U.S. and Mexican policies

Petnas, James and Morris Morley. THE UNITED STATES AND CHILE (1975). This volume investigates the U.S. role in Chile during the Allende years. The author maintains that the American policy of prolonged confrontation was designed to systematically undermine the Allende administration's capacity to govern.

Schoultz, Lars. NATIONAL SECURITY AND UNITED STATES POLICY TOWARD LATIN AMERICA (1987). The author focuses on the sources of instability in Latin America, investigating such issues as poverty, communism, and the Latin American strategic location.

Smith, Gaddis. THE LAST YEARS OF THE MONROE DOCTRINE, 1945-1993 (1994). The thesis of Smith's book is that the end of the Cold War marked the end of the Monroe Doctrine.

Europe

The literature concerning United States relations with Europe during this period investigates the role of Western Europe in the American defense strategy, particularly as it relates to NATO and to the Warsaw Pact. Authors seek to describe the characteristics of the military alliance and to assess and predict its immediate and long-range impact on European nations.

Andrianopoulos, Argyris G. WESTERN EUROPE IN KISSINGER'S GLOBAL STRATEGY (1988). This volume examines the U.S. and Western European partnership as it related to nuclear issues, the presence of U S. troops in Europe, rapprochement with East Germany, and the Nixon-Kissinger approach to the Western alliance. The author addresses the thesis that Kissinger's attention to the Soviet Union, the People's Republic of China, and Vietnam War distracted attention from the Atlantic alliance. He contends that it was national sovereignty and nuclear issues which inhibited bold initiatives in that partnership.

Baylis, John. ANGLO-AMERICAN DEFENSE RELATIONS, 1939-1984: The Special Relationship (1981, 1984). Baylis investigates the origins and characteristics of the American relationship with Britain throughout World War II and up to the present with particular attention to defense. The author forecasts the future of Anglo-American cooperation and suggests that new foci in American foreign policy, recent developments in the international system, and economic factors will alter certain aspects of the special relationship.

Clawson, Robert W. and Lawrence S. Kaplan, eds. THE WARSAW PACT: Political Purpose and Military Means (1982). This collection of essays by specialists on the Warsaw Pact provides a description of that alliance from the perspective of its political objectives, its relationship to NATO, the forces it deploys, and its weapons.

Costigliola, Frank. FRANCE AND THE UNITED STATES: The Cold War Alliance since World War II (1992). Costigliola's thesis is that during the Cold War the U.S. sought loyal followers while France insisted on taking an independent track.

DePorte, A. W. EUROPE BETWEEN THE SUPERPOWERS (1979). This work examines the European state system of the 1970s and analyzes the outcomes of the many challenges to its security. The author contends that the system has been effective in meeting conflict and concludes that the structure is sufficiently effective to promise a stable future

Dimbleby, David and David Reynolds. AN OCEAN APART (1988). This work examines U.S. and U.K. relations during the twentieth century both directly and in other parts of the world and suggests that despite a continued affinity with the United States, Britain's future best interests will require growing political and economic attention to European allies.

Garnet, Richard L. THE ALLIANCE (1983). Barnet identifies the United States, Europe, and Japan as the makers of the postwar world and describes this alliance of industrialized nations as the most ingenious political inventions of the twentieth century.

Garthoff, Raymond L. THE GREAT TRANSITION: American-Soviet Relations at the End of the Cold War (1994). Garthoff analyzes the Soviet-American relationship from 1981 to 1991 and he argues that Reagan's attitude towards the U.S.S.R. changed during his second term thanks to the increasing influence of Secretary of State George Shultz and National Security Advisor Frank Carlucci.

Grosser, Alfred. THE WESTERN ALLIANCE (1980). Grosser presents a European perspective on European-American relations from 1945 to 1978. He concludes that, despite the complexities of the relations among these countries, the alliance endures because of the military and economic advantages, as well as the similarities of cultural values.

Kaplan, Lawrence. NATO AND THE UNITED STATES: The Enduring Alliance (1988). Kaplan offers a concise, chronological presentation of the development of NATO, with attention to the influence of such issues as the role of the Korean War, the French rejection of the military treaty, detente, and arms control.

Kaplan, Lawrence S., et al. NATO AFTER FORTY YEARS (1990). This volume offers a review of the historical record of NATO as well as an assessment of its present and future role after forty years of operation. The work is organized in four main sections examining the alliance in reference to its member states, its role in world politics, its approach to security issues, and speculations about its future.

Korvg, Bennet. THE MYTH OF LIBERATION: East-Central Europe in U.S Diplomacy and Politics Since 1941 (1973). This analysis of U.S. policies regarding East Central Europe deals with the period ranging from the signing of the Atlantic Charter to the invasion of Czechoslovakia

Louts, William Roger and Hedley Bull, eds. THE SPECIAL RELATIONSHIP: Anglo-American Relations Since 1945 (1986). Specialists analyze U.S. and British relations in the postwar era from the approaches of history, economic considerations, defense, and the demands from other areas of the world community

Nelson, Daniel J. A HISTORY OF U.S. MILITARY FORCES IN GERMANY (1987). This book investigates the impact of the American troop presence in Germany on U.S. and West German relations. Nelson believes that it behooves Americans to think as Germans think regarding American troops on German soil.

The Middle East

The significant oil resources of the Middle East focused the attention of the industrialized nations on that area during World War II. The economic importance of the region continued to heighten its influence in global affairs after the war, and the instability produced by conflict between Arab countries and the new State of Israel illustrated the difficulties besetting reliance on Middle East oil supplies and other resources in that region.

Scholarship concerning this aspect of American foreign relations during the 1960s, 1970s, and 1980s seeks to assess the sources of the instability and the relative merit of various United States efforts to maintain peace and security in that part of the globe.

Alexander, Yonah and Allan Nanes, eds. THE UNITED STATES AND IRAN (1980). This volume provides a documentary history with commentary of U.S. and Iranian relations from the mid-nineteenth century through the hostage crisis of 1980.

Bromley, Simon. AMERICAN HEGEMONY AND WORLD OIL: The Industry, the State System, and the World Economy (1991). Bromley devotes much of this book to show how the general realignment of U.S. hegemony, in the 1970s and 1980s, is paralleled in, and thus can be illustrated by, changes to its position in the global oil industry.

Campany, Richard C. TURKEY AND THE UNITED STATES: The Arms Embargo Period (1986). This book deals with the 1974 U.S. arms embargo against Turkey. The author investigates embargo as a diplomatic tool, examines the foreign and domestic relations of Turkey, and discusses the embargo itself. Campany maintains that embargo is overused and ineffectual as a foreign policy measure.

Chomsky, Noam. THE FATEFUL TRIANGLE (1983). Chomsky investigates the relationships among the United States, Israel and the Palestinians from the foundation of the State of Israel until the early 1980s, positing possible future outcomes and assessing their potential impact.

Druks, Herbert. THE U.S. AND ISRAEL: A Diplomatic History 1945-1973 (1979). This brief history of U.S. and Israeli affairs contends that United States assistance to Israel is given only when it serves U.S. interests and can be identified as addressing a worthwhile cause. Druks maintains that the security of Israel's own future will depend upon sound leadership and increased self-reliance.

Gasiorowski, Mark J. U.S. FOREIGN POLICY AND THE SHAH: Building a client state in Iran (1991). Gasiorowski contends that U.S. aid from 1953 to 1963 let the shah become largely immune to domestic pressures when oil revenues were low.

Kuniholm, Bruce R. and Michael Rubner. THE PALESTINIAN PROBLEM AND UNITED STATES POLICY (1986). This guide to the issues which be set the Palestinian situation and the accompanying bibliographical essay on the topic introduce the reader to the recent history of U.S. relations with Arabs and Israelis in the Middle East, suggests options, and discusses their risks and advantages.

Miller, David Aaron. SEARCH FOR SECURITY: Saudi Arabian Oil (1980). This volume provides a general background to U.S. foreign relations concerning Middle Eastern oil but focuses on the special relationship between the United States and Saudi Arabia.

Quandt, William B. DECADE OF DECISION (1977). Quandt investigates American policy toward the Arab and Israeli conflict from 1967 to 1976 and concludes that only those negotiations which are accompanied by considerable presidential commitment, consistent policy, and an orientation toward Middle East issues are apt to meet with lasting success.

Rubin, Barry. PAVED WITH GOOD INTENTIONS: The American Experience in Iran (1980). The author maintains that difficulties arose between the United States and Iran because of mutual ignorance and misperception.

Safran, Nadav. ISRAEL: The Embattled Ally (1978). Safran analyzes in detail the historical factors behind the creation of the State of Israel and traces its development into a key force in the Middle East. The last half of the volume is dedicated to U.S. and Israeli relations. Safran contends that the two countries must continue to commit themselves to settlements of the major issues in the area while recognizing that the United States has interests not only in Israel, but also in the surrounding Arab states

Sheehan, Edward R. THE ARABS, THE ISRAELIS, AND KISSINGER (1976). Sheehan recounts the story of Kissinger's Middle East negotiations of the early 1970s. This work offers an inside view of the conduct of such missions as well as insights into the nature of diplomacy in the Arab and Israeli part of the world. He concludes that the United States and Israel will be forced to a negotiated settlement by the increasing material costs involved in conducting war in the region.

Sick, Gary. ALL FALL DOWN: America's Tragic Encounter with Iran (1985). Sick presents the history of U.S. and Iranian relations under the Shah's regime. His analysis of the events affecting the Iranian revolution and the U.S. diplomatic measures addressing the changes it produced suggests that the United States and other major powers are poorly equipped to deal with societies in revolution.

Spiegel, Steven L. THE OTHER ARAB ISRAELI CONFLICT (1985). Spiegel's examination of U.S. policy in the Middle East focuses on the preconceptions of officials involved in negotiations and analyses the impact of those views on decision-making and policy formulation. His research covers the post-World War II era through the early Reagan administration.

Stookey, Robert W. AMERICA AND THE ARAB STATES: An Uneasy Encounter (1975). Stookey provides an overview of the history of U.S. relations with Arab states and explains the primacy of the oil issue in the post-World War II era.

Tillman, Seth P. THE UNITED STATES AND THE MIDDLE EAST (1982). Tillman examines conflicts in the Middle East and the U.S. role in attempts to resolve them, particularly the Camp David negotiations He concludes that domestic considerations have historically resulted in considerable abstention on the part of the United States from exerting pressure on Israel and predicts that these will continue to foster reserve on the part of Americans involved in Middle East diplomacy.

Yergin, Daniel. THE PRIZE: The Epic Quest for Oil, Money, and Power (1991). Yergin views oil as a commodity intimately intertwined with national strategies and global politics and power.

Asia

The Vietnam conflict of the 1960s and early 1970s tended to dominate research on U.S. relations with Asian countries during the period. Aside from the issues concerning Southeast Asia, major interests of the United States lay in relations with Japan, the Peoples' Republic of China, the Philippines, and the Republic of China. Important strategic location as well as economic significance bolstered these countries in foreign policy priorities and much of the literature dealing with American diplomacy emphasizes these factors, endeavoring to assess the costs and advantages involved.

Banner, Raymond. WALTZING WITH A DICTATOR (1987). Banner reviews the history of U.S. and Filipino relations during the Marcos regime and concludes that it was consistently the United States that acquiesced to Marcos when conflicting positions emerged.

Brands, H. W. BOUND TO EMPIRE: The United States and the Philippines, 1890-1990 (1992). Brands views U.S. and Philippine relations from the vantage point of those individuals and groups, American and Filipinos, who have wielded power.

Chang, Gordon H. FRIENDS AND ENEMIES: The United States, China, and the Soviet Union, 1948-1972 (1990). Change stresses the domination of realistic rather than ideological factors for the U.S. as it formulated its triangular relationship with the Communist powers.

Clapp, Priscella and Morton H. Halperin, eds. UNITED STATES-JAPANESE RELATIONS: The 1970s (1974). This collection of essays by experts examines the state of U.S. and Japanese relations in the early 1970s from a variety of perspectives.

Cohen, Warren I. AMERICA'S RESPONSE TO CHINA: An Interpretative History of Sino-American Relations (1980). Cohen describes U.S. and Chinese relations from the mid-nineteenth century through the 1970s.

Foot, Rosemary. THE PRACTICE OF POWER: U.S. Relations with China Since 1949 (1995). Foot suggests that the Sino-American rapprochement since the early 1970s has been beneficial to the U.S.

Neu, Charles E. THE TROUBLED ENCOUNTER: The United States and Japan (1975). Neu synthesizes the commercial, cultural, and political aspects of twentieth century U.S. and Japanese relations.

Ross, Robert S. NEGOTIATING COOPERATION: The United States and China, 1969-1989 (1995). Ross praises the ability of the U.S. & China to resolve their differences and improve their relationship so that both sides have benefited.

Stanley, Peter W. ed. REAPPRAISING AN EMPIRE: New Perspectives on Philippine-American History (1984). This collection of essays supports the notion that the American impact on the Philippines has been much less substantial than previously imagined.

Westad, Odd Arne. COLD WAR AND REVOLUTION: Soviet-American Rivalry and the Origins of the Chinese Civil War (1993). Westad takes the controversial position that the Cold War caused the civil war in China in 1946.

Wolpert, Stanley. ROOTS OF CONFRONTATION IN SOUTH ASIA (1982). This work investigates the role of India, Pakistan, and Afghanistan in U.S. and Soviet relations. The author places particular emphasis on the role of Islam in the convicts of the region.

Nuclear Issues

The advent of nuclear military power produced considerable debate on the necessity and role of strategic armaments, their relationship to tactical weapons, and their appropriateness in determining national security. Some scholars contend that American possession of nuclear weapons deters aggression against the United States. Others argue that U.S. reliance on such arms actually detracts from the overall military safety of nation.

Ball, Desmond. POLITICS AND FORCE LEVELS (1980). This volume addresses the strategic missile program during the Kennedy years and concludes that the excessively high stockpiles that resulted from that plan suggest the need for a different approach to decisions about future force levels.

Baucom, Donald R. THE ORIGINS OF SDI, 1944-1983 (1992). Baucom concludes that SDI contributed significantly to the West's triumph in the Cold War.

Garnet, Richard J. ROOTS OF WAR (1972). Barnet analyzes the what and the who of the U.S. national interest and concludes that the goal of remaining the leading nation in the world produced the militarization of American society. He contends that the permanent war in which he believes U.S. foreign policy is conducted can only be transformed by fundamental changes in American society.

Blacker, Coit D. RELUCTANT WARRIORS (1987). Blacker examines U.S. and Soviet relations as they pertain to arms control and concludes that neither the restoration of American military superiority nor disarmament are adequate as goals for achieving national security. He offers a modified approach to resolving the issue that relies on an educated public and patience in negotiations.

Divine, Robert A. BLOWING ON THE WIND (1978). Divine investigates the nuclear test ban debate of 1954-1960 and concludes that the Failure to resolve the controversy in the early years had the positive impact of revealing the fundamental lack of trust between the superpowers.

Halloran, Bernard F., ed. ESSAYS ON ARMS CONTROL AND NATIONAL SECURITY (1986). This volume contains a collection of essays dated from 1948 to 1985 and written by experts addressing the issue of arms control and its relationship to U.S. security since the advent of nuclear weapons.

Herken, Gregg. COUNSELS OF WAR (1985). Herken investigates the history of the nuclear debate and contends that it needs to be refocused upon American intentions instead of speculation about Soviet actions.

Howlett, Charles F. and Glen Zeiter. THE AMERICAN PEACE MOVEMENT: History and Historiography (1985). This short work traces the roots of American resistance to war since the early history of the United States and concludes that peace is a necessary reform on which the survival of the modern, nuclear world depends.

Jones, Howard, ed. THE FOREIGN AND DOMESTIC DIMENSIONS OF MODERN WARFARE (1988). This collection of essays addresses American military involvement in Vietnam and in Central America, and investigates the impact of nuclear strategy on modern warfare.

Kincade, William H., et al. NEGOTIATING SECURITY: An Arms Control Reader (1979). This collection of essays addresses the nuclear and conventional arms control debate from various perspectives, providing a substantial orientation to U.S. national security issues as they relate to weapons.

National Academy of Sciences. NUCLEAR ARMS CONTROL (1985). This volume examines the history and 1985 status of nuclear arms control efforts.

Mandelbaum, Michael. THE NUCLEAR QUESTION: The United States and Nuclear Weapons, 194-1976 (1979). Mandelbaum describes the development and application of nuclear weapons in their strategic and diplomatic context and charts the changes in U.S. policy regarding their deployment and use. He contends that through modem diplomacy the world has adjusted to living with the bomb.

Newhouse, John. COLD DAWN: The Story of SALT (1973) Newhouse describes the complex process of negotiations which culminated In the 1972 signing of the first phase of the strategic arms limitations agreements.

Talbott, Strobe. ENDGAME (1979). Talbott researches the evolution of strategic arms limitation talks and follows their development through the signing of the SALT II agreement by Carter and Brezhnev.

Terriff, Terry. THE NIXON ADMINISTRATION AND THE MAKING OF U.S. NUCLEAR STRATEGY (1995). Terriff examines the discussions regarding the strategic nuclear targeting policy of the United States and the ultimate adoption of the Schlessinger Doctrine in 1974.

Winkler, Allan M. LIFE UNDER A CLOUD: American Anxiety about the Atom (1993). Winkler provides an overview of the history of nuclear arms control and explains why fear of nuclear destruction has not yet brought these weapons under effective control.

Wells, Samuel F. and Robert Sleds Litwak. STRATEGIC DEFENSES AND SOVIET-AMERICAN RELATIONS (1987). This collection of essays investigates the historical context of the policy debate over strategic defenses in the 1980s, particularly the Strategic Defense Initiative.

DIPLOMATIC GLOSSARY

abrogate: to abolish by authoritative, official or formal action.

accord: an agreement between two or more states. Once used to refer to subjects less important than those covered by treaties but now employed interchangeably.

admiralty court: a court having jurisdiction of maritime questions.

aide-memoire: a written summary or outline of important items of a proposed agreement.

agreement: general terms for a binding accord of any kind—bilateral or multilateral.

alliance: a promise between two nations to provide diplomatic and military support as need dictates.

ambassador: a minister of the highest rank accredited to a foreign government

amity: friendship and goodwill.

armistice: a suspension of hostilities by mutual agreement. See truce.

asylum: a place exempted by custom or convention from the territorial jurisdiction of a state.

attache: a technical specialist, with diplomatic rank, attached to an embassy or legation.

belligerent: a nation at war with one or more nations. See neutral.

belligerency, recognition of: acceptance, by a nation, that a state of war exists between two or more other states.

bilateral: affecting two nations in a reciprocal manner.

blockade: the isolation of an area by one belligerent so as to hamper entrance or exit by an opponent or other interested parties. Normally involves the use of warships, but may be accomplished by aircraft or land forces.

boycott: a prohibition against commercial activities with a nation or nations. Boycotts may be publicly or privately inspired. See embargo.

capital ship: a warship of the first rank in size and armament.

cartel: agreement among independent states to restrict commercial competition by regulating prices, production or the marketplace.

casus belli: a cause or occasion for war or other strife.

casus foederis: an event covered by the provisions of a treaty or compact.

chancellery: the office of a foreign embassy.

charge d'affaires: a member of the diplomatic corps who directs affairs in the absence of the ambassador or minister.

chief of mission: ranking officer in a permanent diplomatic mission, e.g., the ambassador in an embassy or a minister in a legation.

Cold War: term used to symbolize the conflict betwixt the United States and the Soviet Union following the Second World War.

COMINFORM: Communist Information Bureau (1947).

COMINTERN: Communist International (1919).

comity: courtesies extended by one nation to another.

commonwealth: voluntary federation or association of states who share interests, values or heritage.

communique: an official announcement.

condominium: joint sovereignty by two or more states over a colony or politically dependent territory.

conference: meeting between representatives of more than two states to address specific matters. See also congress.

congress: term customarily used in the nineteenth century to denote a meeting between representatives of more than two states to address specific matters.

consortium: international partnership or association of financial institutions to pursue a joint venture to large for one bank.

consul: an official appointed to represent the interests of citizens of the appointing nation in a foreign country.

contraband of war: items which cannot be shipped to one belligerent except at the risk of seizure by the other.

convention: an agreement between nations for the regulation of specific matters, e.g., a postal convention.

counselor: a diplomatic official ranking just below a minister or ambassador

coup d'etat: a sudden forcible act unseating the personnel of a government.

coup de main: a sudden attack in force.

credentials: documents to demonstrate that a diplomatic agent has the right to exercise official power.

declaration: a joint statement by two or most states. Declarations are frequently as binding as a treaty.

de facto: a government actually functioning but not yet permanently established or recognized.

de jure: the lawful or recognized government—it may or may not be the de facto government.

demarche: a diplomatic move, countermove or maneuver.

denounce: formal proclamation of the termination of an agreement.

detente: a relaxation of strained relations between nations.

diplomatic immunity: freedom of foreign envoys from local jurisdiction.

dispatch: a message, often in code, sent by an agent in the field.

doctrine: in American history a significant presidential statement or initiative

Downing Street: synonym for British Foreign Office or British government.

doyen: the senior male member of the diplomatic corps by reason of longest assignment (doyenne-female).

embargo: an official edict forbidding trade with a country or countries. See boycott.

embassy: the office or residence of an ambassador.

emissary: a diplomatic agent sent as a official messenger by a government or head of state.

entente: a written or unwritten international understanding providing for a common course of action.

envoy: any person reputed to represent a government in its intercourse with another. In specific terms the senior diplomat in a delegation.

executive agent: presidential envoy whose appointment is not subject to legislative approval.

executive agreement: one made by a President which is not subject to approval by the U.S. Senate.

expropriation: confiscation of property by a government extradition: surrender of an alleged criminal by one nation to another.

extradition: the return of person accused of a crime by one nation to another. Such matters are normally subject to previously negotiated agreements.

extraterritoriality: general or partial exemption from the application of local law or jurisdiction of local tribunals.

fait accompli: accomplished fact and presumably irrevocable.

filibuster: to carry out insurrectionist or revolutionary activities in a foreign country.

Foggy Bottom: synonym for U.S. State Department since 1945.

free ships, free goods: nineteen century catchphrase denoting the freedom from seizure of non-contraband enemy goods when carried by a neutral.

freezing: to impound the assets of another nation or its citizens.

good offices: a process whereby a nation serves as a mediator between disputing states.

Group of Five: France, Germany, Japan, the U.K. and the U.S

imbroglio: a complicated or embarrassing misunderstanding between nations.

impasse: a predicament affording no obvious escape.

intern: to confine or impound material or people during wartime.

internuncio: a diplomat, equal to an minister, who represents the Vatican.

jingo: a clamorous or belligerent chauvinist.

justiciable: liable to trial in a court of justice.

Kremlin: synonym for the government of the U.S.S.R. or any subsequent Russian government.

legation: office or residence of a diplomatic minister.

letter of marque: authority for a person to be a privateer.

mandate: territory administered by a nation under authority of an international organization, e.g., the League of Nations.

mediation: involvement of a third party to settle a dispute with the consent of the parties to the conflict.

minister: the chief of a diplomatic mission who heads a legation rather than an embassy. Before 1893, American diplomats were accredited as envoys extraordinary and ministers plenipotentiary, thereby placing them behind ambassadors in any official procession.

mission: group sent to conduct diplomatic negotiations or a permanent embassy or legation.

modus vivendi: a workable compromise on issues in dispute without permanently settling them.

most-favored-nation clause: a provision that grants to a nation any privileges that may be subsequently granted to a third nation.

multilateral: includes participation of more than two nations.

nationalization: the seizure of private or property belonging to foreign nationals by a foreign government—sometimes with compensation.

neutral: a nation that does not participate in a war between other states. Neutrality confers both rights and obligations with respect to belligerents.

nonaligned: term common during the Cold War to describe those nations which pursued a policy of independence from either side to the struggle.

nuncio: a diplomat, equal to an ambassador, who represents the Vatican.

order in council: an executive act by the sovereign and the privy council or cabinet (British).

pact: an agreement or treaty between nations. The term is frequently used to refer to a military alliance.

paper blockade: a blockade which does not effectively interdict an area and thus no penalties for violation.

persona grata: acceptable as an envoy—opposite of persona non grata.

plenipotentiary: a diplomatic agent with full power to negotiate.

privateer: an armed private ship authorized to attack enemy ships, this practice was outlawed by the Declaration of Paris (1856).

prize court: a court having jurisdiction to adjudge upon wartime captures at sea.

protectorate: a circumstance in which one nation exercises authority over another without annexing same. A protectorate state usually takes charge of foreign affairs, defense and public finances.

protocol: a formal agreement similar to a treaty but less important and the ceremonial aspect of diplomacy.

Quai d'Orsay: synonym for French Foreign Office or French government.

quid pro quo: something in exchange for something.

rapprochement: friendly relations between powers.

ratification: act whereby a state formally confirms and approves the terms of a treaty. The United States Senate only approves treaties. They are not ratified until signed by the President.

reciprocity: granting commercial privileges in exchange for similar concessions by another nation.

recognition: acceptance by one nation that a specific government exercises effective control of another nation. Normally accompanies the establishment of diplomatic relations.

reparations: payments, financial or otherwise, by a nation for damage inflicted.

reprisal: retaliatory acts to procure redress of grievances by one nation against another.

reservation: limitations attached to a diplomatic agreement to restrict its scope.

right of visit and search: the right of a belligerent to examine a neutral ship during wartime.

sanctions: coercive measures adopted by a nation or nations to persuade another to fulfill its lawful obligations.

self-determination: the right of a people of a territorial unit or ethnic group to govern themselves.

signatory: a person or nation who has signed and is thus bound by a document.

sine qua non: absolutely necessary.

sovereignty: the idea that an independent state is free from external interference within its own borders.

sphere of influence: exclusive interest in an area granted by other nations to a particular country.

summit: a meeting between two or more heads of state.

status quo: the existing state of affairs.

status quo ante bellum: state of affairs existing before a war.

treaty: a formal mutually binding agreement that defines the obligations and rights of all those signatory to the act.

truce: a suspension of hostilities by mutual agreement.

trusteeship: supervision of an area granted by an international agency.

ultimatum: the best terms that a negotiator will offer, the rejection of which usually ends negotiations.

U.S.S.R.: Union of Soviet Socialist Republics. Official title of the Soviet Union.

unperfected: a treaty that fails to achieve ratification.

visa: passport endorsement allowing the bearer to proceed.

Whitehall: synonym for the British government.

Wilhelmstrasse: synonym for the Imperial German Foreign Office.

INDEX

www.ingramcontent.com/pod-product-compliance
Lightning Source LLC
Chambersburg PA
CBHW060453290526
45791CB00001B/96